The House of Lords

MANCHESTER
1824

Manchester University Press

The House of Lords

Donald Shell

Manchester University Press

Manchester and New York

Distributed exclusively in the USA by Palgrave

The right of Donald Shell to be identified as the author of this work has been asserted by him in accordance with the Copyright, Designs and Patents Act 1988.

Published by Manchester University Press
Oxford Road, Manchester M13 9NR, UK
and Room 400, 175 Fifth Avenue, New York, NY 10010, USA
www.manchesteruniversitypress.co.uk

Distributed exclusively in the USA by
Palgrave, 175 Fifth Avenue, New York,
NY 10010, USA

Distributed exclusively in Canada by
UBC Press, University of British Columbia, 2029 West Mall,
Vancouver, BC, Canada V6T 1Z2

British Library Cataloguing-in-Publication Data
A catalogue record for this book is available from the British Library

Library of Congress Cataloging-in-Publication Data applied for

ISBN   978 0 7190 5443 3 *hardback*

First published 2007

16 15 14 13 12 11 10 09 08 07   10 9 8 7 6 5 4 3 2 1

Typeset in Charter ITC BT 10.5/12.5pt
by Servis Filmsetting Ltd, Manchester
Printed in Great Britain
by Biddles, King's Lynn.

Contents

List of tables		vi
1	The House of Lords and the British constitution	1
2	The House of Lords in the twentieth century	17
3	What is the House of Lords?	47
4	The work of the House	85
5	Second chambers elsewhere	130
6	Reforming the second chamber	149
	Addendum	173
	Appendix: Party manifesto statements on the House of Lords: 1979–2005	176
	Official sources	180
	Select bibliography	181
	Index	184

List of Tables

3.1   Nominal membership of the House of Lords 2006   49
3.2   Creation of life peers 1958 to 2006   57
3.3   Changing party strength in the House of Lords   68
3.4   Activity in the House by category of peer 2003–04   70
4.1   The growth in activity of the House of Lords   86
4.2   How the House of Lords spends its time   91
4.3   Amendments to government bills by parliament
        1970–2004   99
4.4   The European Union Committee in 2006   118

1

The House of Lords and the British constitution

Constitutional reform has been one of the major themes of the Blair-led Labour Governments since 1997. Pride of place in these reforms must go to the establishment of a Scottish Parliament and an Assembly for Wales. The first parliamentary session, 1997–98, saw the legislation for these changes carried following referendums, and the new devolved institutions were brought into being in the summer of 1999, some two years after 'New Labour' arrived in office. That same first session also saw legislation enacted to incorporate into domestic British law the European Convention on Human Rights. Though less high profile than the devolution measures, at least as far as the general public was concerned, the constitutional implications of this change and the enhanced role for the judiciary, especially with the creation of the new Supreme Court in 2009, are likely to prove very considerable. The introduction of new arrangements for the government of London, including a directly elected mayor, were also clearly intended as a possible forerunner to change elsewhere in local government, though in the event little developed from this initiative, with the electorates of only twelve other local authorities choosing in referendums to have elected mayors. And the idea of regional assemblies within England foundered badly with the decisive rejection of the proposed North-East Assembly in a referendum in 2004. The system for electing British members of the European Parliament was altered to a closed-list proportional representation system based on regional constituencies. And within parliament a programme of 'modernisation' was embarked upon, which included the removal of hereditary peers from the House of Lords.

These changes taken together were often referred to as a programme of constitutional reform. In one sense this was obviously true. Legislation introducing constitutional change can easily consume vast quantities of parliamentary time. For that reason alone, if no other, priorities must be set. The reluctance of governments to apply guillotines to bills embodying constitutional reform, and the assumption that such measures should be dealt with in committee of the whole House (rather than in the usual legislative standing committees) accentuate the need for government to consider carefully the pace at which it brings before parliament legislation embodying such reform. There must therefore be a prioritising of change and that fact in itself requires that a programme, a running order, for the introduction of change be set. To some extent these reforms must also be taken in sequence. If steps towards regional government are to be taken in Britain, then starting with Scotland and Wales is natural, just as London is an obvious city for the introduction of a directly elected mayor. And in the case of the House of Lords, if a single comprehensive reform is not to be attempted, then a starting place must be found, and for Labour the removal of hereditary peers seemed an obvious place to commence.

But whether Labour's constitutional reforms represent a programme in a more developed sense of the term is certainly open to question. There is little evidence of government ministers having given much serious thought to the nature of the constitution and the basic principles that might guide change. No fundamental examination of the constitution has taken place and no principles for reform have been set out. There has been no serious attempt to foresee how one reform relates to another, and to orchestrate the changes. Of course, in the back of some ministers' minds there is no doubt the feeling that perhaps reform of the second chamber could be tied in with the introduction of devolved institutions, or the need for parliamentary oversight of the new machinery for monitoring human rights. But no systematic attempt to relate the reforms to each other has taken place.

Certain themes may have been identified. Changes have been presented as transferring power away from the 'centre', and to devolved institutions. But it is much easier to see the introduction of highly asymmetric devolution as driven by political expediency. Labour felt under considerable pressure from the rising tide of nationalist support, especially given the party's reliance on Scottish and Welsh seats. After the Conservative Government had committed itself against making any change it was good electoral politics for Labour to offer a clear alternative. Devolved institutions for the more peripheral parts of the UK were the answer. And if it was deemed necessary to make some counterbalancing adjustment for England, then yet another model of devolution might be advanced for the English regions. But there is no evidence that Tony Blair and his colleagues genuinely saw this as an attempt to devolve power. On the contrary, when the need for coalition government became apparent in Scotland after the first devolved parliamentary elections in 1999, Tony Blair was quoted as saying (over the issue of student fees): 'You can't have Scotland doing something different from the rest of Britain'.[1] As the expectation that Labour would hold the reins of power in Edinburgh and Cardiff as well as in London was disappointed, so the reality of devolution slowly sank in.

Another theme linking these changes was 'modernisation', a conveniently ambiguous term for those who wish to introduce change, but have no clear rationale or sense of direction for that change. Modernisation can simply mean removing some archaic features and making institutions look rather more up-to-date and contemporary in appearance. There are always aspects of behaviour associated with ancient institutions that appear curious to the contemporary onlooker. Some of these can undoubtedly be removed without loss, but others have an instructive symbolic significance. 'New Labour' found it convenient to modernise, but only in a selective manner. As far as parliament was concerned, aspects of dress and procedure could be changed, but the state opening remained untouched because to tamper with that would be to tamper with the monarchy, which for electoral reasons remained – at least for the time being – a politically no-go area. In a superficial sense reforming the House of Lords obviously sat well with a modernisation agenda. Here was a body whose formal membership was still dominated by hereditary peers, with most of its remaining members appointed for life, and not a single one elected. That such a body should share parliamentary power on the eve of the twenty-first century seemed ridiculous. It was an institution ripe for modernisation. But again little thought was given to what that might involve beyond the obvious – the removal of peers by succession.

Devolving power and modernising were essentially selling points to the public. They indicated a marketing strategy for the government's spin-doctors, ever eager to persuade and cajole the electorate into believing the changes were reasoned, wise and sensible, contrary to the negative image presented by the Conservative opposition. But the verdict of Dawn Oliver that 'there has been no master plan or coherent programme for reform of the UK constitution . . . no coherent "vision" of democracy or citizenship or good governance or constitutionalism has informed the various actors' seems sound.[2] Indeed to some observers the absence of guiding principles makes it doubtful whether the UK actually has a constitution at all.[3]

The constitutional changes made since 1997 are best understood as piecemeal, specific and pragmatic. This may sound like a criticism. But it is not necessarily so. Such a style of change has, it can be argued, suited the development of the British constitution rather well. This is how change has taken place in the past. The extension of the franchise took place bit by bit during the nineteenth and twentieth centuries in response to pressures placed on successive governments. The removal of the House of Lords power to veto legislation was the response to the constitutional crisis triggered by the rejection in the upper House of the 1909 budget. Reform of the structure of local government, or a change to the means by which parliament holds the executive to account, are further examples of constitutional adjustment. Many relatively small changes have taken place, sometimes agreed between the major parties, sometimes contested, which cumulatively have represented significant adjustment to the constitution. In this way ancient institutions that have accumulated respect – even veneration – over the centuries, have evolved to fulfil the requirements of a constitution for a modern democratic society. Thus Britain has moved gradually and without any fundamental and enduring upheaval from feudalism and monarchical despotism to popular democracy.

Such a pattern of past change has not been the result of any synoptic overview of the constitution, nor even of deliberate design. In England at least the tendency has been to think and speak of the constitution as a living organism, subject to gradual evolutionary change undertaken for practical reasons, and not as a piece of machinery, subject to periodic redesign, or updated by having new parts fitted from time to time.

An unwritten constitution

Such an approach has resulted in the British constitution remaining 'unwritten'. That term on its own can of course be misleading. The constitution is in existence in the sense that there are rules defining the major institutions of the state and their inter-relationships. At one level it is a trivial point to say these rules are unwritten. The fact that British citizens cannot take a document out of their pockets and say, this is the constitution, unlike for example American or French citizens, does not of itself alter the perception of the way government takes place. But the point has a more profound significance for several reasons. First there is no clear authoritative definition of what the constitution actually states on a range of important matters. Is the House of Lords acting unconstitutionally when it insists on resisting the will of the Commons on a bill? What limit is there, if any, on the right of a prime minister to appoint new peers? How many ministers can a prime minister appoint from the Lords? Can a prime minister remain in office following an election in which his party has won fewer Commons seats than another party? No one can be sure of the answer to such questions. The constitution is what the government of the day does and can get away with, or as Professor John Griffith is quoted as saying: 'the constitution is what happens'.[4]

Politicians frequently accuse their opponents of acting unconstitutionally, and the accusation can be difficult to rebut. Second, the process of
constitutional change can be confusing. On the one hand a change may
result simply from altered practice, a process that may be quite subtle
and largely unnoticed – at least to begin with. The rise of judicial review
in the latter part of the last century would be one example. The developing role of the prime minister would be another. But equally change
may take place quite suddenly and by simple parliamentary process
as the government of the day secures a parliamentary majority to alter
the powers or composition of the House of Lords, or to establish
devolved institutions in part of the UK. There is no requirement that
such legislation should receive enhanced majorities, be subject to a referendum or be taken through parliament in a way different from that of
other legislation.

Third, the unwritten or historic constitution points to the fact that
there has been no defining moment in the life of the British state when
a deliberate and self-conscious attempt has been made to reformulate
our system of government. Instead ancient institutions have simply been
adapted, adjusted here and there, with some allowed to wither and
others flourish, encouraged perhaps to take on new tasks never imagined by our forebears. Britain's constitution is historic. It has just grown,
and as a people we have adapted it when and where necessary to cope
with changed circumstances and ideas. Most other countries have had
a defining moment, perhaps when independence was attained, perhaps
as a result of internal revolution, or maybe after defeat in war and invasion, or even when two or more separate states have come together to
form a federal system. Such moments involve a fresh start and as such
tend to produce new constitutions, newly formulated rules about the
state and its system of government. Such constitutions are codified in
the sense that they have a definite legal basis. This is deemed necessary
to ensure that the rules will be followed and that any future changes will
be made according to some definite criteria.

If the purpose of a constitution is to define the major institutions of a
state and to regulate their inter-relationships, then it is easy to exaggerate
the difference in practice between a written and an unwritten constitution. As far as the exercise of power is concerned, an unwritten constitution may embody understandings that are at least as precise, as clear and
as authoritative to all concerned as any provisions of a written constitution. Indeed, it may well be that the ancient nature of an unwritten constitution, the authority derived from its longevity so to speak, offers a
definite advantage. That at least was often suggested in twentieth-century
Britain. And another advantage, so it was argued, was the flexibility that

an unwritten constitution offered. Understandings could be adjusted so as to cope with changing circumstances whilst specific rules might be incapable of modification except by a complicated and perhaps politically fraught process.

In practice, written or codified constitutions may contain all kinds of statements that are essentially embellishments rather than precise rules about government and its powers. Some constitutions express aims and hopes, goals for a new state, formulated at a moment of high aspiration and intended to point to a new beginning for a society, perhaps one hitherto a colony but now independent, or formerly run by a corrupt oligarchy, but now a democracy of free people. Constitutions may be relatively short-lived. Sometimes old problems quickly re-emerge, and the only solution appears to be another fresh start, not just with a new government, but ostensibly a new way of doing things different from that embodied in the existing constitution. Generally a written constitution will be incomplete in the sense that anyone seeking to understand the system of government will need to know many things about which the constitution itself is silent. Unwritten rules may be every bit as important as that which is written, in the sense of defining what those who run the system need to know. Constitutions may remain deliberately silent about matters which it is very difficult to define precisely, or perhaps where great delicacy is necessary and where the development of an understanding rather than the formulation of a clear rule is deemed to serve the interests of those involved. After all, an understanding can change and adapt to new circumstances. Those affected can build on success, or alternatively can gradually accept some adjustment with dignity rather than facing humiliation. In this sense the line between what is written and what is unwritten may be hard to draw. But where a whole constitution remains unwritten, it is also necessary to describe it as uncodified because no formal procedure exists for amending the constitution.

Adjusting to the rise of democracy

This has been true for the United Kingdom throughout the modern period, ever since the 'glorious revolution' of 1688 and the settlement of 1689 brought the seventeenth-century upheavals to a close. The struggle between king and parliament had led to the execution of the king and the abolition of both Monarchy and House of Lords for the period of the Commonwealth. Translated into modern terms, the Instrument of Government formulated by Cromwell was a written constitution. But from the perspective of British history it is seen as a temporary expedient. The eleven years of the Commonwealth were an interlude, followed by the Restoration, with monarchy and House of Lords brought back. When King James began again to revive the bad old ways that had preceded Cromwell's bloody revolution, parliament responded firmly, and the king fled into exile. At parliament's invitation William of Orange took the throne, but in doing so he accepted a 'Bill of Rights' drawn up by parliament and designed to ensure that never again would the rights of parliament be trampled on by the monarch. This became the 1689 Bill of Rights, and is the nearest Britain has to a written constitution. But as such it is a very incomplete document; it deals not with individual rights but with the rights of parliament *vis a vis* the crown.

With both Monarchy and House of Lords restored, the question might be asked, what had changed? The answer must be that a great deal had changed in terms of the understanding of relationships between the various institutions of the state, especially between the monarch and parliament. It was clear that the monarch would no longer be able to govern without parliament, and that taxes and the keeping of an army would only be possible through parliament, but the modern idea of a constitutional monarch was still far distant. Queen Anne vetoed a bill passed by both Houses of Parliament in 1707, but no one then realised that this was the last time a monarch would feel free directly to veto a bill passed by both Houses. On the other hand no one wished at that stage to try to define too precisely what was or was not possible in the new setting. Better to allow the new relationships gradually to evolve. And this is what happened. The office of prime minister was an eighteenth-century invention, though that word implies a precise for-mulation of the office, which of course did not take place – and never has. It was simply that at the interface between parliament and crown it was necessary for a parliamentary leader to emerge, someone who could command the support of parliament and who could therefore resist pressures from the king.

In this context the House of Lords remained a clear part of parliament, sharing in the power parliament could command. It was true that in the seventeenth century the Commons had passed resolutions, incorporated into the standing orders of the lower House to safeguard its financial privileges. This was to give a clearer formulation to the reason for the original emergence of two separate Houses, and to ensure that the aris-tocratic upper chamber did not interfere with matters of taxation and supply. But this was in essence simply a rule made by one House and accepted by the other. In 1702 the House of Lords amended its own standing orders to ensure that any legislation involving the financial privilege of the Commons was tightly drawn, to avoid the further erosion of the power of the Lords, which in all other respects had co-equal legislative power. These were matters which could have been included in a written constitution had such emerged, but instead they were dealt with in the standing orders of the two Houses.

A classical understanding of the English form of government had seen it as a balance between monarchy, aristocracy and people, represented by king, lords and commons. This was modelled on Aristotle's analysis and first formulated in England in Tudor times. It was an understanding that survived the seventeenth-century revolution. The three elements remained and were all still considered essential, even if the balance between them had altered. Later with the rise of democratic ideas the focus was initially on the need to reform the way the Commons was constituted, to improve if not perfect the democratic element in the constitution without disturbing the other two elements.[5] Reform of the franchise was not advocated in order to ensure the democratic element triumphed over aristocracy and monarchy.

In practice however with the rise of democratic ideas the political supremacy of the Commons was gradually established. The American and the French revolutions, in their very different ways, reinforced this demand, though they also made the aristocratic classes very nervous about where such change might lead. When franchise reform was achieved in the great Reform Act of 1832, it may have altered only very slightly the electorate for the Commons, but far from being seen as a once and for all perfection of the constitution, it was soon recognised as the admission of a principle that would inevitably find fulfilment in much more sweeping extensions of the right to vote. Though after 1832 still only one in six of adult males (and no females) had the vote, a direction of change had been set that would within another 100 years give to all adults a part in the choice of MPs. It was not simply that fact, but also the manner in which the Act was passed, and in particular the way in which opposition from the House of Lords was overcome, that was significant. For in order to secure its passage, notwithstanding Lords hostility, the king agreed to create enough new peers to give the Whigs the majority they needed in the upper House. Implicit in this was the relegation of the House of Lords to a subordinate position within the constitution. Thus it became clear that a consequence would be to elevate the Commons to a position of clear dominance within the constitution. If power was to rest with the people as a whole, then that power would be reflected through the Commons. Both monarch and Lords would have to acknowledge that fact.

Territorial adjustments and the House of Lords

Nor was a new start required when the territorial boundaries of the British state were adjusted. The Act of Union with Scotland in 1707 formally brought together the governments of the two countries. This could have been the moment for promulgating a new constitution, extinguishing the former institutions of both states and bringing into existence new agreed institutions for what was a new state. But the opportunity for this was not taken. It was not deemed necessary, and therefore in a typically English way, what was not necessary was not therefore considered desirable. Instead English institutions were simply extended with slight adaptation to include Scotland. True, Scotland maintained a separate legal system and a distinct established Church. But as far as parliament was concerned the two English Houses were simply extended to include Scotland.

At the time of the Act of Union there were 134 peers of Scotland and 157 peers of England. The English were eager to retain a dominance and so insisted that only sixteen places be made available in the House of Lords for peers of Scotland (to be elected by all Scottish peers, a parliament at a time). The Act of Union also specified a minimum number of seats for Scotland in the House of Commons. Over the years the number of peers qualified to sit in the Lords solely by virtue of their Scottish peerage declined as many sought and were given peerages of Great Britain,[6] until in 1963 the right to sit in the Lords was extended to include the fifteen Scottish peers not already members of the House, a total of thirty-one.

When a century later another Act of Union brought Ireland into what became the United Kingdom, the same pattern of merely extending existing institutions was adopted to include Ireland. By then there were a total of 267 peers – either of England or (since 1707) of Britain. The Irish peers had their own Irish House of Lords, but were given the right to elect twenty-two from their number as representatives to what became the United Kingdom House of Lords. Unlike the Scottish representative peers, who were elected for a parliament at a time, the Irish representative peers were elected for life, an arrangement which continued until the separation of Ireland in 1922. After this no new elections took place, but those already elected remained members of the Lords until they died, the last one not doing so until the 1960s. Unlike Scotland however no provision was made to retain peers of Ireland in the House of Lords. The Peerage Act of 1963 simply confirmed their exclusion.

In this way pragmatic adjustments were made without any apparent feeling that consistency should be maintained. Interestingly, the arrangements for membership of the House of Lords reflected an early form of asymmetric devolution. There was no suggestion when the territorial boundaries of the state were altered that a federal structure of some kind should be created. Had this been the case then it would have been necessary to safeguard such an arrangement by means of a codified constitution. But adaptation was adequate, as it proved to be so again when another century later the larger part of Ireland was detached and became an independent state. At this stage under the 1920 Government of Ireland Act a bicameral parliament for Northern Ireland was created, with a twenty-six member senate largely elected by the lower House. In 1972 these arrangements were abolished when direct rule was imposed, and later as various attempts were made to introduce a devolved Assembly for Northern Ireland, this was always a single chamber body, as of course were the Scottish Parliament and the National Assembly for Wales.

Responding to constitutional change

So the absence of successful revolution in the modern period, the absence of invasion or defeat in war, and the fact that no attempt was made to create a federal union, have all allowed the United Kingdom to develop without the need to formulate a codified constitution. The House of Lords exists within this context. It has a recognisable continuity with the House of 700 years ago. Lords Spiritual (bishops) remain members responding to a writ of summons using the language of the middle ages. Some peers remain eligible to sit in the House by virtue of peerages first granted centuries ago. But of course in practice, in the way the House works, in the relative power it possesses, in its working membership and in other ways the House is utterly different from its predecessor institution of the fourteenth century.

There is a continuity of institutions within which the central power of the crown has never been destroyed. Rather, responsibility for the exercise of that power has been transferred from the person of the monarch to ministers who in turn are responsible to parliament and through parliament in this democratic age to the people. This is the basis of the Westminster model. A government must have the support of a majority in the House of Commons, and it must retain the confidence of the Commons. Ministers must explain themselves to parliament and if they fail to do so adequately and convincingly, they may be removed from office. By this means the elected representatives of the people can probe and scrutinise any area of government activity, and if the government is found wanting, changes can be demanded. This is the theory at least of the Westminster model, within which the House of Lords still plays a subsidiary role as a chamber of scrutiny and influence, but not of real power. The practical reality of the model is heavily conditioned by the dominance of disciplined parties, but it remains a powerful political myth, an idea which guides the minds of those involved and shapes public understanding, even if practical outcomes rarely conform precisely to the theory it embodies.[7]

In modern times the relationship between the two Houses is partly conditioned by law, in particular the Parliament Acts of 1911 and 1949, and partly by convention. On the whole conventions have been very effective in establishing and maintaining norms of behaviour that have provided sufficient regulation without becoming too rigid. Interestingly in 2006 the government set up a joint select committee charged with the task of codifying the supposed conventions, including the Salisbury–Addison agreement concerning the treatment of manifesto bills.[8] Whether it will prove possible to codify these conventions clearly in a way that permits continued desirable flexibility remains to be seen, and is discussed further below.

If conventions are relied upon, one potential difficulty is the direction events take when the conventions are not properly understood or are blatantly broken. In the latter part of the nineteenth century it was widely accepted that the House of Lords did not have the right to resist other than temporarily the clear will of the Commons. Various rationales were found by peers to justify their independent existence at a time when democracy was still viewed with great suspicion. Giving the vote freely to all adults was seen as a highly risky venture. Mill spoke of the danger of 'uncontrolled democracy'.[9] Maintaining an independent House of Lords capable of exercising a constraint on populist opinion was seen as desirable in many quarters. The House could serve the interests of democracy by subscribing to a referendal theory, an idea developed by the third Marquess of Salisbury.[10] Under this it was the duty of the second chamber to delay legislation on which the mind of the country was unclear. Possibly such legislation could be submitted to the verdict of the electorate by means of a referendum. But more usually it would be an election which would reveal the will of the people. This notion that a second chamber should safeguard the country from legislation that otherwise would be thrust upon the nation as the consequence of a single, perhaps rash, decision made at an election no doubt seemed very plausible to the aristocratic class itself. But it failed to carry conviction throughout the body politic.

Nevertheless this was a view sustained for many years. The Bryce Commission in 1918 defined as one function of the second chamber the need to interpose delay in the passage of legislation long enough for the mind of the nation to be ascertained. And in much more recent years the same justification for a second chamber has been advanced. But it is a curious justification. For it makes an unelected chamber a supposedly superior judge of the state of public opinion than an elected chamber. In modern times it is surely those who not only have been elected but who must face re-election who are most likely to take care to judge public opinion accurately.

At the start of the twentieth century the House of Lords was still seen as the preserve of an aristocratic class that had every right to share in the exercise of political power. Ministers including the prime minister could be drawn from either House. Indeed from 1721 (when Walpole first became prime minister) to the end of the nineteenth century prime ministers were frequently members of the House of Lords. The House remained co-equal with the Commons in legal power. And it remained aristocratic. Peerage and property went together. However, tension between the two Houses did from time to time erupt. If peers remained associated with property, MPs were associated more and more with public opinion.

It is worth noting that another understanding of the constitution might have seen parliament as representing the nation as a whole, and recognised that the two houses together had to take note of the rise of democracy. If that were so both might have adjusted their composition in response to democratic feeling. The House of Lords could have responded to the 1832 Reform Act by reforming itself, perhaps maintaining at least for a while representatives of the hereditary peerage, but bringing in life peers and maybe initially indirectly elected members, perhaps representatives of major local authorities and of the colonies. This would have sustained a genuine bicameral parliament. But instead the House of Lords sought to sustain itself as a purely aristocratic house. Proposals for the introduction of life peers were brought forward almost immediately after the 1832 Reform Act, but these were stoutly resisted by the House for over 100 years. It was considered vital that the House maintain its independence, and to this end a hereditary House was seen as imperative.

In some ways this is the more strange because there were precedents for life peerages, for women peers, and indeed for the monarch not issuing writs of summons to all peers. The House could through its own procedures in the nineteenth century have brought itself into much closer harmony with the developing spirit of the age. But it set its face against anything that it feared would compromise its independence. The crown must not be allowed to decide to summon some peers and not others. During the 1909–11 constitutional crisis the possibility of over-coming Tory resistance to the Parliament Bill limiting the power of the Lords through withdrawing writs of summons to some peers was con-sidered. But no modern precedents for such action were available, and it was therefore felt better to go down the route of threatening to create large numbers of new peers to swamp the Tory Unionist majority if the latter proved recalcitrant. When in 1856 the crown sought to strengthen the judicial element in the Lords by giving a senior judge a peerage for his lifetime only, the House resisted this on the grounds that any com-promise in the principle of members holding hereditary peerages would weaken the independence of the House. In 1876 compromise strictly limited to a specified number of senior judges was agreed, but not for almost another 100 years were life peers allowed. When individuals who inherited peerages tried to avoid taking their seats in the House of Lords in order to remain members of the House of Commons, as hap-pened a number of times in the nineteenth century, the upper House resisted this, and through its Committee of Privileges prevented such a development. Then in 1922 the House's Committee of Privileges debarred a hereditary peeress from taking her seat, which it preferred to keep an all male preserve.

It is worth reflecting on the fact that several changes subsequently requiring legislation could have been made by the House of Lords itself had it so wished. These included the introduction of life peers and of women, the withholding of writs of summons from some hereditary peers, perhaps to oblige them to elect from among their number (as had been agreed for Scottish and Irish peers), and allow-ing those who succeeded to peerages not to take their seats. Had this happened the House might well have adjusted to become a second chamber within a genuinely bicameral parliament. But all these changes were at different times resisted. The result was that by the middle of the twentieth century none of them could be made without legislation.

This illustrates that through resisting change in order to maintain its purity as an independent institution, far from safeguarding its strength, the House of Lords became the agent of its own progressive weakening. In effect the House conspired in the creation of a de facto unicameral parliament by refusing to accept change. This was not of course what the House of Lords thought it was doing at the time. On the contrary it thought that it was maintaining its strength through maintaining its independence and this on the basis of an unchanged composition. The House chose to remain an exclusive aristocratic preserve. The price it paid for this was to become marginal in parliamentary terms. To say that it preferred this fate would be a mistake. The House did not understand that this was the consequence of the choice it had made.

The 1909–11 crisis

But what would happen when the aristocratic house collided head-on with the democratic House? The House of Lords did interpose its view on several occasions in the late nineteenth century. It rejected a home rule bill for Ireland in 1893. But no government felt strong enough actually to confront the Lords and face the chamber down. That is until the Liberal government elected in 1906 with a 'New Labour' style landslide majority. This government saw its legislative programme largely destroyed by Unionist peers using the power still vested in the upper House. In doing this the House was arguably ignoring a developing convention that had resulted in its earlier restraint when faced with legislation distasteful to the Tory majority. Perhaps the landed aristocracy that still dominated the House had been emboldened by their success in rejecting home rule for Ireland in 1893. Perhaps the change that had led to the political pre-eminence of the House of Commons had simply not sunk in as far as the bulk of Conservative peers were concerned. Perhaps it was the sheer radicalism (as they saw it) of the Liberal Government measures. Whatever the reasons, they 'found it quite right and natural that they should turn out in enormous numbers to defeat the Government's measures'.[11]

In 1907 the House of Commons passed a resolution emphasising that it was the will of the Commons that had to prevail. But this seemingly had no effect. When in 1909 peers rejected the Finance Bill outright, this was a direct challenge that the government could not ignore. A major constitutional crisis ensued.[12] Two general elections were fought in 1910, with a 'peers versus the people' theme. The Liberal majority in the Commons fell, but the overall majority in the elected House in favour of reform remained solid. The Conservatives divided, between 'hedgers' (who wanted compromise) and 'ditchers' (who wanted to fight to the last ditch). Eventually with the king having indicated that if necessary there would be a mass creation of Liberal peers to overcome Conservative resistance, the House of Lords accepted the Parliament Act. This effectively limited the power of the House to delay legislation to two years (in the case of certified money bills to one month). The House had lost its right of veto. And this had been brought about in circumstances that reflected badly on the House and drained the morale of the aristocracy dominating its membership.[13] This had been an absorbing political crisis, with popular feeling inflamed by the rhetoric of two general elections, fought on a 'peers versus people' theme. It echoed down through the decades, colouring much subsequent thinking in both political and popular circles about the Lords.

Initially Conservative peers were 'little disposed to accept the situation with good grace'.[14] Between 1911 and the outbreak of war in 1914, the upper House four times refused to pass bills brought to it from the Commons. Two of these were eventually enacted under Parliament Act procedures; these were the Government of Ireland Bill and the Established Church (Wales) Bill, and both were suspended as soon as they were given royal assent because of the outbreak of war. Thus the House prevented home rule being given to the whole of Ireland in 1912, an objective achieved ten tears later in a climate made even more dangerous and difficult by the delay. And disestablishment of the Anglican Church in Wales likewise had to await not only Parliament Act procedures but similar suspension until the end of the war – to the displeasure of Welsh nonconformists. On a third bill, dealing with licensing law in Scotland, agreement between the two Houses was reached following its reintroduction under Parliament Act terms in the 1913 session. The fourth Bill – for the abolition of plural voting – was introduced a year later and had failed to complete its Parliament Act obstacle course by the time war broke out. So it was abandoned and this reform had to wait over thirty years for its realisation. Looking back, the part played by the House of Lords in delaying these measures was not something from which the House could derive any real satisfaction.

In using that power it was not thought that the House was behaving unconstitutionally. On the contrary it could be argued that the very passage of the 1911 Act legitimised the use of the power that had been deliberately left with the Lords. But within a few years any such understanding was again to change. The subtleties of an unwritten constitution were once more to assert themselves, as it gradually became accepted that the upper House only had the right to ask the Commons to think again once or twice, or perhaps in special circumstances three times, but thereafter to give way to the will of the lower House rather than use the delaying power it still possessed. In this way the House of Lords acquiesced in the emergence of a de facto unicameral parliament.

Indeed, the House took pride in its role as a chamber of influence rather than one of power. In so doing it made itself unthreatening to both the Commons and the government. It became a political convenience. But it remained an anomaly. And sooner or later, however docile the House might be, some government would get round to altering the place. That eventually happened under New Labour in 1999.

Notes

1 P. Ashdown, *The Ashdown Diaries*, vol. 2 (London, Allen Lane, 2001), p. 446.
2 D. Oliver, *Constitutional Reform in the UK* (Oxford University Press, 2003), p. 3.
3 A. King, *Does the UK Still Have a Constitution?* (London, Sweet & Maxwell, 2001).
4 P. Hennessy, *Whitehall* (London, Secker & Warburg, 1989), p. 306.
5 C. C. Weston, *English Constitutional Theory and the House of Lords 1556–1832* (London, Routledge, 1965).
6 M. W. Cahill, 'The Scottish Peerage and the House of Lords in the Late Eighteenth Century', in C. Jones and D. L. Jones (eds), *Peers, Politics and Power* (London, Hambledon Press, 1968).
7 D. Judge, *Political Institutions in the UK* (Oxford University Press, 2005).
8 First Special Report, Joint Committee on Conventions, HL 189, HC 1151, 2005–06.
9 J. S. Mill, *Representative Government* (London, J. M. Dent, Everyman edition, 1962), p. 324.
10 C. C. Weston, 'Salisbury and the Lords, 1868–1895', in Jones and Jones (eds), *Peers*.
11 P. A. Bromhead, *The House of Lords and Contemporary Politics 1911–1957* (London, Routledge, 1958), p. 135.
12 R. Jenkins, *Mr Balfour's Poodle* (London, Heinemann, 1954).
13 A. Adonis, *Making Aristocracy Work* (Oxford, Clarendon Press, 1993).
14 Bromhead, *The House of Lords*, p. 137.

2

The House of Lords in the twentieth century

When the Parliament Act was passed in 1911 no one could have imagined that the hereditary peerage would survive as the predominant component of the second chamber until the end of the century. The expectation that major reform of the House of Lords would soon occur was widespread, encouraged and encapsulated in the oft-quoted preamble to the 1911 Act: 'whereas it is intended to substitute for the House of Lords as it at present exists a Second Chamber constituted on a popular instead of hereditary basis, but such substitution cannot be immediately brought into operation'. It seemed that the political will fundamentally to reform the House was strong, and certainly proposals for reform, some of them carrying widespread support, abounded. But no such reform took place until the closing year of the century. And even then the 1999 House of Lords Act was a rather timid measure which still failed to eliminate the hereditary principle from the membership of the House.

The long delay in bringing even to modest fruition the aspiration of 1911 is one of the puzzles of the twentieth century. But though no major reform did take place, a great deal of gradual change and adjustment occured. The House at the end of the twentieth century was in practice a totally different institution to what it had been at the commencement of the century. It is the purpose of this Chapter to elucidate both the failure to bring about fundamental reform, of the kind envisaged in the preamble to the Parliament Act, while also explaining the changes that transformed the House from being a leisurely aristocratic chamber of power to a much more hard working chamber of influence, where aristocracy was leavened with meritocracy.

These two points are of course linked. One of the reasons for the survival of hereditary peers as the preponderant group in terms of formal membership of the House until the close of the century was the capacity peers demonstrated to adapt, and to absorb changes necessary to make their part of parliament acceptable within the evolving British political system. In effect the House reinvented itself. From being a chamber of veto it became a chamber of scrutiny. From being a chamber of power, the House settled for being a chamber of influence. From being a chamber prepared to contest the will of the Commons, the Lords became a chamber more intent on complementing the work of the elected House. From being a chamber dominated by landed interests the House became representative of considerable diversity in professional, public and business life. From being a chamber generally conducting business in a leisurely and even haphazard manner the House became hard working with its business much more tightly organised.

But the survival of the House also depended on the fact that for different reasons the leadership of the major parties never had sufficient motive after 1911 to undertake fundamental reform. No government suffered the obduracy of the House as the Liberal Government did leading up to the political crisis of 1909–11. After the first world war the House settled for cooperation rather than confrontation with the Commons. And after the second world war, when another government of the political left came to power with a substantial majority, the House far from contesting the will of the Attlee cabinet sought instead to secure its reputation as a chamber of revision. The heavy programme of legislation emanating from ministers seeking to remodel the role of the state even as post-war reconstruction took place was given more detailed and systematic scrutiny by the House than any previous government's legislative offerings. This growing enhancement of the scrutiny function has continued since.

Of course no government of the left could ignore the curious, undemocratic and seemingly archaic nature of the second chamber. Sentiment within the Labour Party demanded that its leaders endorse a policy of fundamental reform or outright abolition of the House. But for most of the time the practical reality was that Labour ministers, like their Conservative counterparts, recognised the value of a diligent and generally docile revising chamber. When its docility became less evident, the unreformed House could always be threatened, reminded of its lack of legitimacy, and thereby warned of the possible consequences of any sustained intransigence towards government wishes. This would usually have the desired effect of inducing caution and a realistic degree of meekness on the part of peers.

From time to time throughout the century discussions about reform took place and proposals for change were placed on the political agenda. But when this happened one consequence was invariably to remind party leaders how difficult the process of carrying reform was likely to be. Divisions within parties were as great as division between parties.

Party leaders were understandably wary of investing time and effort in solving a problem that was not pressing and could so easily exacerbate tensions within their party ranks. And should time consuming legislation on reform be given priority in a busy parliamentary schedule? If the House of Lords remained from a constitutional point of view a problem, any proposed solutions appeared even more problematic.

The politics of reform never seemed quite right. Labour wanted to avoid doing anything that would enhance the prestige of a basically undemocratic House, preferring to keep its composition quaint if not ridiculous – rather than make it more legitimate. Conservatives were fearful that any fundamental reform initiated by their party could backfire on them, possibly by giving Labour an excuse to neuter or remove the House. In any case all governments tend to be highly ambivalent about parliamentary reform. From a ministerial point of view making either House more effective as a chamber of scrutiny, probing into government policies or the working of the executive, can be expected to take second place to the attempt to make parliament a more efficient machine at processing legislation and one that enables ministers to parade government achievements to better effect.

All this contrasts with the position before 1911. Then there had been a necessity to tackle the second chamber question. A political crisis had erupted over the House of Lords; two general elections were fought and the King's Government could not be carried on unless the problem of the House was addressed. There was an over-riding practical political imperative to confront the constitutional question. This was made inescapable because of the use by the House of its legal power to veto government legislation. But subsequently the House evolved, with understandings, practices and conventions being formulated, which gradually and wholly altered the constitutional understanding of the role of the second chamber.

These are the themes elucidated in this Chapter, which examines both how the House changed, and also considers a selection of the schemes put forward at various times for major reform of the second chamber. First we consider how the House came to terms with the loss of power.

Adjusting to the loss of power

As already indicated, the 1911 Parliament Act brought the curtain down on a dramatic political crisis that had engulfed parliament and the country. Thereafter came war, and throughout the inter-war period the Conservative Party generally dominated government; until 1945 Labour was only in office briefly as a minority government or as a junior partner in a coalition or national government. So their legislative ambitions had to be kept modest, and this being so, the Lords found little they wished to frustrate. Furthermore, an immense amount of time and energy had been expended on the House in the first two decades of the century. With no obviously agreed reform in view, why reopen the question, especially as the House had ceased to be troublesome? Even the Labour Party, which had viewed the Parliament Act with suspicion because it confirmed the power of the existing unreformed and Conservative dominated House, showed little interest in the place. Ostensibly its preferred policy was outright abolition, leaving parliament as a unicameral body, but so long as the House was no real impediment, then why devote precious time and energy to its removal?

When Labour first came to power with a decisive overall majority (a very decisive one of 147) in 1945, the Attlee Government faced a huge agenda of national reconstruction as well as social welfare reform. The Lords could have been a serious obstacle if the House had chosen to flex its muscles and use the power it still retained under the Parliament Act. It was overwhelmingly Conservative in composition; the Labour peers in 1945 numbered only sixteen in a House of over 700.[1] Had the Conservatives chosen to behave towards this radical government as they behaved towards the 1906 Liberal Government, then swift reprisals would no doubt have been taken. But the Conservatives were no longer in the mood for such foolishness. Instead they chose the path of discretion. In the 1945 King's Speech debate their leader in the House, Lord Cranborne (later the fifth Marquis of Salisbury), said: 'I believe it would be constitutionally wrong, when the country has so recently expressed its views, for this House to oppose proposals which have definitely been put before the electorate'.[2] Thus he enunciated the so-called 'Salisbury' doctrine whereby the House refrained from voting against the second reading of legislation clearly foreshadowed in the Labour manifesto. It was accepted that this also covered 'wrecking' amendments that might destroy or alter such bills beyond recognition. As Walters observes, this 'code of conduct' never achieved the 'status of a standing order of the House', but it became widely recognised as a necessary convention.[3]

The Conservatives in the House chose to be a constructive opposition, using the capacity of the second chamber to revise with diligence and without partisanship the lengthy bills brought up from the Commons. In his memoirs Attlee paid tribute to the House of Lords, saying it 'fulfilled a useful role as a debating forum and a revising chamber'.[4] But with the nationalisation of iron and steel looming, the government realised there may be difficulty. In any case the whole doctrine of the mandate wore thin towards the end of a parliament as governments inevitably feel the need to react to events not anticipated at the time of the election. It remained a possibility that in the last two years of the life of a Labour Government the minds of peers might take a different direction. Especially if the government were to face a public loss of support, Conservative peers might perhaps try to hasten it into electoral oblivion by denying it the right to legislate as the parliament drew to a close. Accordingly the government introduced the Parliament Bill of 1947, a limited measure which did no more than amend the 1911 Act so as to cut the delaying power of the House from two years to one. Conservative peers carried a reasoned amendment at second reading calling for talks on reform of the House. A conference of party leaders took place in 1948, which saw a substantial measure of agreement on a range of matters, but on the question of power the two sides could not agree.[5] Even here however, ostensibly, the difference was narrow, a mere matter of three months in the delaying power. But behind this divergence there lurked a more fundamental difference. Was a second chamber really entitled to be a regular and significant player in the exercise of parliamentary power across the whole range of legislation? Conservatives clearly felt that if its composition was to be altered then the pay-off for agreeing to this had to be a real share once more in parliamentary power. Labour were of course unwilling to accept a second chamber that retained power while remaining undemocratic, and there was no desire to make it democratic lest it became a rival to the Commons.

Given this breakdown in inter-party talks, the Labour Government went ahead with their Parliament Bill. Because of Conservative opposition, this had to be enacted under the terms of the 1911 Parliament Act, becoming thereby the first Act to be passed this way since before the first world war. In order to speed its passage to the statute book a special short parliamentary session was devised in 1948, so that the requirement that the Bill be reintroduced in three sessions was complied with. In 1949 the Act became law. It might have been used in order to secure the passage of the bill nationalising iron and steel, but the Labour Government had lost its own momentum on this issue, and agreed to Conservative demands that ensured the vesting date for nationalisation lay beyond the next general election. Labour almost lost its majority in 1950, and did do so in the election of the following year. The House of Lords remained an hereditary body, still with significant powers, but powers that it now knew could only be used with the greatest restraint.

The question of power arose only rarely until the 1970s. Under the Conservative Governments of 1951 to 1964 there were at times differences of view between the Houses, but those that were most notable were in areas of policy where the Conservative Party itself was divided, and where ministers had no wish to use Parliament Act procedures to enforce the will of the Commons. Notable was the abolition of the death penalty. In 1948 MPs had voted for abolition on a free vote on a clause in the Criminal Justice Bill, but when the Lords voted against abolition, the government let the matter drop because senior ministers were much divided on the matter.[6] In 1956 the Commons passed a private member's bill to abolish the death penalty, which was rejected by the Lords. But the Conservative Party was split on the issue and the government had no collective wish to force the Bill, introduced by a Labour MP, onto the statute book. After Labour returned to power in 1964 there were occasions when the House may have used its remaining power. In 1967 Lord Carrington, then leader of the Conservative peers, had suggested that the formal power of the House could only be used once because when this happened the government of the day would remove it.[7] Janet Morgan quotes Lord Salisbury as saying that Conservative peers were constantly being told we had 'only one shot in our locker'; eventually Lord Carrington agreed that the party should be 'allowed to let off steam' on the Southern Rhodesia Sanctions Order 1968.[8] Because the Parliament Acts only dealt with primary legislation, the House retained a veto over all statutory instruments, so the effect of this rejection was potentially fatal to the Order concerned. But the action was more a demonstration by Conservative peers, and in the event one that damaged their reputation because their victory in the division lobby was very narrow, and their party leaders made clear that as soon as the Order was re-laid, they would allow it through. One consequence of this action was to further undermine the chances of an agreed reform taking place along the lines considered by an all-party committee established by the Wilson Government in 1968 (see below, pp. 37–40). However the following year the Conservatives showed every sign of resisting the House of Commons (Redistribution of Seats) Bill to the uttermost of their capacity. But the government avoided this battle by dropping the Bill, having devised another way of securing its objective, the postponement of boundary revisions, until after the 1970 election.[9]

By the early 1970s therefore it seemed clear that the Lords had almost accepted as a new constitutional convention that the House ought not to use its remaining powers to the point of exhaustion. Asking the Commons (and government) to 'think again', possibly doing this several times, may still be acceptable, but delaying a bill so as to oblige the use of the Parliament Acts was no longer truly constitutional, just as using the power of the House to veto subordinate legislation would be outside the understanding of the constitution that had developed.

However, when Labour returned to office in 1974, matters became rather more opaque, in part because the whole parliamentary context was so fraught. The February 1974 election saw Labour emerge as the largest single party but without an overall majority. In October a wafer-thin majority was secured, but by April 1976 the toll of death and by-election defeat put Labour back into a minority in the Commons. Unlike previous Labour governments with very low majorities, this government did not seek to moderate or abate in any way its legislative programme. Several of its bills provoked severe controversy, and only secured their Commons passage by the narrowest of margins. This of course altered very seriously the context in which the House of Lords did its work. For, if the upper House sent bills back to the Commons with amendments that the government resisted, then ministers had to secure a Commons majority for their removal and if this proved impossible the amendments would stand. This happened when wrecking amendments were made both to the Housing Finance Bill of 1975, and then to the Dock Work Regulation Bill of 1976.

On two bills however peers did dig their heels in despite the government maintaining its Commons majority. First was the Trade Union and Labour Relations (Amendment) Bill, introduced in the 1974–75 session, but without an agreed version of the Bill emerging by the end of the session. It was reintroduced the following session certified by the Speaker under Parliament Act procedures, but before these ran their course a compromise was reached, partly because the government changed its mind about part of the Bill. Then in 1976 the Aerospace and Shipbuilding Industries Bill was delayed and reintroduced the following session, but in this case it ran into procedural problems and the government eventually decided to compromise by dropping ship-repairing from the Bill.[10]

The Parliament Acts have never applied to private bills, which therefore leaves the House of Lords with an absolute veto on such bills, promoted by private bodies outside of parliament, (and increasingly rare because public acts of parliament cover the areas which hitherto were dealt with by private bills). In 1976 the Docks and Harbour Board promoted a private bill to take into public ownership the highly successful but privately owned Felixstowe dock, a bill strongly backed by the government. Peers voted it down at second reading, thus killing the measure, thereby frustrating the will of the Commons and the government.

But apart from these examples the House acted with considerable restraint in these fraught years.[11] On almost every occasion when the Commons returned bills with Lords amendments reversed, peers quickly submitted. The House continued with its diligent work of normal legislative revision, taking care to apply itself to this even at times of great inconvenience, notably when the bulk of government legislation arrived from the Commons very late in the session. Far from exploiting the government's weak position, the House was generally a convenience to government in making minor and agreed adjustments to its legislation.

Curiously the 1949 Parliament Act was first used to enact a bill by a Conservative government in 1991. This was the War Crimes Act. It was not a manifesto bill, and nor was it one on which the government imposed a whip. The purpose of the bill was retrospectively to alter the law to allow for the prosecution of individuals for war crimes committed in German-held territory during the second world war. The bill was a government bill that received strong support in the House of Commons, but was twice rejected by the House of Lords. The use of the Parliament Act was perfectly straightforward, though surprising to many because it indicated a willingness on the part of the Conservative Party leadership to ignore the opinion of the House of Lords even on a matter where principle and conscience were so heavily engaged.

However, after Labour returned to power in 1997, the Parliament Act was used three times, but again two of these were on matters passed on a free vote by the Commons, and the other was a special case, the European Parliamentary Elections Bill. This latter bill was introduced in Labour's first session in 1997, to alter the electoral system used for elections to the European Parliament in line with Labour's 1997 manifesto commitment: 'We have long supported a proportional voting system for election to the European Parliament'. The argument between the two Houses was not over the principle of changing from the first-past-the-post system, but over the kind of proportional system to be used. The government opted for a closed party list system; the House of Lords amended the Bill to insert an open list system. The Lords repeatedly voted for an open list system, and eventually after the Bill had shuffled back and forward four times between the Houses without any significant compromise, it was lost at the end of the session, November 1998.

Because the next European elections were due to be held in June 1999, it was essential that any legislation altering the system be enacted by mid-January. The government reintroduced the same Bill very early in the new session – it completed all its Commons stages on 2 December 1998. It was debated at second reading in the Lords on 15 December, with peers aware that the quickest way to place the Bill on the statute book was for them to reject it outright. If it went forward to a committee stage the mid-January deadline would be missed. The debate took place against the background of heightened tensions caused by the inclusion in the Queen's Speech of a bill to remove hereditary peers from the House of Lords. Government spokesmen emphasised that the government would have won all five votes that had taken place in the House rejecting the government's preferred electoral system if hereditary peers had not been voting. The House duly rejected the Bill by 167 votes to 73, and it thereupon went forward immediately for royal assent.

There were several factors relating to this Bill, consideration of which helps to illuminate the use of Parliament Act procedures. First it was a manifesto bill, but the manifesto had said nothing about the kind of proportional electoral system that would be used. Was this therefore a bill covered by the Salisbury doctrine? In the final debate on the European Elections Bill, Lord Jenkins of Hillhead argued that it would be ridiculous to say that the Leader of the Opposition could impose the 'shape' of a manifesto bill, and clearly in his mind this is what the Conservatives were doing by insisting on an amendment substituting an open list for a closed list system.[12] Others however took a contrary view arguing that the commitment was simply to a proportional electoral system; the former cabinet minister Lord Shore of Stepney said it was 'self-evident that we have not breached the Salisbury convention'.[13] The truth of the matter is that the Salisbury convention lacks clarity except in relation to votes at second reading because the definition of a 'wrecking' amendment is always to some degree debatable.

But that leads to a further point illuminated by this Bill, namely what right has the House of Lords to persist in resisting the clearly expressed will of the Commons? Lord Weatherill, former Speaker of the Commons and convenor of the crossbench peers in the Lords, said that he was passionately against a closed list system and voted against the government to begin with, but later he abstained, and then finally he voted with the government arguing that the House of Lords should not 'seek to frustrate the will of the elected House'. Others, such as Lord Graham of Edmonton, a former Labour whip in the Commons, and Lord Garel-Jones, a former Conservative whip, took similar views, the former declaring: 'It is the right of this House to insist upon its views once but not twice'.[14] Others however took the view that the House had every right to stick to its view precisely because the Parliament Act was available to ensure that at the end of the day it was the will of the Commons that would prevail. This highlighted different understandings of the constitutional position that had arisen. Does the existence of the Parliament Act and the removal of a House of Lords absolute veto mean that peers should accept the junior or subordinate status of their House as far as legislation is concerned? Has it by convention only got the right to ask the Commons to reconsider once or twice? Or does the existence of the

Parliament Act protect the members of the Lords from having to deny themselves the right to sustain their own opinions when strongly held, by ensuring that the will of the elected House can prevail when there is continuing disagreement between the two?

A third point illustrated by the saga on this Bill was the effect of division within the governing party. It was clear from debates and votes in the Commons that many Labour MPs were unhappy with the choice of a closed list electoral system. Almost all Labour backbenchers who spoke at any stage on the Bill declined to support the government – a point much emphasised in Lords debates. Furthermore, the commitment to introduce proportional representation for Euro elections had been part of the agreement on constitutional reform made between the Labour and Liberal Democrat Parties before the 1997 election, known as the Cook–Maclennan pact after its two principal authors.[15] Many Labour MPs were unenthusiastic about the pact, just as many Liberal Democrats were unenthusiastic about the closed list system. Lord Russell, a prominent Liberal Democrat, had initially voted for the open list system, and clearly saw this as a matter of principle. But in the final Lords debate at the end of the 1997–98 session, when it was clear that continued insistence on this would lead to the loss of the Bill, he argued that if the closed list system represented a defeat for democracy, the loss of the Bill would represent an even greater defeat. Accordingly he and other Liberal Democrats fell in with the government. From the government point of view the dearth of vocal support from their backbenchers might have been embarrassing, but what really mattered was their Commons majority, and this remained firm.

Finally it is worth raising the question on this Bill as to whether a better way could be found of resolving disputes between the two Houses. At present whenever there is a disagreement one House sends a bill back to the other with a message expressing a reason for the view that has been taken. These are typically cryptic and brief. Thus on the European Elections Bill the Commons message to the Lords simply asked the House not to persist with the amendment because 'it would result in a voting system that was undesirable'. The Lords reason for its persistence was expressed thus: 'Because electors should be able to vote for the individual candidate of their choice'. Of course, members of both Houses can read the speeches made, but it is questionable whether this facilitates the seeking of common ground.

The context within which peers needed to think about the use of the remaining legal powers of the House was altered by the 1999 House of Lords Act, which ejected the great bulk of the peers by succession. At a practical level this wiped out the Conservative Party's preponderant position in the House, where very soon a rough parity in numerical strength between the two major parties prevailed, with both having to reckon with a substantial number of crossbenchers and a significant group of Liberal Democrat peers. It could also be argued that the composition of the House was now the result of a Labour reform, and that this fact gave the House a greater legitimacy than when its membership remained the rather haphazard outcome of history, a view given some support by the statement made by Baroness Jay, Leader of the House: 'I have no hesitation in asserting that the transitional chamber will be more legitimate than that we have today', a view she reiterated a year later after the hereditary peers had gone, saying: 'this House without the majority of hereditary peers is more legitimate'.[16] The House appeared to become more assertive, though it is also fair to point out that a gradual growth in assertiveness had been a characteristic of the House ever since the arrival of significant numbers of life peers in the 1960s.

The first time Parliament Act procedures were used in this new context was in order to pass the Sexual Offences Amendment Act, 2000. The basic purpose of this Bill was to equalise the age of consent for homosexual and heterosexual acts, while also strengthening protection for young people from abuse by someone in a position of trust. In the 1997–98 session the Lords had rejected an amendment to the Crime and Disorder Bill which would have brought about equality on the age of consent. The government did not wish to jeopardise that Bill for the sake of this amendment so let the matter drop, but returned to it the following session with a separate Bill. This passed the Commons but was defeated at second reading in the Lords on an amendment moved by the former Conservative Leader of the House, Baroness Young. The government brought the Bill back in the following session, and peers gave it an unopposed second reading on 11 April 2000, but in committee a series of amendments were made, the effect of which was to allow homosexual acts at sixteen, but keep the age for buggery at eighteen for both males and females. The government thereupon announced it would not be taking the Bill back to the Commons for further consideration, but would rely on the Parliament Acts to secure its passage. On the final day of the 1999–2000 session the Speaker announced that in view of the failure of the Lords to pass the Bill in the form wanted by the Commons, he was certifying it under Parliament Act procedures, whereupon it received royal assent on 30 November 2000.

The final use of the Parliament Act also occurred on another bill that had been the subject of free votes in the Commons, the infamous Hunting Bill, the purpose of which was to ban hunting for wild animals with dogs, an issue that consumed inordinate amounts of parliamentary time. In 1997 the Labour manifesto had promised a 'free vote in Parliament on whether hunting with hounds should be banned by legislation'. A private member's bill in the first session had made clear that an overwhelming majority in favour of a ban existed in the Commons. But equally it was clear that the government was divided on the matter, with some senior ministers very much preferring some form of regulation rather than an outright ban. In the 2000–01 session the government introduced a bill containing three different options. The Commons voted overwhelmingly for an outright ban, and decisively rejected self-regulation, but the Lords did the opposite, voting overwhelmingly for self-regulation. The 2001 election then intervened.

In the new parliament opinion was again tested, this time by the government initiating two days of debate, which confirmed that MPs were still overwhelmingly in favour of a ban, though peers voted for a licensing system (March 18–19 2002). Unusually the minister responsible then held public evidence-taking hearings at Westminster before producing a bill, which was then amended against the government's wishes at report stage to introduce an outright ban, and did not clear the Commons until July. When the Lords debated the Hunting Bill at second reading on 16 September 2003, of the sixty-four peers who spoke only ten supported it. Peers then commenced committee stage, with some intent on amending the Bill to restore the regulation system the government itself had favoured before the report stage ambush in the Commons. But the Lords minister in charge, Lord Whitty, announced that no amendments would be accepted and that the Bill must be returned to the Commons in exactly the same form as it had emerged from that House. On the one hand this simply recognised the political reality that the Commons would overturn any amendments made by the Lords. On the other hand it appeared a high-handed denial to the Lords of its legitimate legislative role, namely to at least have opportunity to put forward amendments to legislation. The Bill fell, but was reintroduced in the new session, though not until September 2004. MPs voted 356 to 166 for the identical Bill to that which had left their House the previous summer. But MPs then accepted a proposal to delay the implementation of the total ban until the end of July 2006.

In order to pass a bill using Parliament Act procedures, the bill concerned must be in the same form in the second session when it is presented to the Lords as it was in the first session, or it must contain only such changes as have been agreed between the two Houses. So the Lords was invited to agree the change postponing implementation until after the following election, but peers declined to do this, preferring what was described as the 'kamikaze' option of early implementation. This meant that the government had to use the Parliament Act to pass the Bill in a different form from that which MPs had most recently supported, namely an early implementation date. The ban took effect in February 2005.

The whole saga in relation to hunting did not reflect well on parliament. An immense amount of time was spent debating the issue. Far from resulting in a meeting of minds, the tactics employed seemed to inflame suspicion and mistrust between the various protagonist groups within parliament. Nor did parliamentary debate achieve much in relation to outside opinion. Far from legitimising the outcome, or mobilising consent among the public, the consequence of parliamentary debate seemed to be to fuel distrust and hostility, especially among those who felt most affected by the ban on fox hunting. Subsequent to the implementation of the ban, various stratagems were used by active huntsfolk to continue hunting while evading or avoiding prosecution under the new law.

A constitutional footnote to the hunting ban was made when pro-hunting groups challenged the use of the 1949 Parliament Act in the courts, arguing that the 1949 Act could not have been validly enacted without the consent of the House of Lords, which had not been given in that the latter Act had been passed using the 1911 Parliament Act procedures. This was not an argument that had commended itself widely to constitutional experts and it was no surprise when the courts rejected it, though the Court of Appeal did warn that there were limits to the scope of change that could be made to the House of Lords against its will under Parliament Act procedures.[17]

In general terms the frequency of government defeat, and the number of occasions on which the Lords sent a bill back to the Commons more than once (engaging in 'ping-pong') increased. It was not surprising that the nature of the so-called Salisbury convention was called into question. This had after all been first propounded in an utterly different parliamentary context to that which now prevailed. And because it had never been precisely formulated, there was uncertainty over the extent of its reach and indeed whether it remained valid at all.[18] The leader of the Liberal Democrat peers, Lord McNally, speaking in the Queen's Speech debate after the 2005 election, to the consternation of ministers said: 'to resurrect a sixty year old convention that was offered by a Conservative dominated hereditary House to a Labour Government with forty-eight per cent of the vote and then to say that that should still apply to a Labour Party that is now the largest Party in this House, but is a government with thirty-six per cent of the vote is stretching the limits of the convention'.[19]

Partly as a response to this the government set up a joint select committee in 2006 to consider how to 'codify the conventions' concerned with the relationship between the two Houses. These were specified as: the Salisbury–Addison doctrine regarding manifesto bills; the practice of the House in not voting down subordinate legislation; the acceptance that the government of the day was always entitled to get its business in reasonable time; and practices concerned with the exchange of amendments ('ping-pong'). Curiously no one seriously alleged that any of these so-called 'conventions' had been broken, but ministers seemed concerned that they might be, or at least concerned to warn the House against developing further the more assertive role it appeared to have adopted since the 1999 reform. Whether or not it is actually prudent or even possible to codify conventions is a moot point. The price of allegedly greater precision may be a loss of flexibility beneficial to all parties at times, not least the government, and possibly a growing political pressure to push behaviour to the boundaries of what is technically allowed rather then keep to reasonable, sensible and workable norms.

Arguably what stands out most in this whole discussion about the power of the House is the restraint with which power has been used. The 1911 Parliament Act firmly relegated the Lords to a junior status. The House has never in the period since showed any sign of seriously challenging the primacy of the Commons. It has however become a more active and assertive chamber in scrutinising legislation and the executive under all governments. Governments appear to have become increasingly resentful of a House which takes its parliamentary role sufficiently seriously to cause it to stick to its guns when in dispute with ministers, a point returned to in the concluding Chapter. This is a matter that relates to the wider political culture within which the work of parliament as a whole has to be considered.

Reforms and attempted reforms

Meanwhile, having considered how the House has adapted in terms of the exercise of power, we turn now to examine those reforms which have taken place and brought adjustments making the House less objectionable to contemporary values, despite the retention of its hereditary membership. These changes were concentrated in the Conservative period of office from 1951 to 1964, though all had been foreshadowed in earlier discussions. For example, during the all-party talks in 1948 there had been agreement in principle on the following points: that life peerages should be introduced; that women should sit in the House; that hereditary peers should be free not to take up their seats (and in particular should therefore be free to sit as MPs); that expenses should be payable for attendance; and that peers should have the opportunity to withdraw from the House if old age, infirmity or disinclination rendered them unable to take part in its business. This set an agenda for practical reform, and although there was no deliberate and systematic effort to implement these changes, all these points were in fact addressed in a piecemeal and haphazard manner during the Conservative period in office from 1951 to 1964. Agreement could not however be reached on the question of power, and in the absence of that, Labour remained unwilling to consider even minor changes in composition, for example to allow those MPs who inherited peerages to remain in the Commons. Among these was the second Viscount Hailsham, who as Quintin Hogg had made clear his desire to remain in the Commons (to which he had been elected in 1939). His personal appeal to Attlee as prime minister to allow hereditary peers to renounce their peerages and remain in the Commons went unheeded and he was transported reluctantly to the Lords on inheriting his viscountcy in 1950.[20]

Reimbursement of travel expenses had been introduced in 1946, but this was limited to rail travel and initially only available to those who attended over one-third of the sittings of the House. Gradually these rules were relaxed, car travel expenses were allowed in 1961 and the assiduity rule was abolished in 1972. Travel costs to attend the House or to take part in parliamentary business elsewhere gradually became payable in full. Payment of expenses was introduced in 1956, at the rate of three guineas (£3.15) per day. Remuneration of expenses thereafter steadily increased (see below, p. 78). While not salaried it is fair to say the payment of expenses has become sufficiently generous to allow peers who want to contribute to the work of the House to receive a very adequate reimbursement of their expenses, a far cry from the 1950s when some Labour peers found it very difficult to attend because of the costs involved.[21]

A further minor reform was the introduction of leave of absence arrangements in 1957 by standing order of the House. This simply enabled peers who so wished to seek a decent indemnity for their non-attendance. They could apply for leave of absence, and so appease their conscience if it were to be troubled by the peremptory demands of the writ of summons (in which Her Majesty commanded them 'waiving all excuses' to attend the House). While on leave they were 'expected' not to attend, but leave could be cancelled at twenty-eight days notice. To begin with a good deal of fuss was made about leave of absence, and up to one-third of the total membership was on leave at any one time. This offered a kind of cosmetic to cover the embarrassment the House occasionally suffered when rare attenders appeared in large numbers to take part in particular divisions (as had happened in 1956 when the House voted to keep the death penalty). But growing awareness of the ineffectiveness of the leave of absence arrangements, together with the increased desire on the part of the respective party whips to keep maximum numbers available for crucial divisions, resulted in declining numbers taking leave. Before the expulsion of most hereditary peers in 1999 only just over sixty peers (some 5 per cent of the House) were on leave of absence. In 2006 only around a dozen peers were on leave.

Much more significant was the introduction in 1957 of the Life Peerages Bill. Though this was preceded by talks between government ministers and Labour leaders, these once again did not lead to sufficient consensus to enable an agreed reform to be introduced. Labour remained very ambivalent about adjusting the composition of the House without also tackling its powers. Labour voted against the Bill at second reading, believing that its main purpose was to enhance the prestige of the House while leaving it otherwise fundamentally unreformed. From the Conservative point of view the Bill was desirable because it provided a means of adding to the working strength of the House without increasing its size for all time to come. The Labour opposition benches in the House had become so seriously depleted that the normal working of the chamber was endangered. Life peers quickly arrived to stave off collapse. As well as the Labour benches in the House, the crossbench numbers also began their steady expansion. Though hereditary peers outnumbered life peers until the ejection of the former in 1999, by the late 1970s life peers were collectively outperforming hereditary peers in terms of contributing to the overall work of the House.

Before 1958 the House was an exclusively male institution. Although very few women inherited peerages it had caused some surprise when in 1922 the Privileges Committee of the House had ruled against the admittance of Viscountess Rhondda on the grounds that no woman had ever sat in the House before, despite the fact that legislation passed in 1919 had enacted that 'a person shall not be disqualified by sex from the exercise of any public function'.[22] During debate on the Life Peerages Bill amendments were moved to exclude women, but these were comfortably defeated. Since 1958 a steady stream of women have entered the House as life peers, resulting in the House of Lords having among its active members at least as many women as does the House of Commons (see Chapter 3, Table 3.2, p. 57). The anomaly whereby women life peers could sit in the House, but women peers by succession could not, was removed as an incidental part of the 1963 Peerage Act.

This measure made provision for peers by succession to renounce their peerages. It was precipitated by the extraordinary case of Anthony Wedgwood Benn, then a youthful and ambitious Labour MP, who upon inheriting a viscountcy, and thereby being debarred from the Commons, determined to avoid incarceration in the Lords. For two years he fought his case, winning a by-election, then seeing an election court seat his defeated opponent in the Commons in his place! This forced the government's hand but as the constitutional conundrum was being considered it became steadily more apparent that there would soon be a vacancy for a new Conservative leader, and that some possible candidates for that post were entrapped in ermine from which they would welcome escape. The Bill was amended during its passage in the Lords to allow for immediate disclaiming rather than delaying this until the end of the current parliament (as originally stipulated). Tony Benn (as he later became known) disclaimed his peerage immediately, but he was rapidly followed by both Lord Hailsham (Quintin Hogg) and Lord Home (Sir Alec Douglas-Home), both contenders for the Conservative Party leadership later in 1963, with the latter actually assuming office as prime minister before completing the formalities of his release from the Lords and his re-entry to the Commons, courtesy of a by-election. Speculation that a sizable number of hereditary peers would disclaim was mistaken; in the event only sixteen individuals have done so, mostly soon after the Act was passed.

Other provisions increasing the number of hereditary peers in the House were tacked onto this measure. As already mentioned all thirty-one holders of Scottish peerages were admitted (instead of just sixteen elected peers as previously). And the anomaly whereby the few women who had inherited peerages in their own right were still excluded from the House was removed, resulting in eighteen women taking their seats for the first time.

A minor change that was never made was the proposal to adjust hereditary membership to allow for greater gender equality. Attempts to alter the law to provide for inheritance by the first born rather than primacy being given to males were made during the period of Conservative Government from 1979 to 1997.[23] At one level this seemed a small change in tune with the values of the time, and indeed one that would terminate gender discrimination in relation to the composition of parliament. On the other hand, peerages were not simply passports to membership of the House of Lords. Some of the arguments resisting change sounded strangely old-fashioned (about property rights inherent in peerages and so on) but none the less some of these had legal validity which it would be complicated to unravel. Again, within the Labour Party there was little real enthusiasm for changing the law in relation to hereditary peerages, when the party was committed to the removal of such peers altogether from the House. While the Macmillan-led Conservative Government made several changes (including the significant introduction of life peers), the Thatcher/Major period from 1979 to 1997 witnessed no change at all. Conservative interest in reform of the House vaporised, as if the party believed the best way of opposing Labour's developing arguments for constitutional reform was to totally ignore the subject.

Increased activity and expanded functions

The activity of the House has expanded greatly, especially in the second part of the twentieth century (see Chapter 4, Table 4.1, p. 86). This has mainly been the result of increased business rather than significant changes to the functions of the House. The latter have expanded, but the range of functions indicated in the Bryce report of 1918 constituted a very good summary for most of the century. These were as follows:

1 The examination and revision of Bills brought from the House of Commons, a function which has become more needed since, on many occasions during the last thirty years, the House of Commons has been obliged to act under special rules limiting debate.
2 The initiation of Bills dealing with subjects of a comparatively non-controversial character which may have an easier passage through the House of Commons if they have been fully discussed and put into a well-considered shape before being submitted to it.
3 The interposition of so much delay (and no more) in the passing of a Bill into law as may be needed to enable the opinion of the nation to be adequately expressed upon it. This would be especially needed as regards Bills which affect the fundamentals of the Constitution or introduce new principles of legislation, or which raise issues whereon the opinion of the country may appear to be almost equally divided.
4 Full and free discussion of large and important questions, such as those of foreign policy, at moments when the House of Commons may happen to be so much occupied that it cannot find sufficient time for them. Such discussions may often be all the more useful if conducted in an Assembly whose debates and divisions do not involve the fate of the Executive Government.[24]

In 1968 the Wilson Government produced a white paper on Lords reform, which endorsed the above functions, but added the consideration of secondary legislation (a major growth area since 1918); scrutiny of private bills (where the Lords did at least as much work as the Commons); and 'the scrutiny of the activities of the executive', referring to questions and debates, perhaps not covered in point (4) above. An appendix to the white paper suggested a reformed House could engage in more select committee work, perhaps including a range of joint select committees.[25] Though the proposals for reform of the House failed, this suggested development of the functions of the House took place, in particular the House developed in the 1970s a sizable select committee operation scrutinising European Community matters, and later science and technology, as well as an increasing range of ad hoc investigatory select committees. The development of select committee work was further endorsed by the Wakeham Commission in 2000.[26] In general terms it may be said that the House of Lords has itself taken the initiative to develop its functions, not in a competitive way to the Commons, but rather in a complementary way, seeking to fill gaps in the work of the lower House and to avoid duplicating the activities of the Commons.

The main task of the Lords has been revising legislation brought from the Commons, where major bills almost always commence their passage. The reference made by Bryce to the use of the guillotine in the Commons has become much more apt, with many bills now passing under tight programme motions. The work of the House is analysed in Chapter 4; here we may simply note that the Lords has taken an increasing share in the parliamentary task of scrutinising draft legislation, the quantity and complexity of which has grown so greatly since 1911. Though not a salaried House of full-time politicians (as the Commons has become) the House of Lords is now close to being a professional parliamentary chamber, with many of its members regarding their activity there as a full-time occupation.

Proposals for radical reform

From examining changes that have taken place in the House, we conclude this Chapter on twentieth-century developments by considering a selection of the proposals that have been put forward for major reform of the House but have not been implemented. No attempt can be made to chronicle the numerous schemes for reform of the House that have been publicly ventilated. Generally these have endorsed the existing functions of the House, and concentrated on composition. However, special attention is given both to the 1918 Bryce report, to the failed attempt to reform the House made by the Wilson-led Government of the late 1960s, and to the report of the Conservative Party review committee led by Lord Home in the 1970s.

At the start of the twentieth century there were two obvious difficulties about the House of Lords. One was its numerical size, the House having expanded from around 150 in 1700 to over 600 members. The second problem lay in the huge political imbalance in the House, which after the great Liberal triumph in the general election of 1906 meant the new government with a 357 majority in the Commons faced an upper House in which the opposition majority was still greater, at 391. The obvious way to arrest the seemingly inexorable growth in the size of the House was to introduce life peerages, a proposal that had been discussed almost throughout the previous century. Several attempts were made to introduce legislation to allow for the creation of life peers, perhaps in strictly limited numbers. But despite some powerful support none succeeded, until the 1958 Life Peerages Act.

In 1907 a Bill to reform the composition of the House led to the whole issue being referred to a select committee under the chairmanship of the former Liberal leader, Lord Roseberry, and including among its members a distinguished cast (the Archbishop of Canterbury, an ex-Speaker, and several leading Conservatives). The report made in 1908 boldly declared that: 'The Committee at an early stage in their proceedings came to the conclusion that, except in the case of peers of Blood Royal, it was undesirable that the possession of a peerage should of itself give the right to sit and vote in the House of Lords'.[27] This simple principle, accorded general acceptance before the first world war, was not acted upon for over ninety years.

The question of reform of the House in a more comprehensive way remained very much alive, however. There was every expectation that such reform would soon take place. In August 1917, as war drew towards a close, Viscount Bryce, formerly a Liberal cabinet member, a constitutional scholar and historian, was invited by the prime minister to chair a conference of over thirty leading men of the time on the future of the second chamber. Their report is a remarkable document which in its understanding of the role of a second chamber (it is quoted above in relation to the functions appropriate for a second chamber) has stood the test of time.[28] Though the Commission was unable to reach full agreement on how the second chamber should be composed, a clear majority favoured a mixed membership scheme with MPs playing a crucial role in indirect elections, and members of the second chamber serving twelve-year terms. It was the need to devise a chamber different in type and composition from the Commons, yet complementary to the lower House, which especially taxed the minds of Commission members.

Though the government set up a cabinet committee to consider reform in the light of the report, there was disagreement and nothing resulted. In 1922 a series of proposals were brought forward on behalf of the coalition government, providing for a tripartite House consisting of elements chosen by hereditary peers, by the crown and by the wider electorate. These were debated for four days, but the debate was then adjourned. Another attempt was made when the Conservative Government published proposals in 1927 for a 350-strong House, some nominated and some elected hereditary members, all serving twelve-year terms renewable by thirds. In 1933 the fourth Marquess of Salisbury brought forward a private member's bill roughly based on the above ideas, but also providing for the restoration of the pre-1911 powers of the House.[29]

All these schemes involved not only retaining a hereditary element in the House, but also retaining its Conservative majority. It was not surprising that outside of the Conservative Party such proposals attracted no significant support. And even within the Conservative Party the leadership had no interest in restoring pre-1911 powers to the House. The wider political context saw the franchise finally extended to all adult citizens, and political power clearly drawn from the electorate and therefore focused on the Commons. After Lord Curzon's failure to attain the Conservative Party leadership in 1923, it was recognised that changed times meant no government could in future be led from the House of Lords.

The most serious attempt at reform was that made by the Labour Government in 1968/69. A bill, the Parliament (No. 2) Bill, was introduced but eventually floundered during its Commons committee stage. Had it been enacted the hereditary element would have been all but entirely eliminated by the time Tony Blair reached Downing Street in 1997. But that was not to be, and the frustration and difficulties the Bill brought in its wake induced great caution throughout the next thirty years in relation to Lords reform. It was a seminal episode in relation to further thinking about the House, and deserves some attention here.

When Labour returned to power in 1964 it found a House of Lords that was very different from the chamber it had last faced when in office thirteen years before. The arrival of life peers had already considerably strengthened the Labour benches. Furthermore, the illiberal attitude of the House had changed greatly. But of course the second chamber remained overwhelmingly hereditary and overwhelmingly Conservative. It may have quickly shown itself useful to the new Labour Government through its capacity to revise the detail of legislation brought to it from the Commons, and to do so even when the principle of that legislation was unwelcome to the great majority of peers. But though the possibility that the House would use its powers to derail Labour's programme

appeared less likely than ever, that possibility still had to be allowed for –
so long as the House remained unreformed. Furthermore, if Labour was
a genuinely reforming government, modernising the country for whose
stewardship it held responsibility, then surely alongside the civil service,
local government and the other great institutions of state, the House of
Lords demanded some attention.

Peers themselves realised reform was again appearing on the agenda
of government. In 1967 during a debate on reform the deputy leader of
the Conservatives, Lord Harlech, conceded that 'the built-in majority for
the Conservative party . . . is . . . in this present day and age not really
a rational basis on which to run a second chamber'. He went on to say
that he thought the hereditary peers should be limited to say fifty or
seventy-five, not chosen by election but according to their frequency of
attendance.[30] It was little surprise when in the Queen's Speech the following November the government announced its intention to set up an
all-party committee to discuss reform, and to bring in a bill later in the
session 'to reduce the powers of the House of Lords and to eliminate its
hereditary basis'. The agenda was set for discussion of both powers and
of composition.[31]

The all-party committee quickly got to work, and found as expected a
large area of common ground. Labour compromised on accepting a six-
month delaying power, but measured from the date of disagreement,
which in practice represented little change from the existing twelve
months from the date of the Commons second reading. The Conservatives
accepted the notion of a two-tier House, consisting of voting and non-
voting peers, the latter including most of the existing hereditary peers,
whose right to sit in the House would remain until they died but not be
passed to their heirs.

The peculiar episode in which Conservative peers voted down the
Order maintaining sanctions against the then rebel colony of Southern
Rhodesia took place in June 1968. This gave the prime minister, Harold
Wilson, the excuse to break off the all-party talks, which had in any case
by this time run into the ground. Within Labour ranks many MPs pressed
for immediate action to remove the remaining powers of the House, or
to abolish it altogether. The result was that the two parties stood apart
when the detailed scheme for reform was introduced later in the year.
Seeds of dissension sufficient to sink the proposals simply through lack
of adequate all-party support had already been sown.

The white paper was published however at the start of the new
session in November and debated in both Houses.[32] In the Lords the proposals were greeted with near enthusiasm, with peers voting 251 to 56
in support. But in the Commons there was no enthusiasm, and indeed

severe pockets of hostility. A substantial number of Labour MPs and a majority of Conservatives who voted were opposed. Many within the Labour Party were far from pleased at the thought of allowing the second chamber to retain real power. And on the Conservative side the eventual elimination of the hereditary peers was a high price to pay for a reform that left a second chamber not only weak, but one whose future legitimacy could certainly not be guaranteed.

Fundamental to the reform was the concept of two-tier membership of the House. Some peers would have full rights of membership while others would be able to attend, speak, take part in business, ask questions, move motions, sit on committees, do anything a peer could do – except take part in divisions in the House. It was proposed that initially non-voting peers would include all peers by succession as well as all created peers who were not 'regular' attenders at the House, or who were over a fixed retirement age. In this way no peer already a member of the House would be immediately and totally excluded from it. But the voting membership would be limited to about 230. Within such a House it was envisaged that the government of the day could have a majority of some 10 per cent over all other parties, but excluding the crossbench peers who would therefore hold the balance. The thinking behind this scheme was therefore to allow for a gradual transition from the present House to a new House.

New peers would continue to be nominated by the prime minister. Other possible ways of constituting the House were considered. Any form of election, direct or indirect was ruled out because of the danger of rivalry with the House of Commons. Nomination for a period less than life, say for a parliament, was ruled out because this would detract from the independence of members. The net result of this would have been that the entire second chamber of parliament would have been composed of prime ministerial nominees, enhancing the patronage power of the prime minister. Fears over this were one of the principal reasons for the scheme not generating sufficient support to see it though the choppy waters of backbench dissent in the Commons. As to powers, as well as proposing that the delaying power for bills be cut to six months, the white paper proposed that for secondary legislation the House should only have the power to ask the Commons to 'think again' once, because 'the concept of a period of delay is not part of the general legislative framework within which subordinate legislation is enacted'.[33]

Looking back, what is interesting is that these proposals were given the degree of support that they did receive. The white paper received massive endorsement in the House of Lords, and the Parliament (No. 2) Bill embodying its proposals was given its second reading in the Commons. No doubt there would have been much debate and many attempts at amendments in respect of details had the Bill reached the Lords. But after ploughing through twelve committee days on the floor of the House of Commons, with pathetically slow progress recorded, the Bill was abandoned. Opposition from the Labour left, including the future party leader Michael Foot, and the Conservative right, notably Enoch Powell, destroyed the Bill's prospects. But these two, though often cited as producing an unholy cross-floor alliance actually had much support from elsewhere in their respective parties. Many Labour MPs shared their party's traditional reluctance to create what might become a more credible second chamber. And not a few Conservatives were reluctant to sign the death warrant of the heredi-tary system, even if its final execution was to be delayed for a gener-ation. But above all the concept of an entirely appointed House and the consolidation of prime ministerial patronage, drew withering crit-icism. This was aggravated by expectations that peers would receive salaries.

The failure of the Bill certainly affected the mood of the upper House. It was not the Lords itself that had frustrated reform. Quite the contrary, the House had bent over backwards to facilitate reform. Peers had swal-lowed many of their misgivings and were prepared to give the propos-als a fair wind. But MPs had destroyed the possibility of reform. A new boldness on the part of peers was quickly apparent in the 1970s. It was not the peers' fault that their House remained as it was. Why should they therefore take special care not to offend the sensibilities of MPs? Furthermore, given the time and effort that had been put into the planned reform, it seemed unlikely that future governments would will-ingly embark on such a task again, at least for many years. Government had burnt its fingers badly. The whole episode had loosened the ties that bind backbenchers to party leaders. Government defeat on House of Lords reform was followed by further ministerial humiliation when leg-islation to reform trade unions and industrial relations was likewise lost later the same session. Few might have thought that it would be thirty years before another government embarked seriously on reform of the House. The continuation of so odd a second chamber, so huge in size, so dominated by hereditary members, and so politically lopsided, seemed ample grounds for taking some sort of action.

Interest in reform of the Lords declined with the return of the Conservatives to power in 1970. For the prime minister, Edward Heath, there were far more important matters for government to be engaged with than reforming the upper House. Even the exercise of patronage in awarding peerages appeared to stir little interest; he was positively parsimonious in the award of honours. Labour too seemed to lose interest in reform in this period, possibly because Labour peers (three times as numerous as they had been when last in opposition) were able to use the House, with its absence of procedural restrictions, to mount sustained attacks on some government legislation. Notable were the 138 divisions during the twenty-nine days spent on the Industrial Relations Bill, where the opposition's tactics tested almost to their limits the traditional flexibility and freedom inherent in the procedures of the House. The government won all those divisions, but it lost twenty-six others and on several occasions gave significant ground in order to avoid more prolonged conflict with the House where the Conservatives no longer enjoyed an overall majority.

However when Labour was back in power the story was quickly very different, as already indicated when considering the use of power by the House. To ministers in office the House of Lords was an irritant. Calls for its abolition grew. In 1976 the party conference carried the following resolution: 'We believe the House of Lords is an outdated institution completely inappropriate to a modern democratic system of government. It should not therefore continue in its present form'. The following year the party conference voted overwhelmingly (by 6,157,000 to 91,000, on the old block vote system) to abolish the House, the relevant motion declaring: 'This Conference believes that the House of Lords is a negation of democracy, and calls upon the Government, the Parliamentary party and the National Executive Committee to take every possible step open to them to secure the total reform of Parliament into an efficient single-chamber legislating body without delay'.[34]

The story of how as prime minister Jim Callaghan fought to prevent this commitment being included in the 1979 party manifesto has often been told.[35] The joint meeting to decide the manifesto between the cabinet and the party national executive committee was forced to accept his veto on this point. When it appeared, the manifesto committed the party simply to the removal of the remaining powers of the House of Lords. Tony Benn and others were furious, but on the eve of an election they could not withstand a determined prime minister who threatened resignation if he did not get his way. Labour of course lost the election, and in opposition went through the party's strangest period. By the time of the next election in 1983 it was led by Michael Foot, a man who had never made any secret of his desire to abolish the House of Lords outright, which was exactly the policy the party declared in its 1983 manifesto. As the party's years in opposition lengthened through the loss of the 1987 and the 1992 elections, so its policy on the House of Lords gradually adjusted. The story of how Labour's policy evolved, and how it came to power in 1997 with a definite commitment to reform the House, is taken up again in the concluding Chapter.

Meanwhile, however, what of the Conservatives? Back in the 1970s, in opposition, serious thoughts of reform were kindled. For the Conservatives the wider context was one in which they felt Labour was subverting the constitution, and many also blamed their own party for acquiescing in this trend when in office. Lord Hailsham summed up these concerns in his much-quoted Dimbleby lecture of 1976 on elective dictatorship.[36] The Labour Government was driving through parliament measures for which it claimed a mandate because it had very slightly more MPs than any other party. But there was plenty of evidence that many of these measures had little support in the country at large. Nevertheless because they had been anointed with the imprimatur of the manifesto, they were supposedly unassailable. Ministers in office took more notice of trade union leaders than they did of parliament. They generated consent for their policies by securing the approval of the Labour Party Trades Union Congress (TUC) Liaison Committee. Even budget changes were made conditional on TUC approval. In all this the House of Lords was effectively powerless. It might dare to use its delaying power, but only on sufferance. The sword of Damocles hung over its head; if it resisted the government it would face abolition.

If this was the Conservative perspective on both the way the country was being governed and the role of the House of Lords, then it behoved the party to think how it should respond to Labour's threat to abolish the upper House. The newly elected Conservative leader, Margaret Thatcher, invited the former party leader and prime minister, Lord Home of the Hirsel (once again back in the Lords, this time as a life peer), to head an inquiry and make recommendations for the future of the House. This could be seen as a kind of preventative move. If Labour did win the next election and proceeded to do something drastic to the House, then the Conservatives would be better placed to fight this if they had a clear alternative, and were not left simply defending the status quo.

The Home Committee report remains one of the most serious contributions to the whole subject of Lords reform that has appeared this century.[37] The report began by emphasising the drift towards unicameralsim, and the rise in what it termed 'mandated majority government', something 'supported on occasion by *all* parties' (the emphasis was in the original). It was therefore necessary to boldly reform the second chamber. This was a matter of ensuring the future of parliamentary government. The Parliament Act of 1911 had led to the acceptance of the view that parliamentary sovereignty adhered to one chamber only, though the exception allowing the Lords an absolute veto still on any proposal to extend the life of a parliament indicated in effect what had been lost, and what needed now to be restored, namely the notion that sovereignty truly attached to both Houses in a bicameral parliament. The House of Lords must have a strong moral authority within the nation in order for it to fulfil its role as a constitutional safeguard.

Reviewing the various ways in which the House could be composed so as to bring this about, both appointment and indirect election were found inadequate, as was the notion that peers could elect from among their own number. This would perpetuate the political imbalance in the existing House. A two-writ scheme was found to be anathema; instead the report stated: 'In the present climate moral authority can only come from the direct election of its members'.[38] However there were dangers in having a wholly elected House and definite advantages in having a measure of continuity with the existing chamber. The danger arose from the possibility that a second chamber possessed both of sufficient power to act as a genuine constitutional watchdog, and one directly elected, could too easily become a damaging rival to the Commons. Hence a two-thirds elected and one-third appointed House was the committee's preferred option. To assist continuity the one-third appointed would initially consist of all life peers (unless they chose to retire) and some fifty hereditary peers elected by the House itself acting as a single electoral college. As these members died off they would be replaced by other appointees, chosen by the prime minister but acting on the advice of a committee of privy counsellors, on which other party leaders would sit and which would give advice based on established criteria. Elections to the House should be by means of a proportional representation system, with elections linked to some existing structure, possibly elections to the European Parliament, or to regional elected institutions if these were created. The committee was however emphatic that second chamber elections should not be linked with elections to the Commons. Election should be for nine-year terms, with one-third being re-elected every three years. Appointed members would also sit for similar terms. Though by no means dogmatic on the detail, the committee envisaged a House containing 268 elected members, 134 appointed, to which would be added sixteen bishops (the same number as had been proposed in the 1968 Bill) and eleven serving law lords, together still with the royal dukes. Peers excluded from the House would of course be able to stand for the Commons.

This was a bold scheme. It was drawn up against a background viewed in somewhat apocalyptic terms. There was in the committee's view an urgency about adopting a scheme of reform; 'at best the present

House of Lords faces gradual but relentless atrophy; at worst it may be swept away by a government impatient of the modest checks it imposes on the passage of legislation'. In conclusion the committee emphasised the need for action: 'we feel obliged to point out again that in our view maintenance of the status quo is not a prudent policy. Indeed we are doubtful whether it is a policy at all'.[39]

Margaret Thatcher was less impressed by the need for action. True to past form the Conservatives, once securely back in office, saw the constitution as safe in their hands. Lord Hailsham fell silent on warnings of elective dictatorship, and the drift towards 'mandated majority government' (in which the Home Committee had felt all parties had acquiesced) was quickly forgotten even as Mrs Thatcher's government rapidly exemplified this very trend. The Conservative 1979 manifesto was vague about the House of Lords. In office the government had plenty of other things to think about. Mrs Thatcher agreed to departmental select committees in the Commons, but even that was seen more as a regrettable necessity, a hostage offered while seeking to be the champions of parliamentary democracy when in opposition, rather than a genuine matter of principle. As for Lords reform, that could only present a colossal distraction from the real business of vanquishing trade unions, subduing the European Community and turning Britain away from an ever-growing reliance on the state and towards the virtues of the free market. Some folk, including cabinet colleagues, sought to stir Margaret Thatcher up on the subject. A party conference debate in 1980 reminded the party of its earlier commitment to reform, and a cabinet committee was established to examine the matter. But nothing came of these initiatives. And in a curious way the House of Lords itself began to offer some support for maintaining the status quo by demonstrating its capacity to act as an alternative opposition to a Conservative Government at a time when the Labour opposition was so strikingly ineffective.[40]

When the Conservatives began their long period in office, House of Lords reform within a wider context of parliamentary reform was under active consideration. Quite quickly however the subject fell by the wayside. By the time the party left office in 1997 it had become committed to upholding the status quo. The obvious reason for this alteration of view was that once in office party leaders found existing arrangements congenial. 'Elective dictatorship' no longer mattered if it was the Conservative Party doing the dictating. The patronage power that the House afforded a prime minister was acceptable if it was wielded by a Conservative leader. Mrs Thatcher showed no embarrassment at reinforcing her party's preponderant position in the Lords by creating twice as many Conservative peers as Labour peers during her time in office. And this scandal received very little public comment.

Conclusion

That the House of Lords was a wholly different chamber in the 1990s to what it had been in the first decade of the twentieth century is self-evident. The fact that no fundamental reform of the House had taken place was not for want of ideas, but rather because no party in office had sufficient incentive or political will to carry through such reform. And given the usefulness of the House, along with its general docility, the balance of advantage remained with avoiding sweeping reform. The survival of the House in a basically unreformed state was made more acceptable because it did adapt in significant ways to the changing political and constitutional landscape. Behind the facade of a predominantly hereditary House much change did take place, at least ensuring that the House could sustain its role as an active junior chamber within the British parliament.

Notes

1 D. Butler and G. Butler, *British Political Facts 1900–2000* (Basingstoke, Macmillan, 2000), p. 228.
2 HL Deb. 16 Aug. 1945, col. 47.
3 R. Walters, 'The House of Lords', in V. Bogdanor (ed.) *The British Constitution in the Twentieth Century* (Oxford University Press, 2003), p. 194.
4 C. R. Attlee, *As it Happened* (London, Heinemann, 1954), p. 167.
5 Agreed statement on conclusion of conference of party leaders on the Parliament Bill, 1948, Cm. 7380.
6 P. A. Bromhead, *The House of Lords and Contemporary Politics 1911–1956* (London, Routledge, 1958), pp. 217–19.
7 HL Deb. 16 Feb. 1967, cols. 419–24.
8 J. Morgan, *The House of Lords and the Labour Government 1964–70* (Oxford University Press, 1975).
9 *Ibid.*
10 D. Shell, *The House of Lords* (Hemel Hempstead, Harvester-Wheatsheaf, 1992), pp. 249–50.
11 N. Baldwin, 'The House of Lords and the Labour Government 1974–79', *Journal of Legislative Studies*, 1:1 (1995) 218–42.
12 HL Deb. 15 Dec. 1998, col. 1316.
13 HL Deb. 18 Nov. 1998, col. 1346.
14 HL Deb. 18 Nov. 1998, cols. 1348, 1350.
15 Report printed in R. Blackburn and R. Plant, *Constitutional Reform: The Labour Government's Constitutional Reform Agenda* (London, Longman, 1999), Appendix 2, pp. 443–67.

16 HL Deb. 14 Oct. 1998, col. 925; 24 Nov. 1999, col. 572.

17 See 7th Report, Select Committee on the Constitution, *Constitutional Aspects of the Challenge to the Hunting Act 2004*. HL 141, 2005–06.

18 See House of Lords Library Note, *The Salisbury Doctrine*, 2005, LLN 2005/004.

19 HL Deb. 6 Jun. 2005, cols. 759–60.

20 G. Lewis, *A Life of Lord Hailsham* (London, Pimlico, 1998), ch. 12 'Reluctant heir'.

21 P. Williams (ed.), *The Diary of Hugh Gaitskell* (London, J. Cape, 1983) pp. 416, 564.

22 E. F. Iwi, 'Women and the House of Lords' in S. Bailey, (ed.) *The Future of the House of Lords* (London, Hansard Society, 1954).

23 HL Deb. 7 Mar. 1994, cols. 1283–330. (Debate on Bill introduced by Lord Diamond).

24 Cd. 9038 (1918).

25 Cmnd. 3799 (1968).

26 Royal Commission on the Reform of the House of Lords, *A House for the Future*, (chm. Lord Wakeham), Cm. 4534 (2000), Recommendations 21, 56.

27 HL 234 (1908).

28 Cd. 9038 (1918).

29 On all this see Bromhead, *House of Lords*, ch. 20.

30 HL Deb. 12 Apr. 1967, cols. 1295–303.

31 On this whole saga, see Morgan, *House of Lords*.

32 Cmnd. 3799 (1968).

33 Cmnd. 3799, para. 35 (1968).

34 Labour Party Conference Report 1977, p. 270. See also on this whole period T. Lamport, *Reform of the House of Lords in British Politics 1970–92*, PhD thesis, (University of London, 2005).

35 See Lamport, *Reform of the House*, also T. Benn, *Conflicts of Interest: Diaries 1977–80* (London, Hutchinson, 1990), pp. 482–3.

36 Lord Hailsham, *Elective Dictatorship* (London, BBC Publications, 1976).

37 Lord Home, *Report of the Review Committee on the Second Chamber* (London, Conservative Political Centre, 1978).

38 *Ibid*, para. 30.

39 *Ibid*, paras. 66 and 68.

40 Shell, *The House of Lords*, ch. 6.

3

What is the House of Lords?

Analysing the membership of the House of Lords is not as straightforward a task as it might at first appear. This is partly because there are
various routes into membership of the House, and partly because almost
all those who arrive in the House remain members for life, though
inevitably some fade away as old age and infirmity take their toll. It is
therefore necessary, in addition to explaining how the formal membership is composed, to examine more closely the question of activity and
the varied forms of participation in the working House, and to what
degree different groups of peers engage in these. While some enter the
House as 'working' peers, with a definite commitment to attend regularly, others arrive there more or less by accident, perhaps through inclusion in an 'honours' list, or because they have taken up another
appointment – as a bishop or a senior judge. Though members can take
formal leave of absence, and so at least for a time be excluded from
effective membership of the House, others attend very rarely, or even
not at all, yet must be included in an analysis of membership. In the
2003–04 session eleven peers never attended the House, while another
twenty-four did so only once or twice. At the other extreme ten peers
attended every single one of the 157 sitting days. All of these are
members of the House, but while for some people membership is clearly
a very marginal feature of their lives, and their contribution to the
House is minimal, for others their role in the House is central to their
lives.

All this makes the House an unusual parliamentary body. Most such
institutions have a common route into membership, usually through
election, and along with membership there is an obligation to attend
that is reinforced by the receipt of a salary for doing so. Peers do not
receive salaries, though the allowances they can now claim are relatively
generous. And though some new arrivals may have been asked for
undertakings about their attendance, for example by their party before
being nominated as a 'working' peer, most make no such commitment.

Furthermore, once there, no commitment regarding attendance can be enforced (as party whips know well!). Nor is there any fixed number of members. As peers die they are not automatically replaced, with the exception of bishops who retire, and – up to now – serving law lords, and curiously (since 2000) elected hereditary peers. New arrivals do not reach the House in a steady stream. Prime ministers vary in the frequency with which they recommend peerages. General election years tend to produce a bumper crop of new recruits as dissolution honours and perhaps resignation honours swell the ranks of new arrivals.

These matters are explored further in this Chapter. It is well however to begin by looking at the formal membership of the House. Table 3.1 gives a snapshot picture of the total membership as it was in July 2006. It is derived from the House website, where from week to week changes in the membership are recorded as peers die, and as new arrivals take their seats.

If peers on leave of absence are included (and such leave can be terminated at twenty-eight days notice) the total size of the House is 753. It is worth noting how rapidly this has grown from the total of 666 members immediately after the removal of most hereditary peers. Of those who were members of the House at the close of the 2003–04 session, no fewer than 688 attended at least once during the session (see below). This does make the House one of the largest legislatures in the world. Table 3.1 shows that one-eighth of the total membership is hereditary, though another fifteen classified in this table as life peers first sat in the House as hereditary peers. Those elected as hereditary peers are on the whole active members, ensuring therefore that the House created by the 1999 Act retains a significant hereditary element.

Hereditary peers

Prior to the 1999 Act hereditary peers were the most numerous in terms of formal membership, comprising just over 750 of the 1330 total. Before the 1958 Life Peerage Act all peers were hereditary except for law lords and bishops, though some – the first holders of hereditary peerages – had themselves been created peers. But gradually since 1958 the proportion of the House composed of life peers has grown, and in terms of active membership by 1999 life peers constituted well over half the House. Some 300 peers by succession either attended very rarely or not at all, but conversely over 100 hereditary members attended for more than two-thirds of the time. The 1999 Act as originally introduced would have removed all hereditary peers. However it had been widely assumed that some of those so removed would remain in the House pending a

Table 3.1 Nominal membership of the House of Lords 2006

Party	Created peers			Hereditary peers			Total
	Life peers (1958)	Life peers appellate	Bishops	Elected by party groups	Elected by the House	Ex officio	
Cons	161			40	9		210
Labour	209			2	2		213
LibDem	74			3	2		79
Crossbench	138			28	2	2	170
Law lords		26					26
Bishops			26				26
Other	15			2			17
Total	597	26	26	75	15	2	741

Notes:

Excludes twelve peers on leave of absence, whose party allegiance in the House had been: Labour six; Conservative four; and crossbench two.

Life peers (1958): Created under Life Peerages Act, 1958.

Life peers appellate: Created under 1876 Appellate Jurisdiction Act as amended.

Source: derived from House of Lords website:
http://www.parliament.uk/about_lords/about_lords.cfm

more comprehensive reform. This was because some hereditary peers did play a key role, as frontbenchers and as office-holders, and others played a significant role in its select committee work. Most of those who had been involved in discussion about House of Lords reform had assumed that a special list of life peers would be announced, possibly running up to about 100, whereby some active hereditary peers would be given life peerages.

Instead however, as is well known, the government agreed to allow for the election of ninety hereditary peers to remain in the House. Government ministers spoke of such as providing continuity, enabling the 'transitional' House to function effectively. But Conservatives referred to such peers as 'representative' peers, a group who would embody the hereditary principle through being chosen by their hereditary brethren. As the House of Lords Bill was going through parliament it was further amended to provide for the indefinite replacement of hereditary members of the House who died. Initially this was through the runner up principle, the nearest loser stepping in, but after the end of the first session of the next parliament (November 2002) it was agreed that new by-elections would be held when vacancies occurred.

The government publicly maintained that stage two of its reform would have taken place by then, and therefore such elections would never take place. But others were more sceptical. The former Conservative Leader in the House, who negotiated the deal to elect hereditary members, spoke of it as being 'sand in the government's shoe' – in other words an irritant that would help ensure further reform would be forthcoming. It has certainly proved an irritant to Labour, but it has so far done nothing to advance further reform; indeed it is probably now an arrangement which many peers would prefer to keep rather than endure unwanted change thrust upon the House by the Commons – such as making it a largely elected chamber!

The number of peers so elected was initially set at 10 per cent of the total of hereditary peers. To this was then added a further fifteen as 'office-holders' (there were at the time fifteen hereditary peers who were deputy speakers), and then two further hereditary peers who held hereditary offices of state were also included, making a total of ninety-two. Curiously in dividing up the seventy-five places allocated to party groups, instead of taking the number of peers in each group who actually attended the House (just under 300 for the Conservatives), the total number of nominal members who subscribed to the party was taken (over 400 for the Conservatives – even including peers who never attended or were on leave of absence). This inflated the Conservative share to forty-two places while Labour got just two.[1] Then once the Act had been passed a special list awarding life peerages to ten of the hereditary members of the House was issued (and the following April seven more former hereditary peers returned to the House in another list of life peerages). This indicated how easily continuity in the work of the House could have been provided by giving life peerages to hereditary peers whose continued presence their party group deemed desirable, with such peers remaining members until further reform, or until they died, without any requirement for cumbersome and frankly ridiculous by-elections that perpetuate the hereditary element in the house!

The initial elections in 1999 were keenly contested, with a total of 223 peers coming forward as candidates. For the fifteen office-holders the electorate was (and remains) all members of the House. For the party groups the electorate consisted of all hereditary peers in the party group concerned, while for subsequent by-elections the electorate since 2002 has been those already elected to the House as hereditary peers who take the party whip concerned. This meant that when a by-election occurred for a Labour place (as it did in 2003), the electorate consisted of the three remaining peers in that group, while in the Liberal Democrat case when a by-election occurred in 2004 there were four Liberal Democrat peers entrusted with the choice! So far there have been seven by-elections. Far from ensuring continuity in the House, two of these have been won by candidates who had never previously sat in the House, thereby entrenching the Conservative characterisation of this group as representative hereditary peers. The Clerk of the Parliaments keeps a register of hereditary peers who may wish to stand for election (containing the names of 137 peers in 2006). Competition in by-elections so far has been keen; there were thirty-six candidates for the first by-election held in 2003. A preferential voting system is used so the count can be quite complicated, with many redistributions of votes taking place.

The two other hereditary peers who retained their seats in the House ex officio were the Lord Great Chamberlain, the Marquess of Cholmondeley, and the Earl Marshal, the Duke of Norfolk. When the latter, the seventeenth duke, died in 2003, his son immediately entered the House, making his maiden speech shortly afterwards. This survival of the hereditary system is a very curious outcome of the 1999 legislation. Given the exceptions made for these two, one might almost have anticipated exceptions being made for royal peers too! Prince Charles and the Duke of Gloucester had both taken their seats and made speeches in the House, but the royal family made clear that none of its members would remain in the House.[2] Just before the 1999 House of Lords Act reached the statute book, the government offered life peerages to all remaining hereditary peers who had themselves been created peers, and though the royal family declined, the Earl of Snowdon, who had been created an earl upon his marriage to Princess Margaret, accepted a life peerage – as Lord Armstrong-Jones.

New hereditary peerages had been created regularly until 1964. But following the arrival of a Labour Government that year the prime minister, Harold Wilson, announced he would not be recommending any new hereditary peerages. His Conservative successor, Edward Heath, did not do so either, so that by the time Margaret Thatcher became prime minister a period of fifteen years had elapsed during which all new creations had been life peerages. However, following her second election victory in 1983, she reintroduced hereditary creations. Her deputy, William Whitelaw, and the former Speaker of the Commons, George Thomas, both became hereditary viscounts. The following year Harold Macmillan, who had remained a commoner for the twenty years since his retirement from the premiership in 1963, received a hereditary Earldom. William Whitelaw and George Thomas both died without heirs, but when Macmillan died in 1987 his grandson inherited his peerage. Margaret Thatcher did not take a hereditary peerage, though her husband did receive a hereditary baronetcy, (inherited by her son).

The 1999 Act imposed no limitation on the right of the crown to create further hereditary peers, and indeed while the Bill was proceeding through parliament the Queen's youngest son was created Earl of Wessex on the occasion of his marriage. The convention established earlier this century whereby retiring prime ministers take earldoms could be revived! But no new hereditary peer would have any right to a seat in the second chamber unless also awarded a life peerage.

Because of the way peerage law favoured succession through male lines, almost all hereditary peerages have been held by men. The removal of most hereditary peers therefore led to a considerable improvement in the gender balance within the House, the proportion of female members rising from less than 8 per cent to around 15 percent, without the actual number of women altering. That parliament, which had in recent decades invested much legislative effort in removing gender discrimination elsewhere, should have allowed the perpetuation of such a blatant form of discrimination in regard to its own membership was absurd.

All hereditary peerages awarded in the twentieth century were peerages of the United Kingdom, but Irish peerages used to be awarded, and prior to the Act of Union in 1707 peerages of Scotland were also awarded. As explained in Chapter 2, the 1963 Peerages Act confirmed the permanent exclusion of Irish peers, but resulted in the inclusion of all remaining thirty-one holders of Scottish peerages. During the passage of the House of Lords Bill in 1999 there was some debate over whether the proposed exclusion of Scottish hereditary peers involved a breach of the Act of Union. The fact that this Bill followed so soon after the establishment of the single chamber Scottish Parliament aggravated the minds of some hereditary peers. But attempts by some backbenchers to make special provision for peers of Scotland were resisted.

Hereditary peers are divided by rank. In November 1998 there were twenty-five dukes, thirty-four marquesses, 174 earls and countesses, 103 viscounts and 415 at the rank of baron. For many years these distinctions have had no practical significance in the work of the House. Peers are all equal as regards participation in debate and in the business of the House. Among elected hereditary peers, in 2006 there were two dukes, one marquess, twenty-five earls and seventeen viscounts, with the remaining forty-seven being barons, making elected hereditaries a slightly more aristocratic lot than the total group from which they are chosen.

The House of Lords Act removes from hereditary peers their previous disabilities in relation to the House of Commons. All except those who are elected to membership of the House of Lords now have the right to vote in parliamentary elections and themselves to become members of the Commons. In 2001 Viscount Thurso, who had become a member of the Lords when he succeeded to his peerage in 1995, and had left the House in 1999, became the first evicted hereditary peer to become a member of the Commons when he won the seat of Caithness, Sutherland and Easter Ross as a Liberal Democrat. Two other senior Conservative MPs have inherited peerages since the 1999 Act was passed, Michael Ancram becoming the thirteenth Marquess of Lothian and Douglas Hogg the third Viscount Hailsham. Both remained as MPs without needing to renounce their peerages as MPs had to do in the past if they wished to stay in the House. It is worth noting that the hereditary peerage does contain many families with a marked tradition of political involvement. This is not likely suddenly to cease.

The legislation removing hereditary peers from the Lords is silent on the matter of titles. Individuals still inherit peerages and (as already noted) new hereditary peerages could still be created. No doubt many will continue to use their titles, and some will certainly be active in political life. Where disputes arise as to who is the rightful heir to a hereditary peerage, these will still be resolved by the House of Lords Committee of Privileges – as has been the case hitherto. The question of what rights (if any) former peers by succession should have in relation to the Palace of Westminster remained vexed throughout the passage of the House of Lords Act. On the one hand some argued that it would be wrong not to accord any special privileges to hereditary peers who have served the house, government and country with distinction. But others argued no 'club rights' should be given to former members of the House precisely because the House was not a club, but a working part of Parliament. The fact that retired bishops have dining rights, and that they along with Irish peers (excluded from the House since 1921) have the right to sit in the chamber on the steps of the throne, were cited in debate as precedents that might be followed in relation to hereditary peers who were former members. It was decided to allow excluded hereditary peers these limited rights too.

Bishops and law lords

Turning to the created peers, we will first consider the bishops, the Lords Spiritual. These are the two archbishops together with the Bishops of London, Durham and Winchester who sit as of right, together with the most senior twenty-one of the forty-six other diocesan bishops, seniority being determined by date of first appointment to a diocesan see. This has in recent years meant that a newly appointed diocesan bishop has waited some five years before entering the House. Representation of the Church goes back to the very origins of the House of Lords. Before the reformation the Lords Spiritual outnumbered the Lords Temporal. Though today greatly reduced in number the bishops are nevertheless an important element in the House. Table 3.4 shows that although all bishops do attend the House, few attend regularly. Unlike the Commons, where the Speaker's chaplain reads prayers, bishops take it in turns to read prayers in the Lords, and this ensures the presence of a bishop for at least part of each day's proceedings. But for many bishops commitments elsewhere clearly take priority over their membership of the House. Collectively the bishops may take their membership of the House seriously and make every effort to ensure that contributions from their benches are made when these seem appropriate, especially on matters of obvious moral or ethical concern. The bishops take briefing for their contributions from professional staff within Church House, and more widely seek to be representative of other churches too through a representative body known as the Churches Main Committee. A bishop on a prayer week rota will probably be called upon to speak during that week.

Because the Church of England remains an established church, certain matters of church government have to come before parliament. In the House of Lords bishops introduce 'Measures' (the technical term for such items of legislation). But bishops may also use their position in the House to initiate other items of business, for example to ask questions or put down motions. The Archbishop of Canterbury, Rowan Williams, initiated a debate on the social purpose of sentencing policy in 2004, where his own opening speech was followed by one from the Lord Chief Justice.[3] Bishops are not averse to taking part in legislative business too, though they do not necessarily speak with one voice. When Lord Lestor opposed the Employment Equality (Sexual Orientation) Regulations 2003 because they allowed religious bodies to impose requirements in relation to a person's practice of their sexuality, one bishop spoke on each side in the debate and then two voted in each lobby at the end of it; the government defeated Lord Lestor's motion by eighty-five votes to fifty.[4] The Bishop of Portsmouth moved an amendment to the Nationality, Immigration and Asylum Bill in 2002 to reverse the government's proposal preventing children of asylum seekers in accommodation centres from attending local schools. On this occasion three bishops voted in the same lobby, against the government, with one of them (Winchester) acting as a teller, and the government lost by a single vote.[5] Richard Harries, Bishop of Oxford, chaired one of the ad hoc select committees set up by the House, into stem cell research, which reported in 2002. In recent years the bishops have had a recognised convenor in the House, a role assumed in 1998 by Richard Harries, who had first entered the House five years earlier. The convenor simply acts as a kind of recognised spokesman for the bishops in the House. When Richard Harries retired in 2006 he was created a life peer, and his place as convenor was taken by Kenneth Stevenson, Bishop of Portsmouth.

The fact that the Church of England retains a monopoly of official Church representation in the House is an historical anomaly, but it arises out of the continued status of the Church as established. If the present Archbishop of Canterbury, Rowan Williams, had remained Archbishop of Wales he would never have sat as of right in the House (though his predecessors before the disestablishment of the Church in Wales in 1920 did so). All recent proposals for reform of the House have tried to address the anomaly of having official Church representatives drawn exclusively from one church within one part only of the United Kingdom – England. The Wakeham Commission, which included the Bishop of Oxford as a member, proposed that representation from the Church of England be cut to sixteen places, but that sitting alongside the bishops should be representatives of other churches throughout the United Kingdom, as well as representatives of other faith groups. With the Wakeham proposals being allowed to languish little more has been heard of this idea, which would certainly have been complicated to implement.

The role played by the bishops may offer some clues as to how a chamber composed on an ex officio principle might operate. The obvious problem concerns the many other pressing demands made on busy people. The business of the House is arranged at relatively short notice and those whose diaries fill up months ahead therefore find attendance at particular debates is often difficult to arrange. And just when they become free from their heavy professional commitments they cease to be members of the House. Bishops must now retire from their sees at the age of seventy and when they do so they also leave the House, though recent archbishops have been awarded life peerages, as was the Bishop of Oxford upon his retirement in 2006.

Senior judges sit in the Lords because it has had a judicial role as the supreme court of appeal as well as its parliamentary role. Those appointed as judges have been known as 'Lords of Appeal in Ordinary', and have been given peerages; until 1876 these were hereditary peerages, but since that date they have been life peerages. Gradually the number of serving law lords has crept up, reaching the present figure of twelve in 1994. The total who have entered the House by this route includes those who have retired because unlike bishops law lords don't have to leave the House upon retirement. Some are very active members after retirement, which now must take place at seventy, though with the possibility of continuing to sit to hear appeals until seventy-five. A few other peers who have held high judicial office are qualified to sit judicially, and are therefore usually also described as law lords.

However, these arrangements are in the throes of change. When Lord Falconer was appointed Lord Chancellor in 2003, the prime minister announced that the appellate functions of the House of Lords would be transferred to a new supreme court, the post of Lord Chancellor would be abolished, and a new judicial appointments commission would take over the responsibility for nominating senior judges. All this caused a good deal of turbulence because though long discussed in general terms, these proposals had not been the subject of consultation either with the judiciary or with the House of Lords. When the necessary legislation, the Constitutional Reform Bill, appeared, peers voted (against the wishes of the government) to send it to a special select committee.[6] This resulted in the Bill being carried over into the following session and not being enacted until just before the 2005 election. Under its provisions the serving Lords of Appeal in Ordinary will be renamed Justices of the Supreme Court and will cease to be members of the House of Lords. But this will not come into effect until the new Supreme Court building (formerly Middlesex Town Hall, across the square from parliament) has been refurbished, probably in 2009. Those who have already retired will however continue as members of the House, and as things stand in 2006 the new Supreme Court judges will be eligible for appointment as life peers after they retire.

Serving law lords in the past have taken part in the ordinary business of the House, frequently speaking in debates, especially on criminal justice and the penal system, and sometimes taking part in legislation, especially where this has concerned the administration of the courts. Generally they have avoided political controversy. It has been suggested that the anger felt and expressed by several law lords on the Courts and Legal Services Bill in 1990 marked something of a turning point in relation to their participation in the business of the House.[7] On this Bill, with the Lord Chancellor speaking from his place beside the Woolsack and the serried ranks of judges facing him from the crossbenches, it seemed as if the normal axis through which government faced opposition had shifted through ninety degrees. In recent years some law lords have been outspoken critics on aspects of government policy, but the proportion of serving law lords who take part in the work in the chamber has declined. A serving law lord has usually been chairman of the European Union subcommittee dealing with law and institutions, and several have been involved in other select committee work. The prospect of their removal from the House has brought considerable expressions of regret from some other peers, who emphasise that their role in the past has not caused difficulty, that they bring valuable expertise to the House, and that both members of the House generally and the law lords themselves have benefited from the experience of working together in developing understanding of one another's roles.

Life peers created under the 1958 Life Peerages Act

As Table 3.1 shows the great majority of members of the house are life peers created under the 1958 Life Peerage Act. Table 3.2 analyses the creation of life peers between the announcement of the first life peers in July 1958 and the end of June 2006, and shows that just over 1100 life peers have been created. This excludes the fifty-one law lords created in the same period, who are also peers for life, and it also excludes those

Table 3.2 Creation of life peers 1958 to 2006

Prime minister	Cons	Lab	LibDem	Crossbench	Total	Number female	Average per 12 months
Macmillan/ Douglas-Home 1958–64	16 (24)	29	0	18 (23)	63 (47)	9	17
Wilson 1964–70	14 (6)	62	2	53	131 (6)	14	25
Heath 1970–74	8	9	2	26	45	8	13
Wilson/ Callaghan 1974–79	27	68	7	36	138	16	27
Thatcher 1979–90	96 (2)	56	10	39 (2)	201 (4)	27	18
Major 1990–97	75	40	17	28	160	29	25
Blair 1997–2006	61	163	53	89 (1)	366 (1)	87	40
Total	297 (32)	427	91	289 (26)	1104 (58)	190	22 (23)

Notes:
Figures for hereditary peers are given in brackets. Average per 12 months includes hereditary creations.
Excludes creations under 1876 Appellate Jurisdiction Act as amended.

who have been newly created hereditary peers in this period, mainly between 1958 and 1964.

The overall rate at which new peerages have been created has been over twenty per year since 1958. This is something over twice the rate at which creations had been made throughout the earlier part of this century. The early Blair years saw an unprecedented number of new life peers, partly due to the fact that the Labour Government was seeking to gain a greater degree of parity with the Conservatives in the House. Before analysing further the peerages created, some comment on the processes involved seems appropriate.

The creation of peers

The sovereign, on the advice of the prime minister, formally confers all peerages. There is no statutory limit on the number of new peerages, just as there is no limit on the size of the House of Lords. It is the prime minister who decides what number is appropriate. By convention when recommending peerages for members of political parties other than their own, prime ministers take advice from the leader of that party, and in practice it is that party leader who is recognised as having made the decisions. As prime minister Tony Blair set up a non-statutory House of Lords Appointments Commission, which since 2001 has had particular responsibility for making recommendations for non-party nominations. The work of the Commission is discussed below.

Most people probably still think of peerages as first and foremost an honour. But while some are awarded as honours, others are awarded in order to bring particular individuals into the House of Lords where they are needed to do a job of work. The fact that the honours system is inextricably mixed up with recruitment to a working second chamber does cause confusion. And while it is possible to differentiate these two aspects they cannot be thought of as entirely separate from one another. Undoubtedly the present House derives its character in part from the mixture of the 'great and the good' who have arrived there because of their eminence in some field, probably unrelated to politics, and the party work-horses who are sent to the House to reinforce party strength. Some of course may reasonably be thought of as belonging in both camps.

There are regular occasions on which honours are announced, notably new year and on the Queen's official birthday in June. Until very recently such lists almost invariably had at their head the names of a few individuals who were awarded peerages. This links the House of Lords to the honours system. In addition to these twice yearly lists, honours may occasionally be announced at other times, for example to mark victory in war (as was the case after the Falklands war in 1982 and after the Gulf war in 1991), or to mark some other event such as the Queen's jubilee. People who receive peerages in these lists are certainly not asked in advance to give any undertakings about frequency of attendance in the House of Lords. The evidence suggests that prime ministers had a keen eye for who would support their party if elevated in these twice-yearly honours lists, further illustrating the difficulty in disentangling the factors leading to the award of peerages. Between 1958 and 1997, of those given peerages in these lists when the Conservatives were in office, fifty-one subsequently took the Conservative whip in the House, and eleven the Labour whip. But of those elevated during Labour's periods in office, only one took the Conservative whip and thirty the Labour whip.[8] Since 1997 almost all peers elevated in these honours lists have gone to the crossbenches (perhaps reflecting growing disdain for political parties). All those recommended by the Appointments Commission have taken seats on the crossbenches.

Honours lists are also issued around the time of a general election or when there is a change of prime minister. Prior to a general election there is usually a dissolution list, and following an election, if a change of government has resulted, there will be a resignation list. In 1997 twenty-one individuals, all retiring MPs, were included in the dissolution list issued in April, then after Labour's victory a further resignation honours list containing the names of ten Conservatives was issued in August. The latter included nine former MPs and the former head of the policy unit at 10 Downing Street. All told, peerages for eighty-nine individuals were announced during 1997. A resignation honours list also follows a change of prime minister mid-parliament. In 1990 Margaret Thatcher's resignation list contained the names of seven new peers (and many other less exalted honours), but because it was mid-parliament it did not contain the names of any MPs; had it done so unwelcome by-elections would have followed. Instead it was mainly composed of friendly business figures. The responsibility for the names contained in a resignation list belongs to the departing prime minister, even though the peerages are announced some time after his or her successor has taken office. John Major's failure in 1997 to include his former Chancellor, Norman Lamont, was clearly his personal decision.

As well as all these, from time to time special lists have been issued the purpose of which has been avowedly to increase the 'working strength' of the upper House. Such lists often include former MPs who have missed out on dissolution or resignation lists. Norman Lamont was included in a 1998 list. In 2006 a list of twenty-three 'working peers' including six former MPs was announced in April. Generally press statements at the time a working peers list is issued will give information about the state of the parties in the House as a kind of justification for the new creations. Precisely when the phrase 'working peer' crept into use is unclear. Some peers resent its use because it implies either that those who arrive at the House by other means do not really work there (plainly false in many cases), or conversely it implies that working peerages are somehow less of an honour. This resentment became clear when a question was asked about the phrase in the House in 1992. The answer implied that the phrase had first been used in 1975, but emphasis was also placed on the fact that it had no constitutional validity.[9] It is worth noting that if a peerage is awarded as a 'working peerage' there is no way that an obligation to attend the House can subsequently be enforced. Some businessmen who appeared on lists of so-called working peers in the 1980s were much less assiduous in attending the House than Margaret Thatcher had hoped. In June 1998, when a list of new working peers was announced it was reported that Labour members on the list were 'forced to give an unprecedented undertaking that they would make regular appearances in the House as a condition of accepting their titles'.[10] This was apparently because of the poor voting record of some of the previous year's entrants to the chamber.

New peerages can be announced at any time. In particular if a prime minister wishes to appoint someone to a ministerial post who is not already a member of either House, the individual concerned may be given a peerage. This enables them to join the government frontbench in the Lords, and in so doing ensure a degree of parliamentary accountability through being answerable to that House. Mr Blair did this in May 1997 when peerages were announced for four individuals as he constructed his government. One of these was for the chairman of BP, who became Lord Simon of Highbury and Minister for Trade and Competitiveness in Europe. Another was Dr John Gilbert who had left the Commons but who was brought back into government as Minister of State at Defence, a post he had held when Labour had last been in power prior to 1979. In 2001 the prime minister's political secretary Sally Morgan became Baroness Morgan of Huyton on appointment as Minister of State at the Cabinet Office and Minister for Women, a post she held for five months, before effectively dropping out of the Lords to become government director of communications. In 2005 a former prime ministerial adviser, Andrew Adonis suddenly metamorphosed into Lord Adonis of Camden Town and took a junior ministerial post at Education.

Finally we need to consider those who arrive at the House through nomination via the Appointments Commission set up in 2000. The story of the Commission is really all of a piece with the confusion and muddle the government has displayed in relation to the wider question of House of Lords reform. It was set up according to rigorous post-Nolan criteria involving the use of 'PricewaterhouseCoopers Executive Search and Selection', and then from among the 239 applicants for Commission membership, some were selected for interview by a panel chaired by the cabinet secretary. Lord Stevenson, a businessman and rarely attending crossbench peer, was appointed chairman, along with three party nominees and three other non-party members. When the membership was announced the prime minister claimed it would remove patronage from his hands because in future 'independent peers will be recommended by an independent commission'. He went on to explain the pro-active role the Commission would take, 'looking for suitable candidates in a wider field than up to now', and ensuring that 'the process of appointing non-political peers to the House of Lords will be open and transparent'.[11] The Commission set to work, holding meetings to stir up interest across the country, and writing to some 10,000 organisations to spread awareness of its role and the new opportunity it was bringing to the citizenry of the UK who might wish to serve their country by joining the House of Lords. Over 3000 nominations were made, with 'six trained sifting teams' producing a short list of candidates for interview by Commission members. Eventually the first list containing fifteen new peers was published in April 2001. This was greeted with general derision for two reasons. First, those chosen were exactly the same kind of people as emerged under the old system; seven already had knighthoods, one was the wife of a peer, three more were professors and four were described in the press as 'charity grandees'. Second, when questioned about this, Lord Stevenson was reported as saying: 'You haven't got your hairdresser in this list, but if you go back to our criteria one of them is that the human being will be comfortable operating in the House of Lords'. This was quoted in a Commons debate in which the work of the Commission was heavily criticised, even ridiculed.[12]

No further list appeared for over three years. Robin Cook commented on this in his memoirs, saying that given the public relations disaster of the first list, there was ministerial pressure to postpone the next list for as long as possible.[13] Meanwhile evidence accumulated to show that at least some of the new independent peers bothered very little about attending the House of Lords.[14] Subsequently the Commission has made four further lists of nominations, containing in total twenty-one more names. But the prime minister has also continued to nominate independent peers, bypassing the Commission in doing so. The Commission itself was reportedly not pleased with this. Subsequently the prime minister announced that he would limit his independent nominations to ten in each parliament![15]

When the Commission was established a body known as the Political Honours Scrutiny Committee was still in existence, charged with the task of ensuring those who received peerages had not acted corruptly in order to obtain them. The origins of this body lay in the scandal associated with Lloyd George's sale of honours in the 1920s. Its effectiveness was always difficult to assess. From time to time peerages were awarded to dubious characters who have subsequently gone to prison or otherwise been disgraced. Lord Kagan, who was given a peerage in Wilson's resignation honours list (one of the most notorious lists ever issued) was convicted of fraud a short while later. In 1990 newspaper reports claimed that the name of Jeffrey Archer had been omitted from Mrs Thatcher's resignation honours list because of doubts raised by this committee, but two years later he was awarded a peerage in a list of 'working peers', before being convicted of perjury and going to prison. The House of Commons Public Administration Select Committee reported on the honours system in 2004, recommending that the lingering work of the Scrutiny Committee be transferred to the new Appointments Commission, a view endorsed by the chairman of the committee who pointed out that two of its members also happened to be members of the Commission.[16] This was done amidst continuing criticism of the extent to which financial donors to political parties had been subsequently the recipients of peerages, a concern that had been frequently expressed since the 1980s. Labour in opposition before 1997 had been very critical of the Conservatives, but after 1997 Labour incurred equal criticism.

In 2000 new legislation had required all significant financial donations to parties to be declared. When vetting candidates for peerages the Committee and later the Commission had relied on certificates of disclosure signed by party office holders. In early 2006 newspaper reports suggested an honours list had been held up because the Commission objected to several of the names.[17] It emerged that five names were removed from the list of new peers because these individuals had made large loans to political parties, which unlike donations escaped the requirement for formal declaration. As more was revealed the waters became ever more murky. The police began inquiries and arrested Lord Levy, a friend of the prime minister who had a role in raising money for the party. The Public Administration Select Committee as part of an inquiry into ethics in public life returned to this subject, but only to reveal through its hearings how much confusion there was in this area. When Lord Stevenson was asked whether the Commission would vet resignation honours he didn't know the answer. Asked whether it was satisfactory for 'a completely undistinguished party hack' to be promised a peerage in return for standing down from a Commons seat in favour of a candidate whose presence in the Commons was eagerly sought by the party leadership, he prevaricated.[18] The openness and transparency the prime minister had promised when the Commission was set up seemed in short supply.

The effect of this unseemliness is clearly of serious concern. For the moment we simply note that the Commission remains non-statutory, appointed by the prime minister and reporting on the suitability of candidates in confidence to the prime minister. It would be possible to remodel the arrangements for scrutiny, just as it would be possible to remodel the arrangements for making nominations. But whether this would now be sufficient to restore public confidence in a system of nomination, or whether it reinforces the view that some other way of composing the House must be found is debatable.

The background of new peers

What kind of people become peers? From being an aristocratic chamber the House has become in part meritocratic, though what exactly is meant by that term is problematic. Working peers lists may contain the names of folk whose achievements seem modest, and have not thus far, for example, earned them an entry in *Who's Who*. (As soon as they become peers they are included!). Increasingly the representative quality of the House is being discussed. But the meaning of this term is also problematic, a point we return to in the conclusion. Meanwhile we may try and indicate something more of the nature of the present membership.

The largest single identifiable group is former MPs, who numbered almost 200 in 2006, or just over a quarter of the total membership. Almost all those who rise to cabinet rank take a peerage, as do a minority of junior ministers and a few backbenchers. Departure from ministerial office and from the House of Commons does not necessarily entail a wish to renounce politics altogether. Membership of the upper House, with the opportunities so afforded to contribute to debates there, may well make withdrawal from the Commons easier to contemplate. It is probably hard to overestimate the attractiveness of the House to most former MPs. There is still the proximity to the Commons, the sense of atmosphere to be found at Westminster, old friends to consort with and the possibility of doing a little useful political work from a base in the second chamber. These advantages are available without the demands of constituents to attend to, nor the strain of an election campaign to contemplate. Furthermore, while in the Commons failure to respond as required to the party whip brings all kinds of dangers, in the Lords the entreaties of whips can be regarded with relative equanimity. Tony Benn who was so resolute in avoiding entry to the House when he inherited his peerage in 1961 wrote in his diary on March 1995: 'It's an awful thing to admit, but you can see how attractive the House of Lords is: to be without a constituency, without elections, just making the occasional speech . . . I couldn't ever take one of Mr Blair's peerages, but I can see the appeal'.[19]

A few other former senior ministers have misgivings about going to the Lords, and some never do so. Michael Foot decided not to when he retired from the Commons in 1987 despite having been Leader of the Opposition. Sir John Nott, who retired in 1983 soon after leaving office as Secretary of State for Defence during the Falklands war, never took a peerage. Some former senior ministers wait a while before entering the House, perhaps because they entertain hopes of returning to the Commons. In 1997 it was reported that two defeated Conservative cabinet ministers, Michael Forsyth and William Waldegrave, had both declined peerages because they hoped to return to the Commons. But two years later they both took peerages. Roy Hattersley, formerly deputy leader of the Labour Party, retired from the Commons in 1997, and was included in that year's dissolution honours list. But he had been heavily critical of the House of Lords and in a newspaper article said he simply could not imagine himself discussing the matter of style and title with someone called Garter King of Arms. However after a seven-month delay he relented and decided to take his seat, though he never became an active member. Some who do take peerages appear to want very little to do with the place. Lord Moore, formerly John Moore and a member of Margaret Thatcher's cabinet, became a peer in 1992 but has seldom attended and in 2006 had yet to make his maiden speech.

Some former MPs enter the Lords in the hope of continuing their political career having suffered rejection from the Commons. When in 1983 at the age of fifty-seven David Stoddart lost the Commons seat he had held for thirteen years, he straightaway became Lord Stoddart of Swindon, and began a second parliamentary career in the upper House. Here he became an active peer, sometimes pursuing causes decidedly out of favour with his party, which he eventually left in 2001 to become an 'Independent Labour' member. Exceptionally, a minister losing a seat in an election may even continue their ministerial career uninterrupted through being rapidly translated to the Lords. This happened in 1992 when Lynda Chalker, Minister for Overseas Development since 1989 lost her Commons seat, but became Baroness Chalker and continued in the same ministerial post until 1997.

Alongside ex-MPs are some whose main career has been in politics, though they have never sat in the Commons. Lord Rennard has worked for many years for the Liberal Democrat Party, being campaign director when he became a youthful peer (aged thirty-eight) in 1999 and later becoming chief executive of the party. Another Liberal Democrat, Celia Thomas, had worked for the Liberal peers for almost forty years before she became a life peer in 2006. Others have a party career within local government, and in some cases may have stood for election to the Commons but without success. Lord Carter who became Government Chief Whip in the Lords in 1997 was active within the Labour Party for many years, standing unsuccessfully as a Labour candidate before becoming a life peer in 1987. Baroness Llewelyn-Davies of Hastoe became a peer in 1967 having four times unsuccessfully stood for election to the Commons, and feeling at the age of fifty-two that she had missed the boat in politics. In the Lords however she became her party's Chief Whip in 1973, a post she held for nine years including a five-year spell as Government Chief Whip. A small number of former members of the European Parliament have gone to the Lords, as have former European Commissioners (who are also customarily former MPs), most recently Lords Kinnock and Patten.

Peers have been recruited from a much wider background since the advent of life peerages in 1958. In particular more trade unionists, more from the universities and from more varied points within the public service and the voluntary sector have entered the House. Peerages invariably are awarded to former cabinet secretaries, almost always to retired heads of the diplomatic service, and sometimes former permanent secretaries in other departments. Such folk almost invariably sit on the crossbenches in the House, though some become adept campaigners on behalf of causes the strength of whose case they may recognise from their own former professional work within the civil service. Advisers to ministers, including former heads of the prime minister's policy unit (Lords Donoughue, Griffiths, Blackwell and Baroness Hogg) have entered the House. It has become usual for Britain's top policeman, the head of the Metropolitan Police Force, to be awarded a peerage on retirement. All recent Chiefs of Defence staff have gone to the Lords as soon as they retire. It has been the former holders of these posts that the prime minister has decided should receive peerages bypassing the Appointments Commission.

As well as some vice-chancellors and heads of colleges, those drawn from universities have included academics that have become associated with a political party and have found their way into the Lords as so-called 'working peers'. Such peers may to some extent represent those who work in education, but it is notable that very few head teachers have entered the Lords, and the frequent debates on schools that take place there are marked by an absence of contributions from peers who have actually worked in schools. The world of industry and finance has always been a plentiful source of recruits to the Lords. Again the changing nature of Britain's industrial base, and the shift from heavy industry to the service sector has been reflected in peerage creations.

Prime ministers have always been ready to reward powerful figures in the world of the media. Newspaper magnates received hereditary peerages and since 1958 some have received life peerages. But editors and some working journalists have also been ennobled in recent years. A smattering of people who represent the arts, for example Lord Lloyd-Webber and Lord Puttnam, have received peerages. A few ministers of religion have entered the Lords, some archbishops on retirement but others have included the former Chief Rabbi, Lord Jakobovits, the Moderator of the Free Church Council, Baroness Richardson of Calow, the Anglican primate of Ireland, Lord Eames, and in 2004 the leading Methodist, Lord Griffiths of Burry Port.

It is noticeable that some professions and some areas of the public service seem under-represented in the House, notably engineers of all kinds. According to a study in 2000, 16 per cent of the House were lawyers, but less than 3 per cent were engineers, and only just over 1 per cent were classified as scientists.[20] The paucity of engineers and the abundance of lawyers may be understandable to anyone who knows anything about parliaments anywhere in the world. Yet in so far as claims have been made about the remarkable range of expertise represented in the chamber, it is worth also taking note of the imbalances that exist.

The proportion of women in the House has been rising, mainly through a gradually rising proportion of new life peerages going to women. As Table 3.2 shows, 190 women have been created life peers, 15 per cent of the total number of such creations. Almost a quarter of Blair's life peers have been female but fewer than one in ten of Callaghan's creations were women. The first ever female law lord, Baroness Hale of Richmond, was appointed in 2004, but there are still no women bishops (the only group in the House entirely devoid of females), and as already mentioned there are very few female hereditary peers (only three of the ninety-two hereditary members are female). However, if the total number of women in the House has been modest, the part they have played has been significant. Baroness Young was Leader of the House from 1981 to 1983, and in 2004 Baroness Amos became the first black female cabinet minister when she was appointed

Leader of the House. In 2006 the House elected the Labour member, Baroness Hayman, as the first ever Speaker in a contest where she was one of two women out of nine candidates.[21] Baroness Hayman had been an MP from 1974–79, but her main experience (apart from being the mother of four boys!) was in the charity and voluntary sector. She entered the House in 1996, and served on the Labour frontbench as an opposition spokeswoman and then a minister until 2001. The proportion of women among active peers has compared very favourably with the proportion of women who have been members of the House of Commons. Likewise even though the proportion of members of the Lords drawn from ethnic minorities has been lower than in the population as a whole, the House has had at least as high a proportion as the Commons. Lord Taylor of Warwick entered the House shortly after he was defeated as Conservative candidate for Cheltenham in 1992, his selection as Conservative candidate for that seat having caused considerable controversy within the local Conservative Party on account of his West Indian origins.

Given lifelong membership it is inevitable that the House will tend to be an elderly body. In 2006 the average age was sixty-eight, with the Conservative and crossbench peers the oldest (average age almost seventy) and the Liberal Democrats the youngest (average age sixty-five!). The oldest member was Lord Renton, born in 1908; he had been in one or other House since he was first elected to the Commons in 1945. In 2006 the 'Father of the House' was Lord Jellicoe who took his seat as an hereditary peer at the minimum age of twenty-one in 1939; he was Leader of the House for a time in the 1970s, and as an ex-Leader was given a life peerage when most hereditary peers lost their seats in 1999. The youngest member in 2006 was an elected hereditary peer, Lord Freyberg, born in 1970. The expulsion of hereditary peers did raise the average age. The youngest person so far to have been appointed a life peer was Lord Mitford in 2000 at the age of thirty-two; curiously he was a hereditary peer without a seat, but was chosen in the internal party ballot Liberal Democrats hold to decide nominations for working peerages. Harold Wilson recommended a life peerage for a thirty-four year old woman disabled in a riding accident (Baroness Masham of Ilton), and in 1998 Tony Blair recommended Waheed Alli, the thirty-four year old founder of Planet 24 television. But these are very much the exceptions. Fewer than 10 per cent of life peers enter the House under the age of fifty. Prime ministers have also had to bear in mind that if they bring people who are relatively young into the House, they may be there a very long time. If the basis of membership is not changed Waheed Alli could easily still be there in 2050.

The party balance

Prior to the removal of most hereditary peers the imbalance between the major parties in the Lords was much emphasised. The Life Peerage Act increased substantially the flow of new Labour recruits, but Table 3.3 shows Conservatives remained the dominant party in the House, a position reinforced by the lengthy periods the Conservatives spent in office. When the Conservatives came to power in 1979 just over 60 per cent of peers taking a party whip were Conservative. By the time the Conservatives left office in 1997 almost 70 per cent of those taking a party whip were Conservative. Margaret Thatcher as prime minister ensured that Conservative supremacy in the House was reinforced by always creating more Conservative life peers than peers of other parties. Labour's loss of members through death during the 1980s was added to by defection to the Social Democrats, founded in 1981 and eventually merged with the Liberals in 1989. Table 3.3 shows how the party balance has altered over the last thirty years.

The ejection of hereditary peers was the decisive factor in establishing a rough parity between the main parties, though this was assisted by the speed with which Blair created new Labour peers (fifty-five in his first eighteen months). As can be seen since 1999 there have been three roughly equal groups in the House, the two main parties and the cross-bench peers. But of course the crossbench peers are emphatically not a party. However, what is striking in Table 3.3 is that the Labour whip is taken in the House by fewer than 30 per cent of its members. Effectively the balance of power is held by the Liberal Democrats, the fourth largest group. They have become the 'pivotal party', a role reinforced by the assiduity with which they attend and vote. Before discussing the

Table 3.3 Changing party strength in the House of Lords

	Cons	Lab	LibDem	Crossbench	Cons as % of party peers
1967–68	314	113	37	215	67.6
1975–76	292	149	30	281	62.2
1984–85	376	122	76	245	65.5
1989–90	397	104	65	260	70.1
1994–95	411	103	51	287	72.7
1997–98	441	174	69	330	64.7
2005–06	204	207	74	227	28.7

Note:
Figures are for peers who attended at least once in the relevant session.

implications of this further and examining the role of parties in the house, we need to analyse activity levels.

Active and less active peers

It has been in the nature of the House hitherto that some of its members have had little or nothing to do with the place, while others make their work in the House a full-time occupation. While it is possible to measure the quantity of activity, in terms of the number of days on which a peer attends the House, or the number of times a peer votes, or indeed the number of interventions made in debates, none of these of themselves provide any assessment of the quality of a particular peer's activity. Table 3.4 does however set out the bare bones so to speak of attendance, speaking and voting in the House. For the purposes of this analysis we have taken the 2003–04 session, which at the time of writing is the latest completed normal length session (the following session was foreshortened by the calling of an election in May 2005, and the 2005–06 session is unfinished at the time of writing and in any case is unusually long running from May 2005 to November 2006).

Attendance figures for all peers are now published, and made freely available on the parliamentary website. But these of course simply tell us the number of days on which a particular peer entered the chamber of the House during business, or attended an official committee of the House. As any visitor to the public gallery will have noticed peers come and go from the chamber the whole time; a peer who simply looks in for a few moments is recorded as having attended. An appearance is enough to entitle a peer to collect a tax-free expenses allowance, and no doubt this is a factor which boosts attendance figures. But attendance is clearly a starting point for the analysis of activity. This table records attendances in the chamber. It does not include committee attendances, though many of these no doubt took place on days when peers also attended the chamber. However, it is reasonable to think peers do at times attend committee meetings without necessarily also attending the chamber. Their daily attendance allowance is payable for committee attendance without the necessity of putting in an appearance in the chamber. All told in the 2003–04 session, 3387 committee attendances were recorded, an average of around six per peer (though of course this average will conceal a wide variation). The work of committees is discussed in the next Chapter. For the moment we simply take note that a great deal of work is done in select committees, and it would be wrong to overlook the fact that our tables do not reflect this. Interventions in debates vary from brief interventions to lengthy speeches. Some peers

Table 3.4 Activity in the House by category of peer 2003–04

		Eligible	Attendance		Voting		Speaking	
			Number	Average	Number	Average	Number	Average
Cons	LP	157	156	80	153	51	113	26
	Her.	47	47	114	47	76	42	44
Labour	LP	198	193	100	191	86	165	48
	Her.	4	4	126	4	93	3	30
LibDem	LP	64	64	101	64	77	61	38
	Her.	4	4	134	4	102	4	94
Crossbench	LP	135	130	60	103	20	101	19
	Her.	35	35	99	32	44	33	32
Bishops		26	26	26	22	5	21	10
Law lords		29	29	18	12	2	15	6
Total		699	688	83	632	52	558	33

Notes:

LP: Life peers

Her: Hereditary peers

Peers: Total number is number of members at the end of the session excluding those on leave of absence, but including those who became members during the session.

Average: Average of those eligible throughout the session, ie excluding those who died during the session and those who became members of the House during the session.

Attendance: As recorded by the House of Lords Information Office (excluding committee attendances).

Voting: Derived from information provided by Information Office on number of votes cast by every peer.

Interventions: As recorded in the Hansard sessional index, with interventions on the same day on the same item of business, or the same stage of a bill, counted as a single intervention.

habitually intervene frequently, while others make only occasional speeches. Speeches too vary from the platitudinous and ill-informed, to the truly authoritative speech that commands attention both within the chamber and beyond it. Nevertheless having made these qualifications, we examine these varied forms of activity in the House.

Since 1999 very few members of the House are entirely absent. Table 3.4 shows that the overall average attendance by peers was in excess of half the sitting days. All the hereditary peers who remain (excluding the two ex officio office holders) have presented themselves for election, and undoubtedly feel an obligation to participate in the work of the House. This is reflected in their high average levels of attendance and speaking. Crossbench life peers have a low average attendance rate, just below one-third, with Conservative life peers averaging just over half, while Labour and Liberal Democrats attend over two-thirds of the days. The table also reveals that crossbench peers vote much less often than all other groups. Indeed of the sixty-four peers who attended but never voted, fifty-seven were crossbenchers. Uniquely among the different groups a larger number of crossbenchers spoke in debates than voted in divisions. Peers who do not take a party whip do not have the same encouragement to vote, or indeed guidance about how to vote. Not surprisingly they vote much less than peers who are members of political parties. The implications of some of these points are discussed further when we return to consider the role of parties in the House.

When contemplating these figures it is well to remember that the House remains essentially a part-time and semi-professional house. Peers are not paid as such for their work. They are not accountable to constituents, or indeed to anybody else. Many still earn a living elsewhere, and of those who don't many are elderly and may find regular attendance at the House too burdensome, especially if they live a long way from London. This does raise the problem inherent in a part-time non-professional House that has legislative power. To what extent ought its members to be required to see themselves as professionals, giving priority over all their other commitments and interests to attendance at the House? In considering nominations to the House a party leader could decide to nominate only those whose ability and willingness to attend were obvious and whose loyalty in the division lobby would be unquestioned. But this would overpopulate the House with retired people who lived in London, and who might crudely be described as 'party hacks'. On the other hand giving life peerages to individuals who are younger, perhaps mid-career, and who have major responsibilities elsewhere in society, probably enriches the counsels of the House (providing such folk do attend sometimes), but also diminishes the average attendance and voting figures. This point we return to in the concluding Chapter.

Before 1999 there was always a reserve force of Conservative hereditary peers who could be summoned whenever the Chief Whip blew his bugle hard enough to bring them in from the shires. Most notorious was the huge turnout Margaret Thatcher secured to crush (by 317 votes to 183) a rebellion led by a Conservative backbench peer on the poll tax legislation in 1984. John Major used the same tactic in 1996 when the government was anxious to reverse a defeat it had suffered over its plans to sell off housing owned by the Ministry of Defence. This it succeeded in doing by 256 votes to 176, but among the 256 voting with the

government were fifteen who had not attended once in the previous
session, and sixteen more for whom this was their only vote of the
session.

Party organisation and government representation

Parties are the all pervasive institutions of modern politics. Because the
government must get its business through the House of Lords it is necessary for it to organise its support there, and this it does through the
party whip. But because the House is essentially a reviewing and revising chamber, and the right of the party to hold office as the government
is not being contested there, parties operate in a more muted way in the
Lords than in the Commons. The life of the government is never at stake
in the upper House, and very seldom is the fate of significant legislation
decided there. Peers themselves do not have to face the electorate, and
if they disagree with their party policy, they can sit rather loose to their
party attachment. And the fact that unlike the Commons the withdrawal
of the party whip carries with it no possibility of the loss of a seat again
diminishes the force of parties. The presence of a large body of crossbench peers further dilutes the impact and pervasiveness of party politics in the House. Nevertheless the government is answerable in the
Lords and ministers must steer legislation through the House. Hence the
need for party organisation, including the maintenance of frontbench
teams and the organisation of support in the division lobbies.

At the commencement of the twentieth century the prime minister
and half the cabinet had seats in the Lords. But the 1911 Parliament Act
confirmed the junior status of the Lords. The proportion of ministerial
posts held by peers fell. Churchill in the early 1950s had seven peers in
his cabinet, but no prime minister since has had more than four, and the
usual number has been two – the Lord Chancellor and the Leader of the
House. In Margaret Thatcher's administration, Lord Carrington was
Foreign Secretary until he resigned over the Falklands invasion in 1982,
and Lord Young of Graffham held cabinet posts until 1989. While under
Major there were never more than two cabinet ministers in the Lords,
Tony Blair did for a few months in 2003 have three full cabinet ministers ensconced on the red leather benches when Baroness Amos was
International Development Secretary before becoming Leader of the
House when Lord Williams of Mostyn, the previous holder of this office,
suddenly died. The Chief Whip in the House has been listed as attending cabinet meetings since 2000, no doubt to assist with consideration of
the government's parliamentary business, as has the Attorney General,
a peer since 1999.

For a senior departmental minister, being in the Lords rather than the Commons may seem an advantage, but there are also potential political difficulties. When Lord Carrington was Foreign Secretary from 1979 to 1982, his ability to absent himself from Westminster was useful, not least for the protracted negotiations that brought Zimbabwe to birth as a fully independent state. The sight of the Foreign Secretary having to abandon overseas visits to rush home for a division in the Commons is rather ridiculous. On the other hand to be one remove from the theatre of power can present problems, as Lord Carrington found when the Foreign Office came under severe political fire in the Commons following the Argentinean invasion of the Falkland Islands. Had he been able to answer his critics directly in the Commons he may not have felt it necessary to resign. It is also true that MPs tend to see appointments to ministerial posts from the upper House as taking good jobs away from those who have borne the heat and battle of campaigning to bring electoral success. The prime minister needs to focus his power of patronage on the Commons much more than he does the Lords!

The office of Lord Chancellor has always hitherto been held by a peer, who at one and the same time presided over debates, was head of the judiciary and a member of the cabinet. While such a multiplicity of roles in the Executive, the Legislature and the judiciary was recognised as anomalous, no serious practical difficulties had arisen, and to many the linkage so provided seemed advantageous. Though the abolition of this office had been announced in 2003, the Constitutional Reform Bill was amended so that the title 'Lord Chancellor' remains, but the holder of this title will no longer necessarily be a peer, or be legally qualified. The role of head of the judiciary has passed to the Lord Chief Justice and peers will from now on elect their own presiding officer. Lord Falconer, who had been Lord Chancellor since 2003, remained in the cabinet as Secretary of State for Constitutional affairs (and Lord Chancellor), but in future the post may be held by an MP. This could mean only one peer may remain in the cabinet, the Leader of the House. The presence of the Chief Whip at cabinet meetings is likely to be of increasing importance, especially as getting business through the House becomes more troublesome. In assessing the relative importance of peers being in the cabinet one has to keep in mind the way the role of the cabinet has itself changed, indicated by the diminished frequency and shortened length of its meetings.

Generally there have been five or six ministers of state and perhaps ten junior ministers, with half a dozen or so whips making up a team of between twenty and twenty-five on the government frontbench. Compared to the Commons this is a relatively small number, which nevertheless must answer for the government on all items of business that come before the House. Almost every department has one minister in the Lords, but unlike their Commons counterparts whips also act as spokesmen for departments. A minister in a department which has a heavy programme of legislation may be kept very busy in the House. Furthermore, ministers or whips must answer questions, and again unlike the Commons ministers do not have set days when they do this. Rather they simply answer when a question within their area of responsibility is asked. Some frontbenchers are clearly no more than spokesmen for the departments for which they answer. But others do have very clearly identified areas of responsibility. For example Lord Simon of Highbury had responsibility for business preparations for European Monetary Union and chaired the interdepartmental taskforce on competitiveness in Europe while a minister from 1997 to 1999. Labour's frontbench team in 2006 consisted entirely of life peers but whereas in the 1970s about half the frontbench were former MPs, by 2006 only three out of twenty-one had previously sat in the Commons.

On the Conservative side hereditary peers always dominated the frontbench until the 1990s, but by 1999 a majority were life peers, and this remained so after the 1999 Act. In 2006 there were nine hereditary elected peers out of twenty-nine on the opposition frontbench, a further indication of the comparatively active role played by elected hereditary peers. Life peers dominate the Liberal Democrat frontbench. Despite being the smallest party in the House they have the longest list of frontbench spokesmen (thirty-eight all told!) because their practice has been to name as spokesmen any member prepared to take on the role.

Work on the opposition frontbench may seem a pretty thankless task; opposition peers do not exactly queue up for appointment! In 1996, aware of the difficulties faced by the opposition frontbench in the House, the then Leader, Lord Cranborne introduced funding for the opposition parties in the House, now known as 'Cranborne money' (paralleling 'Short' money introduced for opposition parties in the Commons by Edward Short when Leader of that House in 1975). Though not generous this has eased the position frontbench peers found themselves in compared to when they had to rely entirely on their own peers' allowances for any assistance they needed.[22] In 1999 this funding was extended to defray secretarial expenses incurred by the convenor of the crossbench peers.

Parties hold weekly meetings, which allow frontbenchers to outline the following week's business, and more generally allow party members to consider their strategy. They also afford opportunities for peers sometimes to hear from their party frontbenchers in the Commons, and probably once a year from their party leader.

As already implied, crossbench peers have also developed an organised structure in the House. They began to meet regularly in the 1960s, when Lord Strang, a former diplomat, emerged as convenor, linking them to the 'usual channels', especially in relation to such matters as the allocation of resources within the House and ensuring that crossbenchers who might wish to be considered for appointments to committees of the House were given this opportunity. He was succeeded by Baroness Hylton-Foster, widow of a former Speaker of the Commons, who devoted herself to this role for twenty-one years up to 1995. Since then it has been understood that the appointment is for a maximum of five years, and has been held successively by Lord Weatherill, former Speaker of the Commons; Lord Craig of Radley, former Chief of Defence Staff; and since 2004 Lord Williamson of Horton, a former career civil servant who became Secretary General to the European Commission. Though crossbench peers eschew the notion that they have a party line on any policy issue, they have collectively given much consideration to proposals for reform of the House. During the passage of the 1999 Act it was their convenor, Lord Weatherill, who took responsibility for piloting through the amendment agreed between Lord Cranborne and Lord Irvine of Lairg, then Lord Chancellor, leading to the election of hereditary peers, often as a result referred to as 'Weatherill' peers.

Voting

There is a paradox about voting in the House. In one sense it is such a trivial activity. The division bells ring and peers come scurrying from all corners of the Palace of Westminster (and from outside it), endeavouring to reach the lobby to have their names recorded as taking sides on an issue about which they may well know next to nothing.[23] Ever vigilant party whips are on hand to ensure peers are shepherded in the right direction. As they tramp through the lobbies they chatter about a hundred and one things, and then within minutes most are scattered again to the varied haunts from which they have just been summoned. Party whips may tell them if and when further divisions are expected, or such information may be conveyed on the pagers they are now encouraged to carry.

But in another sense voting is the most vital activity in which the House engages. For it is this that decides whether a bill is amended against the will of the government or not, and if legislation is changed then ministers must respond. It is government defeats that get noticed. They take up the time of ministers, civil servants and not least of MPs. It is easy to count the number of defeats and a short step from that to formulating conclusions about the assertiveness of the House or its impact on legislation. And of course some defeats are very significant. But in assessing the influence of the House defeats are by no means the whole story, as the next Chapter hopefully makes clear.

In analysing voting as an activity in the House, we need to consider both the frequency with which peers vote and the degree of party cohesion that is demonstrated in the division lobbies. As to frequency we have already commented on the much lower level of voting among crossbench peers. This is not surprising when their circumstances are considered. Crossbench peers have no friendly whip to guide them into an appropriate lobby. When it comes to voting they are on their own. They have to think and decide for themselves, perfectly reasonable if they happen to be following the progress of a particular bill closely, but if not then abstention is understandable. And most of the time crossbenchers do just that – they abstain. Meg Russell found that in all whipped divisions between 1999 and 2005 their turnout was 10 per cent, compared with 34 per cent for Conservatives, 51 per cent for the Liberal Democrats and 53 per cent for Labour.[24] Sometimes crossbenchers have been criticised for their apparently poor voting record. But party politicians who do this should reflect how often when they vote, if it wasn't for that friendly whip telling them which way to go, how would they decide? It seems likely that as often as not they have little if any idea of the actual point being contested in the division lobby.

But of course for party members there is no need for them to know the detail of every matter. Generally they have over many years given loyalty to their party. They support its basic principles and its ideological outlook. And even when they have wobbles about a particular policy, voting against colleagues (many of whom are also probably friends) can seem like an act of betrayal. Loyalty is not just cerebral; it is emotional. It is the loyalty of the tribe.[25] Voting in the House is based on cohesion rather than discipline, and cohesion in the division lobbies is high. Philip Norton found that in 70 per cent of all whipped divisions in the three sessions from 1999 to 2002 there were no dissenting votes. Meg Russell found that in the 806 divisions where the government had a whip from 1999 to 2005, there were no dissenting votes in 600. In divisions where dissent was recorded the number of rebel Labour peers was generally low; in only thirteen did the number reach double figures.[26]

Such cohesion is not a new phenomenon in the Lords: in the 1994–95 session less than 3 per cent of all votes cast by Conservative peers in whipped divisions were against the Conservative Government, while in the same session only six out of 4655 votes cast by Labour peers in whipped divisions were against the party whip. Of course peers who may be reluctant to support their party can simply abstain, and unlike the Commons, no 'pairing' arrangements exist, so there is no clear means by which the level of abstention can be assessed, though sometimes the very low level of support for the government is obvious. Peers threatening to vote against their party are undoubtedly sometimes persuaded by their whip simply to stay away. At least if they do so one less vote is needed to win than if they had voted in the opposite lobby.

The party whips in the Lords have very few sanctions that can be employed against peers who vote against the party line. If in the Commons it is appropriate to talk about sticks and carrots, or even the 'black arts of whipping', this is not so in the Lords. The sticks are 'more like twigs',[27] and the supply of carrots virtually nonexistent. For most peers ambitions are either fulfilled or have mellowed to the point where party whips find them too barren to cultivate. Persuasion and in many cases appeals to party loyalty developed over many years are probably their most useful strategies. These strategies can clearly be effective. Lord Lipsey, a backbench Labour peer, has taken a rather different view from Lord Norton, saying that Labour peers have 'iron whipping, backed by the strongest of all sanctions, which is social disapproval'.[28] Occasionally the whip is withdrawn for obvious breaches of party discipline. In 1996 the former Conservative party treasurer, Lord MacAlpine of West Green had the whip withdrawn because of his very public support for the Referendum Party.

Expectations of frontbenchers are more demanding. If a party spokesman in the House expresses views out of line with party policy then removal from the frontbench may well result. Lord Skidelsky was dropped from the Conservative frontbench because of views expressed on the Allied action in Kosovo. The Labour peer Lord Desai caused his party leader in the Commons embarrassment in 1993 when his views on the extension of VAT were quoted with approval by John Major, and he was dropped for a time. Most notable recently was the sacking in 1998 of Lord Cranborne as Conservative leader in the Lords for negotiating with the prime minister over the future of the House of Lords behind the backs of William Hague and other colleagues in the Conservative shadow cabinet.

Given the cohesion within the main parties, and the low level of voting by crossbenchers (who in any case vote in different directions), the pivotal position of the Liberal Democrats becomes obvious. Russell found that Liberal Democrats voted against the government in 264 of the 283 defeats that the Labour Government suffered in the House between 1999 and 2005, and only sided with the government twelve times when it went down to defeat. But whereas in the first Blair parliament the Liberal Democrats supported the government in well over half whipped divisions, by the last two sessions of the following parliament (2003–04 and 2004–05), they supported the government in fewer than one fifth of whipped divisions.[29] Liberal Democrats have for years yearned for real political power, and the other two parties have on the whole delighted to relegate them to the sidelines of British politics. Tony Blair and Paddy Ashdown may have courted one another before the 1997 election, but once Labour were firmly in the seat of power, the logic of two-party politics rapidly pushed the Liberal Democrats to the margins again. But in the House of Lords the Liberal Democrats find themselves with real power – but ironically only in a chamber of influence.

A part professional House?

The House has stumbled towards a greater professionalism. More peers are more committed to the work of the House than ever before. From the perspective of earlier years, prior to 1997, what is striking about the tables showing attendance and voting is the frequency with which most peers do attend and do vote. In 2003–04 the mean attendance level for all peers was well over half the sitting days; in 1989–90 it was less than a quarter. The House is not a professional House of full-time parliamentarians, but it is much closer to that than it used to be. The hereditary peers who remain feel an obligation to be active, though unless removed by further legislation, their inability to vacate the places they occupy on behalf of their hereditary brethren and their parties will for some become a difficult burden as they face old age and failing health. A far higher proportion of newly arriving life peers feel an obligation to participate regularly in the work of the House than used to be the case. And though there are still no salaries for members, expense allowances have become very much more generous both in the scope of what they cover and the amount that is payable.

The introduction of an expense allowance in 1957 has been referred to in the previous Chapter. Gradually over the years the basis on which the expense allowance is paid has broadened. Costs that can now be claimed include not only subsistence but office costs, travel within the UK on parliamentary business, travel for spouses and travel to EU institutions.[30] A peer who attended every day and claimed all the allowances would receive around £50,000 in a year, and as expenses this sum would be tax free. The Freedom of Information Act has resulted in details of the totals claimed under each heading by every peer being published on the House website. For 2003–04 (since when the level of expenses payable has risen) this shows twenty-seven members claimed over £50,000 and a further eighty-five members claimed over £40,000. Totalling all expenses (including travel costs) claimed for every peer and then dividing by the number of days attended shows that the average claimed by all peers worked out at something over £200 per peer per day attended.

Nevertheless compared to other parliamentary institutions the House of Lords is relatively inexpensive. The total costs of running the House have doubled in the last five years, reaching just over £118 million in 2004–05, though this included an exceptional item, the purchase of the Millbank Island site. Following the acquisition of another nearby property in 2001, this has eased the problem of office space for peers, almost all of whom now have desk spaces. Peers themselves are very fond of emphasising that in terms of annual costs per member, their House is a bargain at £131,000 compared to £489,000 per MP.

Ministers of course receive a ministerial salary, but because the total remuneration for Commons ministers includes an element of the parliamentary salary (not available to Lords ministers), for a long time ministers in the upper House have appeared badly paid. In 1999 most Lords ministers received a 20 per cent plus rise to rectify this. The Leader of the Opposition and the Opposition Chief Whip have also received a salary, as have the chairman of committees and the principal deputy chairman. But no other peers are paid for the work they do in the House. The absence of any salary for the convenor of the crossbench peers, or for the leader of the Liberal Democrats has certainly caused comment. If further reform of the House does take place no doubt the unsatisfactory nature of remuneration arrangements would then be addressed. Until then there is not likely to be a better solution than the situation that currently prevails.

When in the early 1990s scandal appeared to engulf the House of Commons the rules governing the declaration of interests by MPs were made more stringent. The concerns raised had repercussions for the House of Lords. Back in 1974 the Procedure Committee of the House had come down against any compulsory register, partly on the grounds that not only were members not paid, but 'many peers are members of the House involuntarily'; it recommended that self-discipline and personal honour should continue to guide members.[31] In 1995 a committee chaired by a law lord (Lord Griffiths) was established, and this again emphasised the differences between the Commons and the Lords, but did recommend that it should be mandatory for peers to declare paid parliamentary consultancies and financial interests in lobbying companies. This reflected recognition not only of the growing importance of

professional parliamentary lobbyists, but also of the fact that the House
of Lords frequently presented a more worthwhile target than the
Commons for lobbyists eager to secure small adjustments to legislation.
This was a point that had received some endorsement in academic
studies which showed that lobbyists of all kinds were increasingly tar-
geting the upper House.[32] The Committee on Standards of Conduct in
Public Life under its second chairman, Lord Neill, reported on the House
of Lords in 2000.[33] This recommended that mandatory registration
should be extended to cover all relevant interests. In doing so it emphasised that membership of the House could no longer be described as
'involuntary', and that the non-payment of salaries to members was
much less relevant than the fact that peers could and did frequently
influence the content of legislation. At the request of the then Leader of
the House, Baroness Jay, Lord Williams of Mostyn (her successor as
Leader) chaired a small committee of peers to consider how to implement the recommendations. This proposed a code which included a
requirement to register the 'financial interest of a spouse, relative or
friend' where these might be relevant, a phrase which caused particular
perplexity when the draft code was debated. An amendment moved
from the opposition frontbench was very narrowly defeated (152 votes
to 149).[34] This more wide ranging mandatory register came into effect
the following year, and is now published on the House website. If a peer
is unwilling to comply he or she can take leave of absence, which is what
the former Leader of the House, Lord Cranborne, did. In 2004 the sub-
committee on Lords' Interests reported that the code had not led to any
significant problems. The House seems to have settled down into acceptance of the code, and the resulting register of interests may be regarded
as a necessary feature of any contemporary parliamentary body. The
way the House is gradually evolving towards being a modern profes-
sionalised legislature is illustrated in the way it now accepts the requirement for a mandatory and wide ranging register of members' interests.

Lords and Commons compared

There are several significant ways in which the membership of the
House of Lords differs from that of the House of Commons. In terms of
occupational background, gender and ethnicity the differences are not
great. But in other respects the differences are considerable. Among life
peers there may be a similar proportion of lawyers in both Houses, but
an important minority of lawyers in the Lords are actually serving or
former senior judges, and many others are at the senior end of their profession. As noted above judges have been outspoken in the House when

they have felt the role of the judiciary or indeed the resources made available to the courts system have been under attack.

The number of doctors may be roughly similar in the two Houses but those in the Lords as life peers tend to be very senior figures at the peak of the profession, while those in the Commons are generally younger and more junior. Trade union-sponsored MPs are more likely to be young researchers or junior officials of their unions, while trade union peers will be very senior union figures. Of course hereditary peers have in the past altered the picture a certain amount. There have been ordinary working dentists and solicitors, middle managers and even the odd bus driver or toilet attendant, arrived in the upper House through the hereditary system. But the hereditary peers as a body have now departed, and the idiosyncratic members as well as the much more numerous old Etonians now no longer sit as of right.

An important contrast between the Houses is that the Lords has not become dominated by the full-time professional politician in the way the Commons has. There has been a gradual rise in the number of peers who do approach their work in the House in at least a semi-professional way. But the majority even among the active peers still regard their work in the House as part-time. They may see themselves as semi-retired, or they may reckon that much or most of their time has to be devoted to their employment or their business. Some may for a time be very active in the House, and then subside into a very marginal role.

The fact that, hitherto at least, once a member always a member, further differentiates them from MPs. A few people become members in order to do a particular job, usually on one of the party frontbenches. Some undoubtedly strive for a peerage, the attainment of which deposits them in the House. For others membership is a status ascribed to them rather than one they have sought as a deliberate act of will. After years of public service or the attainment of great distinction in some walk of life, they find themselves put forward for a peerage. It may be that in accepting a peerage they intend to contribute to the work of the House. But such an intention may after a few years be exhausted; yet once there members stay for life. Others who accept peerages may simply do so because this is a greater honour than a knighthood, the latter honour being one they may well already hold. Others become members because they reach the top of a professional tree, either in the judiciary or in the established Church; they bring an ex officio quality to the membership of the House. Bishops apart, there is no provision for retirement. Many become very old, and often old age and infirmity greatly impair their capacity to contribute to the work of the House. Yet they remain members. No act of will is required in order to sustain their membership, and no act of will can bring about their removal from membership.

MPs by contrast are all in the House of Commons because they have stood for election and emerged victorious from that process. In modern times this involves a very considerable act of will, perhaps mainly in securing a party nomination but also in winning popular support expressed in the ballot box. Furthermore MPs all know that they must decide within the lifetime of a parliament, a maximum period of five years, whether to stand again for election or whether to retire. Peers never retire – as peers, though they may well fade away from the House. And the professional career politician once a member of the Commons generally aspires to frontbench and hopefully ministerial status. There is always a long line of MPs seeking promotion, and a prime minister's patronage power is strengthened accordingly. But not so in the Lords.

The House of Lords does mobilise into parliamentary activity a range of people who would never be likely to enter the Commons. And the fact that peers do not have constituents alters their perspective on their work. Some take very little part when they first join, perhaps because of heavy business or professional commitments, or maybe sheer disinclination. But later they become much more involved. Not only is the House a House of contrasts in itself, but it is also a chamber very distinctive in its membership, its manners, its ethos and character to that of the Commons.

Notes

1	On this see D. Shell, 'Labour and the House of Lords: A Case Study in Constitutional Reform', *Parliamentary Affairs*, 53:2 (2000) 290–310.
2	As well as Prince Charles, created Duke of Cornwall in 1949, these were the Duke of Edinburgh (1947), the Duke of York (1986) and as peers by succession the Duke of Gloucester and the Duke of Kent.
3	HL Deb. 26 Mar. 2004, cols. 947–1003.
4	HL Deb. 17 Jun. 2003, cols. 751–85.
5	HL Deb. 9 Oct. 2002, cols. 325–53. The result was 83 to 82 against the government.
6	*Select Committee on the Constitutional Reform Bill*, HL 125, 2003–04.
7	G. Drewry and L. Blom-Cooper, 'The Appellate Function', in B. Dickson and P. Carmichael (eds), *The House of Lords: Its Parliamentary and Judicial Roles* (Oxford, Hart Publishing, 1999).
8	Calculated from information contained in House of Lords Library Note on Peerage Creation, LLN 98/005.
9	HL Deb. 7 Jul. 1992, cols. 1055–7.
10	*The Times*, 20 June 1999.

11 Prime Minister Press Notice, 4 May 2000.

12 HC Deb. 9 May 2001, cols. WH71-113.

13 R. Cook, *Point of Departure* (London, Simon & Schuster, 2003), p. 87.

14 Eg. *The Times*, 10 Nov. 2003, 'People's Peers Who Rarely Take Part in Votes'.

15 HC Deb. 25 Jan. 2005, col. 10ws.

16 Fifth Report, Public Administration Select Committee, *A Matter of Honour*, HC 212, 2003–04.

17 For example, *The Times*, 6 Mar. 2006.

18 HC 1119-I, 2005–06, Q. 21-2, 66–8.

19 Tony Benn, *Free at Last: Diaries 1991–2001* (London, Hutchinson, 2002), p. 362; see also p. 294.

20 J. C. McNeill, 'Is the Reformed House of Lords a More Representative Chamber?' unpublished, quoted in B. Criddle, S. Childs and P. Norton, 'The Make-up of Parliament', P. Giddings (ed.) *The Future of Parliament* (Basingstoke, Palgrave Macmillan, 2005).

21 The runner up was Lord Grenfell, a crossbench hereditary peer, who entered the House in 1976, but was not very active until he retired from his career in the World Bank in 1995. At the time of the election he was chairman of the European Communities Committee. The only other female candidate was Baroness Fookes, a former Conservative MP and Deputy Speaker in the Commons, who was the first eliminated in the preferential voting system used for this contest.

22 In 2004–05 the Conservatives received £413,131, the Liberal Democrats £206,272, and £37,023 was paid for crossbench peers expenses.

23 One peer observed that there was usually far less than a quarter of the peers who vote in a division present in the chamber immediately before the vote to hear the arguments being deployed. See P. Norton 'Cohesion without Discipline: Party Voting in the House of Lords', *Journal of Legislative Studies*, 9:4 (2003) 57–72.

24 M. Russell and M. Sciara, 'The Lords, the Party System and British Politics', *British Politics*, 2:3 (2007).

25 See especially E. Crewe, *Lords of Parliament* (Manchester University Press, 2005), ch. 8, pp. 130–59.

26 Russell and Sciara, 'Why Does the Government get Defeated?'; Norton, 'Cohesion without Discipline'.

27 Norton, 'Cohesion without Discipline'.

28 Select Committee on Public Administration, HC 494-II, 2001–02, Qs 139 and 158.

29 Russell and Sciara, 'Why Does the Government get Defeated?'.

30 In 2006 £154.50 for overnight subsistence (which can go towards the cost of a London residence if 'maintained for the purpose of attending sittings of the House'), day subsistence £77 (for meals and incidental travel), £67 per sitting day and up to forty further days for secretarial and office costs.

31 HL 51, 1974.

32 See especially M. Rush (ed.), *Parliament and Pressure Politics* (Oxford, Clarendon Press, 1990).

33 Seventh Report from the Committee on Standards of Conduct in Public Life, *Standards of Conduct in the House of Lords*, 2000, Cm. 4903-I & II.

34 HL Deb. 2 Jul. 2001, cols. 630–87.

4

The work of the House

The House of Lords makes a substantial contribution to the work of the British parliament. Though unquestionably the junior chamber, and not since the 1909–11 constitutional crisis showing any serious sign of forgetting that fact, it is nevertheless constitutionally part of parliament, and must therefore approve all legislation. Though its powers are constrained both by the Parliament Acts and by convention, it shares in the responsibility of parliament to scrutinise all draft legislation. In practice the House is responsible for a great many of the changes made as legislation wends its way through parliament, much of this the result of persuasion rather than through the exercise of power. The House also takes part in the classic scrutiny functions exercised by parliament, through affording opportunities for government spokesmen to be questioned and for debate to take place. Through select committee inquiries too the House contributes to the parliamentary function of holding the executive to account.

It is important to begin by emphasising this because some discussion about the House seems to start from the assumption that its role is actually very marginal. In part such a view may arise out of confusion between assessing on the one hand activity and function, and on the other effectiveness in terms of influence and power. While functions can be described and numerous statistics produced to indicate activity, and indeed the very considerable increase in activity that has taken place in the House in recent decades, these of themselves say nothing about effectiveness. It may be that the House makes hundreds of amendments to bills, but are they really made by the House, or simply processed through the House? Select committee reports may be the vehicle through which interesting and pertinent evidence is gathered, and they may make a strong case for some change in government policy. But how is their effectiveness to be assessed if no change of policy occurs? Likewise debate on the floor of the House may produce powerful and eloquent speeches, but equally it may be difficult to identify anybody – within government or without – that appears to have taken any notice.

Such questions about effectiveness may with equal pertinence be asked about the House of Commons. Opinions vary widely about the value of select committee carried out by MPs. Many people question how worthwhile debate on the floor of the House is. Criticism of the House of Commons has been widespread and much of it well-founded, chiefly because its role in holding the executive to account seems so often vitiated by party majority and the dominance of the government within the House. More will be said about this when we discuss reform of the Lords. But here it is important simply to put into perspective criticisms that are made of the work of the House of Lords. The role of parliament is subtle. Devising performance indicators for any parliamentary body, especially those which do not operate in a system embodying a clear separation of powers, is difficult. It is necessary to keep criticisms of the role of the House of Lords in perspective by keeping in mind both the difficulty of measurement and the fluctuating assessments made of other parliamentary bodies, including the frequently feeble performance of the Commons.

It is worth noting as a starting point that the House has certainly become a very much more active chamber in recent decades. Table 4.1 indicates this.

The changes that have taken place since the arrival of life peers are consistent with the argument developed in the previous Chapter that the House has become more professional. Three-day weeks were the

Table 4.1 The growth in activity of the House of Lords

Session	Peers*	Number who attended	Average daily atten- dance	Hours house sat+	Number of divisions	Number of QWA	Sittings after 10 pm	Amdts to govt bills
1959–60	907	542	136	450	16	48	1	N/A
1971–72	1073	698	250	813	171	315	28	924
1981–82	1174	790	284	930	146	1098	41	1309
1989–90	1186	826	318	1072	186	1204	74	2526
1995–96	1135	853	372	935	110	2471	60	1593
2003–04	707	688	368	1094	176	4524	46	3344

Notes:
QWA: Questions for written answer.
* Number of peers includes those who took seats during the session, but excludes those who died during the session; includes those on leave of absence.
+Number of hours House sat: Hours in chamber only.

norm until the 1960s when Monday became a regular sitting day. By the 1990s Friday sittings were not unusual. In the 1960s the House rarely sat after 10 pm but by the late 1990s more often than not the House worked beyond 10 pm, though subsequently (as in the Commons) the introduction of some morning sittings and other changes have been designed to avoid late sittings. The number of peers attending grew greatly. In the long post-election 1997–98 session over 1000 different peers attended and the average daily attendance rose to over 400 for the first time. The reduction in the size of the House brought about by the exclusion of most hereditary peers in 1999 caused a dip, with average attendance falling from 446 in 1998–99 to 352 the following session, but by 2006 the average was again exceeding 400; the House also sat rather longer than before after peers by succession had departed. Thus the loss of over 600 members caused average daily attendance to fall by less than 100. The frequency with which the House votes increased markedly in the 1960s and 1970s, and has fluctuated since. Whereas up until the 1970s the quota of four starred questions per day was often not filled, from the 1980s onwards all available slots for such questions are usually taken. Questions for written answer were put down at the rate of about two a week in the 1950s. By the late 1990s over 100 a week were being asked, and by 2006 this had risen to over 140 a week.

This growth of activity has clearly placed strains on the House and its customary ways of working. While many adaptations have taken place to cope with the increased pressures, the House has struggled to avoid any fundamental departure from its central traditions. Thus no procedure for introducing 'guillotines' or Commons style programme motions has been introduced, even if the pressures exerted by the 'usual channels' (the party whips acting together in their role as managers of business in the House) have greatly increased. Nor has the House introduced a Commons style Speaker. When the customary role of the Lord Chancellor as Speaker was terminated by the government as part of the 2005–06 judicial reforms, most peers expressed antipathy for the idea of a Speaker empowered to keep order in the House.[1] The model for 'Speakership' that was agreed emphasised that the new presiding officer would have no more authority than other peers in keeping order in the House, and that where difficulties arose responsibility for maintaining order would continue to rest with peers collectively. It is characteristic of the House that the first source of guidance to which it looks, for example when several peers are trying to intervene simultaneously at question time, is still the senior government minister, the Leader of the House. In other respects the House has avoided fundamental change. The House has eschewed Commons style standing committees. Proposals to concentrate divisions in so-called 'prime time' have likewise been resisted. Nor have restrictions been introduced on the right of peers to speak in the House.

However, if fundamental change has been resisted, many adjustments of various kinds have been made as the House has sought to balance the conflicting demands placed upon it. For example, though any peer may speak in a debate, time is generally now strictly rationed, with the usual channels agreeing how long a debate will last and the time available being divided by the number of peers wishing to speak, sometimes giving only a very few minutes for each individual speaker. Though no Commons style standing committees have been introduced, frequent use is now made of a 'Grand Committee', especially for the committee stage of bills (discussed below). Various tensions are evident, perhaps the foremost being the obvious tension between a government eager to get its business through the House quickly and efficiently, and the other parties in the House who feel a responsibility to subject that business to thorough and critical scrutiny. That is a characteristic feature of parliamentary bodies, as perhaps is the tension between the old and the new, between the traditionalists and the modernisers. In the Lords the former tend to believe that traditional and rather elaborate courtesies and procedures add to the dignity of the House and help to ensure that debate is conducted with cool reason rather than raucous passion, pithy incisiveness rather than political invective. The latter want to see some of the rituals of the House and the freedoms enjoyed by peers dispensed with, and rather more predictability about the timing of divisions and the daily finishing time. To some extent this tension overlaps with one between the former MPs in the House, the ex-professional politicians who instinctively bring to the chamber the ways of the Commons, and those who have only ever been House of Lords people, many of whom deprecate what they see as the rowdiness and endless politicking at the other end of Westminster. However, former MPs usually adjust to the ways of the Lords, and not a few become ardent champions of the House, readily declaring its superiority to the Commons as a chamber of debate and critical scrutiny of government. Finally there is a tension between those who treat their work in the House as more or less a full-time occupation and are quite ready to be there as much as necessary, and those for whom it is a subsidiary activity to their professional or business involvement elsewhere, and who wish to timetable their visits quite precisely.

Periodically the working practices of the House have received examination by groups of peers, most recently in 2004, but earlier in 1999 and again in 2002.[2] Changes have included the introduction of Thursday morning sittings, and variations in the time spent on oral questions. The most controversial change has been the alteration of the day for general debates. For many years a feature of the House has been the 'Wednesday' debates. Peers have offered their wisdom on all kinds of topics, with a government spokesman making a reply, but no votes being taken. In 1999 the Labour Chief Whip, Lord Carter, proposed that the day for such debates be moved from Wednesday to Thursday. The reasoning behind this was to concentrate legislative work of the House, upon which important divisions could be called, into the middle part of the week, and enable peers who lived at a distance from London to leave for home (with their party whip's approval!) at an earlier hour on Thursday. However the House as a whole decisively rejected the proposal (by 225 votes to 87, with the minority almost entirely made up of Labour peers). The main argument against the change arose out of concern not to see such debates marginalised. In the background was the feeling that the Commons, by altering its procedures to ensure that no important business requiring votes was taken on a Thursday evening, had effectively shortened its working week. The matter was again considered in 2001 when the majority against the change fell to two (130 to 128). Then in 2005 peers agreed the change by 135 votes to 98.[3]

In 2006 the Procedure Committee conducted an analysis and concluded that Thursday attendance had not declined nor had the number of peers wishing to speak in general debates fallen. But when this was debated several peers asserted that attendance was concentrated on the earlier part of the day, with peers disappearing unless they actually wanted to speak in the debate taking place, and the House being pretty dead by about 3 pm. However the House agreed to make the two-year experiment permanent, with some peers, including Lord Rodgers of Quarry Bank, the former Liberal Democrat leader in the House, who had led opposition to the change, still protesting that all the predicted disadvantages had come about.[4]

Advocacy of modernisation in the House reached a high point in a report made in 2004 by a group of Labour backbench peers entitled 'Reform of the Powers, Procedures and Conventions'. Recommendations included the formalising of conventions, confining votes to set times and introducing delayed divisions, investing powers in a Speaker and other points. When this was debated in January 2005 these recommendations received very little support outside the ranks of the governing party. Indeed most peers were heavily critical of the managerialist and controlling nature of these proposals, which seemed designed simply to make life easier for the government.[5]

Sometimes to outsiders attachment to traditions seems positively quaint. A select committee was appointed in 1998 to consider the ceremony for the introduction of new peers. This recommended shortening the ceremony in order both to save some time, and also to make it less opaque in meaning. The House debated its recommendations for three and a half hours before approving these by 150 votes to 98.[6] Later that year Lord Ferrers initiated a two hour debate on recommendations to alter the formal dress of the Lord Chancellor (allowing him to remove 'breeches, tights and buckled shoes'), a proposal approved against Lord Ferrers wishes by 145 votes to 115.[7] Perhaps even more bizarre was a debate on whether or not peers should be allowed to speak with their hands in their pockets, and if so did this include jacket pockets as well as trouser pockets![8]

An area where some change has occurred (and more has been advocated) has been in the committee stage of bills. Traditionally the committee stage of all bills has been taken on the floor of the House rather than in anything equivalent to Commons standing committees. But in recent years the House has begun to make greater use of committees for legislative work, in particular since 1994 by referring some bills for their committee stage to sittings in the Moses Room. This became known as the 'Grand Committee', and is in effect a parallel chamber the use of which has grown greatly in recent years. The committee has no fixed membership; any peer may attend and take part in business there, but no divisions take place, and sittings are suspended when divisions occur in the main chamber. The use of the 'Grand Committee' procedure has grown greatly, especially in 2003–04 when the number of hours doubled from the preceding session to 246. Some peers have viewed the absence of votes in grand committee as a handicap to effective scrutiny, believing that on important and controversial bills this limits the opportunity to press the government to make adjustments to bills. But others have argued that the committee stage should essentially be seen as an exploratory stage with contested amendments being dealt with by the whole House on report.[9] While the major reason for this change has been to increase the capacity of the House, some peers have argued that it enables a more effective committee stage to take place because the physical arrangements induce greater informality, not least because of reduced physical distance between ministers and their officials, who are seated alongside one another.[10] In 2005 the House agreed to broaden the range of business taken in grand committee, which now includes debates on select committee reports, unstarred questions (short debates) and statutory instruments. This procedure simply doubles up the capacity of the House by in effect using a second chamber, though with restrictions on what can actually be done there. Some peers heavily involved in select committee work have been reluctant to see their committee reports debated there, feeling that this was tantamount to marginalising them.[11]

Forms of Business

Table 4.2 indicates how the House spent its time in the 2003–04 session. No session is entirely typical, but this was a normal length session, that is, one not shortened by the calling of an election (as in 2004–05) or extra long following an election (2005–06).

Table 4.2 divides the various categories of business into legislative and non-legislative, or what might be termed deliberative. This reflects

Table 4.2 How the House of Lords spends its time

	% of total time	Number of hours
Legislation		
Public bills:	54.6	598
Lords bills	21.2	232
Commons bills	33.4	366
Government Bills	52.7	577
Private members' bills	1.9	21
Private bills:	0.4	4
Statutory instruments	5.6	61
Total Legislation	60.6	663
General debates, questions, statements		
Motions for Debate:	17.3	189
Debates on select committee reports	2.8	31
Mini-debates (unstarred questions)	4.8	52
Starred (oral) questions	7.4	82
Statements	3.6	40
Total non-legislative debates and questions	35.9	394
Other (Prayers, introductions, adjournments during pleasure, private notice questions, measures)	3.5	28
Total in chamber	100.0	1085
Grand Committee (committee stage of 18 bills)		246

Notes:
Source: Derived from information supplied by House of Lords Information Office.
Figures are rounded so may not add up to precise totals given.

the basic distinction between the work of the House in dealing with leg-islation of all kinds, and time spent on procedures that are not directly related to legislation, but seek to enhance in some way the account-ability of government. The most important task by common consent is the scrutiny of draft legislation, which as can be seen took around 55 per cent of the time of the House, a proportion that has become normal in recent sessions. Bills vary a great deal in their size, complexity and importance. They may be introduced first into either House, but those of greatest importance are usually taken first to the Commons because it is there that the battle of political will between the parties must be fought out, and that is the House that contains most senior ministers. The consideration of which House to send a bill to first may also be influ-enced by the fact that the Parliament Acts are only applicable to bills taken first through the Commons. Resort to the Parliament Acts may have been unusual, but if such a possibility is precluded then this alters the context within which debate and dispute over a bill takes place. In 2000 a bill to limit the right to trial by jury was introduced into the Lords, but a wrecking amendment was passed by peers, whereupon the government dropped the bill. However later that same session the Home Secretary introduced the Criminal Justice (Mode of Trail) (No. 2) Bill into the Commons, intending if necessary to force it through using the Parliament Act. When the Bill arrived in the Lords however peers rejected it outright at second reading in a remarkably heavy government defeat (184 votes to 88). Having also experienced significant opposition to this measure in the Commons the government decided to shelve the Bill.

If the most time consuming bills are all introduced first into the Commons, this can result in the flow of legislative work for the Lords being very uneven, sometimes giving peers a great deal to do towards the end of the session. The House has frequently returned before the Commons for the autumn spill-over, and has found itself sitting through at least part of the party conference season on several occasions in recent years. In 2003 proceedings on seven major bills were still in progress until the last days of the session.

While major bills involving substantial controversy usually go first to the Commons, there are certain kinds of bills that the Lords expect to deal with first. All consolidation bills are introduced first into the upper House, these being measures which consolidate rather than change the law; usually these take little time. Bills prepared by the Law Commission embodying law reform are usually dealt with first in the Lords. Frequently, but by no means always, criminal justice bills go first to the Lords. Other bills where controversy is more technical than directly political may be introduced in the Lords first. As part of its programme to modernise parliament the Labour Government gave the go ahead for some bills to be carried over from one session to the next. Generally in the past there has been reluctance to allow this because pressures brought to bear on governments by the sessional cut-off on all legislation have been considered helpful to oppositions seeking to wring at least some concessions from government. But if the price paid for this is that parliament's scrutiny function, and perhaps the revising role of the second chamber in particular, are to some extent vitiated, then allowing a limited carry-over seems appropriate. If applied too generously carry-over could clog up the government's legislative programme, but so far the procedure has had very limited use, and is dependent on approval being given by the House on a bill-by-bill basis.

We discuss the effectiveness of the legislative process in relation to government bills in more detail later. Here we may note the relatively small amount of time given to private members' bills. These may be introduced into either House, but must of course pass both before being enacted. Given the reluctance of government to allow extra time for these bills in the Commons, it has become very difficult for private members' bills introduced by peers to complete their passage through the Commons. The same difficulty over time has in recent years imposed a severe inhibition on the ability of the Lords to amend private members' bills brought from the Commons. Any amendment requires approval by the Commons and this inevitably involves some time, even if very little. But late in the session often no time at all is available. Hence peers may express frustration at being unable to amend a Commons private members' bill because to do so would almost certainly lead to the loss of the bill.

In the 2001–04 period, of the forty-five private members' bills introduced by peers only two received royal assent. Both of these were in the 2001–02 session, one being a special case, the Tobacco Advertising and Promotion Bill, introduced by Lord Clement-Jones, following the demise of government legislation in this area the previous session. After the Bill had passed the Lords the government took it over in the Commons. The other was the National Heritage Bill, typical of the very minor changes in the law that a particular peer decides to try and make through introducing legislation, which can then be taken very quickly or purely formally through the Commons. By way of contrast some peers have used the private members' bill procedure to ensure debate takes place on some issue they think important, while well aware that the bill concerned will not progress far. For example, Lord Lestor of Herne Hill introduced an Executive Powers and Civil Service Bill in 2004 and a

Constitutional Reform (Prerogative Powers and Civil Service etc) Bill, dealing with crown prerogative powers in 2006, both of which allowed for substantial second reading debates, with the latter proceeding through its Lords stages. Lord Baker of Dorking did pilot through all stages in the House a bill to curtail the voting rights of MPs from Scottish constituencies on English matters (the 'West Lothian' question) in 2006, while Lord Dubs introduced a Succession to the Crown Bill in 2005 tackling both male primogeniture and religious affiliation (and in so doing drawing contributions taking opposing views from the bishops' bench). One should not overlook the fact that some matters that are ventilated through such a bill are then taken up elsewhere, perhaps by government or perhaps by a private member's bill in the Commons.

It is worth remembering that at times in the past private members' bills have been much more important. In the late 1960s the Lords took a lead in tackling some of the so-called issues of conscience that MPs and government were reluctant to face because of the existing state of public opinion, notably the decriminalisation of homosexuality.[12] More recently the House has attracted considerable public attention through debating issues surrounding the end of life, with Lord Joffe in 2003 introducing the Patient (Assisted Dying) Bill, which was referred by the House to a select committee, the report from which then received debate amidst much publicity.[13] In general terms the whole private members' bill procedure has in recent years lost its effectiveness as MPs have become increasingly adept at exploiting procedural devices to oppose such bills. Issues of conscience are now more commonly dealt with by means of a free vote on a clause in a government bill.[14] However, debate in the Lords at least allows for discussion, hopefully well-informed, on some such matters to take place, with government ministers obliged to define the government's position.

Private legislation (not to be confused with private members' legislation) has been in decline for many years from its nineteenth-century heyday. In some areas it is still necessary for a body outside parliament to promote a private bill because no procedure is available under a public Act of parliament to achieve the desired objective. The most significant private bill in the 2003–04 session was the Mersey Tunnels Bill, which among other things allowed for tolls through the Mersey tunnel to be increased by the rate of inflation without the need for a cumbersome public inquiry.

Statutory instruments (SIs) are often referred to as delegated legislation because the authority for them derives from primary legislation – Acts of Parliament. A minority are known as affirmative instruments because parliament has to approve them before they come into effect, but most are negative instruments, which means that they automatically come into effect without being debated unless one or other House specifically votes them down on a motion known as a 'Prayer'. The two Houses have equal powers in relation to SIs. Since a direct vote on an instrument if carried would veto it, the House of Lords has generally found other ways to register its disapproval of those to which it is opposed. What is known as a non-fatal motion may be moved seeking the withdrawal of an instrument or calling on the government not to proceed with it, but at the same time the motion formally approving the order will be allowed to pass. A non-fatal motion on cannabis reclassification was carried by seventy-eight votes to sixty-one on 12 November 2003, while a motion to approve the relevant order was carried at the same time by sixty-three votes to thirty-seven. In this instance the mover of the motion, explained that he wished to 'send a clear signal to the Government'.[15] Sometimes the only parliamentary debate an order receives will be in the House of Lords. In May 2002 peers held a two-hour debate on the Health Service (Control of Patient Information) Regulations 2002, which had passed the Commons the previous day without debate.[16] Very occasionally the House has rejected an SI. On 22 February 2000 peers supported a Prayer moved against the Greater London Authority Elections Order by 206 votes to 143; this concerned the provision of free delivery of candidates' election material, with the government subsequently announcing a change of policy on this, causing Lord Goodhart to say the sequence of events reflected 'considerable credit' on the House of Lords.[17]

Procedure on statutory instruments has been criticised a good deal recently, and proposals to allow for the amendment of SIs, or for the second chamber to be able to delay rather than veto them, have been put forward. When the Parliament Act of 1911 was passed, little if any thought was given to SIs because there were comparatively few and they were of little significance. But since then, and in particular in the postwar period, they have become not only much more numerous, but also many are now of real importance. In 1911 there were 330 pages of SIs; by the 1990s and since, there were frequently over 10,000 pages of SIs per year.[18] Partly for this reason the House of Lords set up a select committee in 1992 to examine the order making powers contained in bills, while in 2003 the House established a Merits of Statutory Instruments Committee. The work of these committees is considered further below.

Measures are similar to statutory instruments, being formulated by the established Church of England to give statutory authority where this is necessary for changes in Church practice. They are considered by the Ecclesiastical Committee, a large joint committee, before being introduced in both Houses. Generally they take very little time, though occasionally they still excite controversy. It would however seem strange today for parliament to over-rule the carefully prepared proposals put forward by the Church authorities.

The division between legislative and deliberative work is rather artificial at the margin (for example motions calling for the withdrawal of an affirmative SI have been included as part of the legislative proceedings in Table 4.2), but nonetheless it is helpful in terms of identifying procedures under which the House engages in non-legislative activity. The most time-consuming activity is debates on motions. Available days are allocated between the main party groups in the House, including government backbenchers and the crossbenchers. A peer with a concern to initiate a debate on a particular topic may persuade his party group to allocate a slot for this. But backbench peers may also enter a ballot to decide which motions listed on the order paper will be debated on one day a month. The formula usually used for these debates involves calling attention to a particular topic and ends with the words 'and move for papers'. This gives the mover of the motion the right of reply, but the motion is then withdrawn. Unlike the Commons all peers who wish to speak in a debate simply hand in their names to the Chief Whip's office and a 'batting order' of speakers is prepared. This way of arranging matters does detract rather from the notion of debate; peers intervene in each other's speeches much less than MPs do. Peers take pride in making speeches that express eloquently and precisely a point of view. Speeches are works of art, which can be easily spoilt if interrupted.

The House may also debate motions for resolution, and the government frequently uses the formula to 'take note', for example of the situation in Iraq, or of the annual defence white paper, or the report of some official committee, for example the Hutton Report. Debates on select committee reports also use the 'take note' formula and are fitted in around other business. Opportunities particularly exist early in the session before time consuming legislation reaches the House. Unlike the Commons almost any select committee that wishes to have its report debated will be afforded an opportunity for this, though sometimes only after delay. How valuable such debates are is a moot point. As in the Commons they are not infrequently dominated by those who have sat on the committee concerned. They do however permit some exploration of the report's findings and some probing of the government to see what response might be forthcoming.

Unstarred questions are also a procedure under which debates may take place. Under standing orders these are questions asked of the government, but in asking the question the peer concerned is permitted to make a speech and others also may make speeches before the appointed minister replies. But unlike a motion the peer initiating the debate has no right of reply at the end. The general rule is that unstarred questions come last in the day's business, but the practice has developed of using the 'dinner hour' for such debates during proceedings on bills. This gives a break to peers involved in the legislation being considered, and allows debate of about one hour. The nearest equivalent in the Commons is a daily adjournment debate, though the unstarred question is a more flexible procedure. Occasionally in the past, debate on an unstarred question ran on for up to three hours, though it has now been accepted that debates using this procedure should not last more than ninety minutes.

Starred questions are oral questions, with which each day's business commences. Unlike the Commons, where the time devoted to questions is strictly limited, and oral questions each day are to a particular department, in the Lords there is a limit on the number of questions which may be put down for answer on any day, and questions are simply addressed to the government. This limit was fixed at four in 1959, and though experimentally it has been altered since, in 2005 it was decided to revert to the four per day maximum. Over the years the House has adopted various devices to alleviate the pressure placed on spaces for oral questions, for example restricting the number of questions any peer may have on the order paper at any one time. In order to facilitate topical questions, one slot on Tuesdays, Wednesdays and Thursdays is now reserved for questions tabled no more than two sitting days ahead, with the clerks holding a ballot to determine the choice of question if necessary. The House is usually very full during oral questions, with many peers vying to put supplementaries. A limit of thirty minutes for four questions has now been accepted, with the Leader of the House responsible for trying to keep business moving along, and sometimes ruffling feathers a bit in so doing![19] But with seven minutes allowed for each question, and sometimes longer, it is obvious that the exercise takes a different form from that of the Commons. Supplementaries may come from peers who know a great deal about the subject raised, and there is enough time for supplementaries to be pressed home from various angles and by different peers. When question time in the Commons has become such an exercise in partisan point scoring, the practice of the Lords is in many respects a welcome contrast.[20]

Most ministerial statements are made first in the Commons because most senior ministers are in that House. But Commons statements are usually repeated in the Lords, though by agreement, within the 'usual channels' statements may be simply printed in Hansard. However the attractiveness to ministers of this procedure, which enables them to appear to be taking the initiative, and is regarded as a 'prime time' opportunity in the Commons (a convenient time for media coverage), has led to an increase in the number of statements made. With the opportunity for brief responses from other party spokesmen and for questions from all sides of the House, the procedure represents for many parliamentarians an agreeable contrast to full debates, though the tendency for peers to try to make short speeches following statements regularly draws forth exhortations for brevity. In 2003–04 fifty-one statements were made, ten of them on Iraq.

Following this brief overview of the various procedures that exist and the kinds of business that can be considered, we now examine more specifically the role of the House in relation to government legislation, and then the deliberative (or non-legislative) debating role, and the work of select committees.

The House of Lords and government bills

By common consent the work of the House of Lords in revising govern-ment bills is its most important task. The question of how effectively the House does this is not an easy one to answer. A starting point is to examine statistics for the number of amendments made, though this is a very crude measure of effectiveness because amendments vary greatly in importance. Some are described as purely drafting, which means that they do not in any way alter the substance of the bill but simply seek to clarify its wording. Other amendments may be described as technical or substantive and these do make changes, perhaps making the impact of the bill more precise, or maybe conceding some point, but without alter-ing the basic purpose of the bill. Finally are wrecking amendments, so-called because they do alter the basic nature of the bill. Of course there is a good deal of subjectivity in the judgement as to which category any particular amendment falls. A wrecking amendment is sometimes defined as any change that the government does not want.

Over the whole period since the 1950s the number of amendments made by the House has grown considerably. This is partly because the House has simply become much more active, as indicated in the previ-ous Chapter. But it is also because government legislation has become more prolix and more complex. In the 1950s governments added about 1000 pages a year to the statute book; by the 1980s governments were adding two and a half times as much per year. And from making about 1000 amendments per session to government bills in the late 1960s, the House of Lords by the 1990s was making well over 2000 amendments per session, and the number has continued to rise since.

Table 4.3 Amendments to government bills by parliament 1970–2004*

Sessions	Bills introduced into the House of Commons			Bills introduced into the House of Lords		
	Total number of bills*	Number of bills amended	Number of amendments made	Total number of bills	Number of bills amended	Number of amendments made
1970–73	79	31	2366	39	29	488
1974–77	68	49	1859	58	38	1594
1979–82	82	39	2231	33	20	1604
1983–86	69	43	4137	42	28	1373
1987–90	61	38	5181	29	18	2687
1992–95	46	24	3664	29	22	1812
1997–2000	67	50	7815	38	35	2581
2001–04	61	47	5240	32	26	2747

Note:
* Excludes supply and money bills.

Table 4.3 indicates the number of amendments made in the first three sessions of each parliament since 1970. The inclusion of sessions terminated early because of an election can produce a distorted picture because in such circumstances arrangements are made for the rapid enactment of some legislation and the abandonment of other items.

As this table shows many bills are not amended by the House of Lords. Money and supply bills have already been excluded from this analysis, but a good many other bills have as their main object the creation of a charge on the public purse, and though sometimes the House of Lords does amend such bills, it generally leaves them alone. Other bills which are very minor may not be amended in the House of Commons either, or receive very limited amendment there. Government bills do vary enormously in size and importance. Thus of the twenty-two bills brought from the Commons in the 2003–04 session, four accounted for 1286, or some 72 per cent, of the 1795 amendments made that session, while eleven other bills accounted for the remaining 271 amendments. A few major bills usually involve fierce political controversy. They are the measures upon which the media focus, and against which the opposition campaign. These were the bills that used to attract guillotine motions, and now of course they are routinely subject to programme motions moved immediately after second reading. Their passage through the Commons frequently resembles prolonged trench warfare between the parties. This kind of treatment may certainly be defended.

It is the way in which conflict over fundamental policies takes place in our kind of society. Better that there should be verbal warfare in the Commons than violence in the streets. But such bills do also require rather more calm and considered criticism. Parliament needs to be both the forum in which the battle of political will takes place, as well as the institution which provides careful and reasoned public scrutiny of draft legislation. The nature of debate in the House of Lords is different from that in the Commons, and arguably this provides appraisal of a complementary kind to that given by the Commons.

The great majority of amendments made to bills by the House of Lords are introduced from the government frontbench – more than nineteen out of every twenty in the 1988–89 session, though some of these result from pressure and persuasion brought to bear from other quarters in both Houses and indeed from outside of parliament altogether. Also in the 1988–89 session over 99 per cent of the amendments moved from the government frontbench were agreed by the House, whereas only just over 6 per cent of those moved from all other quarters were agreed.[21] What this bears out is that the legislative process in Britain is very much within the control of the executive. Any government with a party majority in the Commons can in effect insist on getting its way. But parliament is there as a sounding board and as a forum in which the opposition can argue its case against what the government proposes. And the government may decide it is expedient to give ground and amend its draft legislation.

Major bills are usually dealt with first, and often at considerable length, in the Commons; but frequently they leave that House in a form that demands improvement. Sometimes large parts of a bill have been undebated in detail in the Commons, and on other occasions the government itself may wish to add substantial amounts of material in the Lords. This may be to clarify points that have been raised there or indeed by interested parties outside parliament. It may be to make adjustments of some significance for which the need has become clear to ministers and civil servants, or in some cases it may be to extend the scope of a bill to cover concerns that have suddenly erupted. The political struggle over a bill may continue in the Lords, perhaps on territory already marked out in the Commons, or maybe over points that have hitherto escaped much attention. The very fact that the legislative process is drawn out over several stages in two Houses allows time for reconsideration, not so much of the principle of a major bill (the government having committed itself to this) but of the detail. But the detail may be significant and may raise again issues of principle. When the government suffers defeats in the Lords it has to decide whether to give way and accept the change thrust upon its bill, or whether to resist and use its Commons majority to overturn the defeat, or to bring forward some compromise. This becomes for ministers a matter of political calculation. If there has already been backbench dissent in the Commons on the matter in question, then the government may prefer to give way or compromise rather than endure the publicity of further rebellion. But it is easy to give too much attention to the defeats the government suffers in the Lords. Many of the changes made to bills are made without recourse to the division lobby.

One may generalise by saying the House of Lords makes its distinctive impact on legislation by means of both persuasion and pressure. The actual mix between these two depends on the circumstances of each bill. Persuasion may be effective because of the recognised expertise and authority of those spearheading the persuasion. For example if the Lord Chief Justice takes issue with ministers, his views must be given careful attention. Other peers who sit on the crossbenches, be they Nobel Prize winners or former senior public servants, will on appropriate subjects command attention. Likewise peers who have held high political office, including former prime ministers and other cabinet ministers, may command the attention of present day ministers. The persuasion that is exerted may genuinely convince ministers and senior civil servants that the change so advocated ought to be included in their bill. But it may also be related to the pressure the House can exert. The fact that debate is taking place in a House of parliament and not in a seminar or at some conference makes a difference. The House can vote to amend a bill, and thus focus pressure on government. The threat of a division and the possibility of defeat for the government in the division lobby is always there in the background. Persuasion can be made more persuasive when the potential for pressure also exists. If this happens then ministers either have to spend time and effort getting the matter overturned in the Commons, with the inherent risks involved, including the possibility of giving further publicity to divisions within their own party ranks, or else they have to give ground. Once clearly defeated, and if reluctant to use their Commons majority to overturn the defeat, ministers will almost certainly have to offer a significant compromise. There are therefore real incentives on ministers to avoid defeats. If during debate it becomes apparent that opinion in the house is such that a division is likely to go against the government, ministers may well promise to 'look again' at the matter under consideration.

If amendments are made in the Lords the bill concerned is returned to the Commons. Here the government has to decide what to do about changes made by peers against its will. If it wishes to delete the amendment or to introduce its own amendment to cover the point (perhaps as a compromise) then providing the Commons agree this, the bill will return again to the Lords. Peers must then decide whether to accept the bill as it then stands or whether to continue to press their own amendments. If they do the latter, parliamentary ping-pong begins. A bill may continue to move back and forward between the two Houses, with either House proposing some variation on previous amendments until one House agrees the version of the bill sent to it by the other, or until a 'double insistence' occurs, in which case disagreement is taken as confirmed and the bill falls unless and until reintroduced under Parliament Act procedures. Examples of the use of the Parliament Act were given in Chapter 2 when considering the way understanding of the use of power by the House has changed over the past century. The rules surrounding these procedures are complex, with parliamentary clerks guiding peers through what appears a procedural minefield. When the clerks in the two Houses disagree the consequences can be fraught, but typically when this happened over the Planning and Compulsory Purchase Bill in 2004 the opposition frontbench in the House, instead of taking advantage of the government's embarrassment, actually helped the government sort out the resulting difficulties.[22]

Especially when the end of session deadline is rapidly approaching, exchanges between the Houses on a disputed matter can become quite frenetic; the speed of the 'ping-pong' increases. Rarely however do exchanges continue for more than two or three rounds, though the frequency of multiple exchanges has increased recently. In 2006 Lord Grocott, Chief Whip, pointed out that in the eighteen years of Conservative Government from 1979 to 1997 'there were only three occasions when there were more than three exchanges or ping-pong between the Houses', but that in the 1997 to 2005 period 'thirteen bills went into protracted exchanges'.[23]

The impact of the House of Lords on government legislation is conditioned by the overall parliamentary and political situation, which itself is dependent on various factors. First is the size of the government majority in the Commons. A very low majority will instil caution in ministers. Overturning Lords amendments may be hazardous, as was certainly the case in the 1974 to 1979 period. This can intensify the pressure on ministers to compromise. Equally however, a very low Commons majority can instil caution on the part of peers because they know that government defeats may stick, or at least prove difficult to overturn. Certainly when the House of Lords was very lopsided politically the Conservative opposition, while it would routinely defeat the government, would equally routinely give way when asked to do so by the Commons. In the 1970s the Conservatives were highly selective in deciding when to start parliamentary ping-pong. Labour's much reduced Commons majority following the 2005 election altered the context within which the House of Lords operates, making defeat in the House more irksome to the government, and making the reversal of such defeat in the Commons more hazardous. This was exemplified in January 2006 when the government was twice defeated in the Commons while trying to overturn Lords amendments on the Racial and Religious Hatred Bill, a measure that evoked very considerable dissent within Labour's ranks during its parliamentary passage.[24]

This points us to a second important factor, the relative cohesion of the governing party within both houses. In the immediate aftermath of election victory, especially where the government have won a large majority and returned to office after a period in opposition, dissent is likely to be minimal. The authority of the leadership that has piloted the party to electoral success is considerable. This was certainly true for 'New Labour' under Blair after 1997. But by 2006 things looked very different. Dissent within the parliamentary party became much more significant, and on a wide range of issues. The authority of the government seemed to be ebbing away, as those dismissed from office and those disappointed never to have achieved office were added to the ranks of natural dissenters.[25] And though the political dynamic is very different in the Lords, the mood of the party in the Commons brings repercussions in terms of peers' behaviour. As indicated in the previous Chapter party cohesion is generally high in the Lords, where the habits of party loyalty have often been nurtured over many years. But the readiness of peers actually to make themselves available to vote may diminish, and turnout can be very important for the governing party. Government backbenchers who have lost their ardour for policies being pursued by their party leadership may calculate that defeat in the Lords will actually bring change, and be the more ready to precipitate this.

A third factor is the party balance in the Lords itself. The political dynamic is very different since the 1999 removal of hereditary peers, with the two main parties roughly equal in numbers, compared to the earlier Conservative predominance. In the 1970s the Conservatives in opposition defeated the government in the great bulk of all the divisions that took place (over 80 per cent of the time), but peers themselves tended to think of real government defeats as only having occurred if the opposition voted again and won a division after a matter had been returned from the Commons. That is clearly no longer the case; any defeat is therefore more significant. And it is no longer simply the Conservatives that decide the outcome of divisions. Indeed as seen in the previous Chapter more often than not the decisive role is played by the Liberal Democrats.

Finally, the overall context within which the House votes has been altered by the greater perceived legitimacy the House now enjoys.[26] The emphasis this receives may be misplaced in that a substantial number of hereditary peers remain, and all other peers are appointed, mostly by processes that lack any obvious transparency. But many peers themselves feel that the composition of their House is now in an important sense the outcome of recent government legislation – the 1999 House of Lords Act, and perhaps the outcome of a failure on the part of the government and the Commons to settle on further reform. Their self-confidence has been boosted, and this is further reinforced when they find not insignificant numbers of backbench MPs rebelling against their party whip in order to support stances the House of Lords has taken.

However, the House of Lords is not in a position to oblige the government to give way on significant issues which have assumed political importance to the government and upon which its House of Commons majority shows every sign of holding firm. A compromise could have been reached on the European Elections issue (as discussed in Chapter 2), and one might reasonably argue that the system chosen by the Blair Government had failed to convince public and parliamentary opinion of its superiority to other possible systems. The lack of vocal support for the government, indeed the expression of clear opposition to it, from its own backbenches in both Houses, was one pointer to this. But ministers remained in an unusually (perhaps one should say an unhealthily) strong position. There was little if any effective opposition. The Conservatives lacked credibility partly because the party only seemed to tumble to the significance of the issue at a late stage, having failed to oppose the system in the Commons. And the Liberal Democrats were so mightily relieved to have actually secured a government commitment to proportional representation that ultimately they were prepared to support whatever variant ministers proposed.

There are other examples where it is clear that only the House of Commons can oblige the government to ditch a policy upon which it has set itself. In 1986 the Thatcher Government set itself to reform the law on Sunday trading, putting a bill through the Lords first, where considerable misgivings were evident. But it was the Commons that put an abrupt stop to the legislation when it voted the bill down at second reading. Only the Commons could have stopped the Blair Government from introducing student tuition fees – and nearly did so when the government's second reading majority on the Higher Education Bill fell to five in the Commons in January 2004. But once the government had won that vote, the Lords could only hope to try and get the details of the proposed scheme adjusted.

There are many examples of major policy issues on which the government of the day refuses to give way, and where it retains a sufficient Commons majority to allow it to take an intransigent line. When the House of Lords set up a select committee on the sentence for murder, which in 1989 unequivocally recommended abolition of the life sentence, the government remained adamant against change.[27] When peers debated the 1991 Criminal Justice Bill, an all-party amendment with the Lord Chief Justice as one of its sponsors was carried by 177 votes to 79; on this occasion only a single non-Conservative peer supported the government minority, while thirty-four Conservatives and forty-four cross-benchers joined the opposition. The government refused to give way. In 1994 the matter came up again during proceedings on the Criminal Justice and Public Order Bill, and again the government would not budge.[28] A different example of government intransigence was provided in 1993 when the Major Government refused to change its policy on its chosen method for privatising the railways, despite strong cross-party pressure from the Lords, which continued until the very end of the session.

Sometimes legislation is required quickly in order to achieve its purpose. Thus when the Lords refused to endorse the Thatcher Government's legislation to cancel elections to the Greater London Council (GLC) due to be held in 1985, (the year before her legislation to abolish the GLC itself would come into effect), a compromise had to be found. If the Parliament Act had been used, by the time the period of delay stipulated under the Acts had run its course, the GLC elections would have taken place. Furthermore, because this was an issue involving elections and was therefore deemed constitutional, the Lords felt emboldened to stand firm. But having forced the government to change the strategy it had for the abolition of the GLC, the House was unable to alter the government's basic decision to do away with the GLC itself. The government had a clear manifesto commitment to abolish the GLC and the metropolitan counties and this the House felt unable to impede.

In assessing the impact of the House it is a mistake to concentrate too much attention on the outcome of divisions and government defeats. In 1994 the Major Government came under great pressure in the Lords on its proposal to increase the power of the Home Secretary in relation to police authorities. Two former Conservative Home Secretaries led over thirty other peers in castigating this policy during the second reading of the Police and Magistrates Courts Bill, with the result that the then Home Secretary, Michael Howard, gave way before the committee stage began. A first hand observer of these events, Lord Windlesham, wrote of this Bill as providing 'a classic demonstration of the negotiated concession as a tactic superior to defeating the Government in the division lobby'.[29] When in 2004 a Labour peer recited figures showing the percentage of divisions in which the government had been defeated in the House since 1970, Lord Elton intervened to say that the figures concealed the significant influence the House had on Conservative Government policy, because the government (in which he had been a minister) not infrequently gave way without a vote taking place.[30] An example of this under Labour occurred when it became known that the former Lord Chancellor, Lord Irvine of Lairg, would be speaking (along with other senior legal figures including the Lord Chief Justice) against the government's proposal to replace judicial review with administrative oversight in the Asylum and Immigration (Treatment of Claimants) Bill. The government announced its climbdown just before the debate took place on 15 May 2004, whereupon Lord Irvine withdrew his name from the list of speakers.

Sometimes securing a crushing defeat for rebels in the Lords has been important to a government. The travails of the Major Government seeking to secure the passage of the European Communities Bill in 1994 were severe. When the Bill reached the Lords a campaign was under way to force a referendum, and among others the former prime minister Baroness Thatcher came to the House and spoke forcefully in favour of a referendum. The largest ever division recorded in the House took place on 14 July 1993 when 691 peers were present, with 621 voting, giving the government the favourable verdict they wanted as the amendment seeking a referendum was defeated by 445 votes to 176. Such a massive victory for the government served ministers well. Mr Major's immediate predecessor had done her utmost to force a referendum on the government, but had conspicuously failed.

The Blair Government

Within the scope of this Chapter it is only possible to make some generalisations and give a few examples of the impact of the House on the Blair Government's legislation since 1997. The fact that New Labour when it came to office had a manifesto commitment to reform the House of Lords obviously affected the mood of the House. The fact too that the Labour Government had a huge majority in the Commons, but constituted less than 20 per cent of the membership of the upper House, made the House potentially problematic for Labour. To begin with the government seemed determined simply to overturn without compromise every defeat it suffered in the Lords. The long term gradual growth in assertiveness that the House had experienced since the arrival of life peers continued, and was given added force by the removal of hereditary peers (as discussed above). Concern that the government was developing an increasing hubris in its dealings with the Commons probably further emboldened peers.

The long-standing concern the House has shown for issues that may be described as constitutional was accentuated by the Blair Government's emphasis on constitutional reform after 1997. The case of the European Parliamentary Elections Bill has already been discussed. The House gave careful scrutiny to the devolution legislation, spending over 100 hours on the Scotland Act, and making over 300 amendments. On the devolution paving bill, peers wanted the referendums in Scotland and Wales to be held on the same day, not a week apart as proposed by the government. When the Commons reversed their amendment on this point peers accepted the result, thereby allowing the bandwagon effect of a favourable result in Scotland to influence the much closer contest in Wales. An amendment made against the wishes of the government was to prevent the Scottish Parliament being reduced in size when Westminster constituencies in Scotland were reduced in number. The Commons deleted this change. Perhaps peers should have dug their heels in because when the prospect of such a reduction loomed up, a special amending bill was needed to do exactly what the Lords had proposed in the first place, namely keep the parliament the same size.

This was not the only bill related to devolution where the Lords made amendments that later proved prescient but at the time were rejected. The introduction of university tuition fees under the Teaching and Higher Education Bill 1997–98 highlighted the distinctiveness of Scottish universities with their typical four year rather than three year degree structure. The effect of this and the Scottish Executive's policy (with which the government disagreed) would make degrees at Scottish universities more expensive than in the remainder of the UK (though oddly enough not for students from other European Union countries!). The government went down to a very heavy defeat on this seeming anomaly (on 2 March 1998, by 212 votes to 89), but at prime minister's question time later that week Tony Blair insisted the Lord's amendment would not stand. When the matter returned to the Lords peers again defeated the government, by 319 votes to 108. The possibility of deadlock loomed, but the government then agreed to a review to see what effect the fee differential would have, and this was a sufficient compromise to get the Bill through. When two years later the outcome of the review (the Quigley Review) was published the government announced that UK students from outside Scotland would have the fourth year tuition fees paid. The ripples of devolution spread to other bills. The Lords amended the Bank of England Bill to specify that one member of the new monetary policy committee should be nominated by the first minister of Scotland, but this was quickly deleted by the Commons.

The Lords gave considerable attention to a range of bills dealing with constitutional issues, including the 1998 Human Rights Bill, and the 2000 Political Parties, Elections and Referendums Bill establishing the Electoral Commission. It is at least arguable that a second chamber should have special concern for such legislation given that it is introduced by a government that may have a controlling majority in the Commons that is based on minority support from the electorate. But in practice there has been an unwillingness on the part of the Blair-led Government to recognise this fact. Lords views on constitutional bills have been over-ridden with as much determination as their views on other legislation. An example of this was the treatment of the 2003 European Parliament and Local Elections (Pilots) Bill, where ping-pong between the Houses extended to no less than five rounds. Some local elections had been conducted on all-postal ballots in 2002 and 2003, but concerns about possible fraud had been widely expressed. The 2003 Bill stipulated that the Electoral Commission had to be consulted regarding the choice of regions, but when the government did this, the Commission recommended only two regions as definitely suitable, though it added that others might be potentially suitable. By the time the Bill reached the Lords the government had made public its intention to extend pilots to four regions (some 28 per cent of the whole electorate). This drew criticism from both opposition parties, who at report stage voted to limit pilots to two regions, and to tighten up the rules on postal voters' declaration of identity. Two weeks later both these changes were overturned in the Commons, with the junior constitutional affairs minister saying: 'although we must listen to the views of the other place [the Lords] as a revising chamber, we must also uphold the fact that we are accountable for parliament's decisions, and they are not'.[31] A week later peers voted to insist, whereupon the Commons presented a compromise on voter identity procedures. The Lords accepted the compromise but continued to insist that pilots should only take place where the Electoral Commission had specifically recommended regions as suitable. This third round of ping-pong ended with the Commons again rejecting the Lords view on 24 March. The fourth round saw a Lords compromise allowing pilots in three regions rejected by the Commons, with the Lords then voting to insist on 30 March, a position overturned by the Commons on the same day four hours later. After this fifth round, Conservative peers decided to give up the fight and the government got its way by 138 votes to 108 despite continued opposition from the Liberal Democrats. Subsequently the problems of fraud in all postal ballots were found to be much more extensive, with the government having to respond to highly critical comments from the judiciary over its 'complacency' in relation to electoral fraud.[32]

An area of similar concern centres on civil liberties. Here, especially with the government's responses to the threat of terrorism, the Lords has increasingly run into protracted conflicts with ministers. But apart from anti-terrorism legislation, issues arose in a wide range of bills, for example the Regulation of Investigatory Powers Bill in the 1999–2000 session on the sharing of information; the Football Disorder Bill in the same session on a sunset clause; on the 2002 Animal Health Bill over rules relating to entry of premises and compulsory slaughter of animals; and on the 2003 Crime (International Co-operation) Bill over rights given to foreign investigators. Matters relating to immigration and asylum have often involved civil liberty questions, as has criminal justice legislation. Reference has already been made to the response of the House to government attempts to limit the right to jury trial. The 1999 Access to Justice Bill involved a stand-off between the Houses on the employment of salaried lawyers by the new Criminal Defence Service, eventually leading to a compromise. In the 2001–02 session the Proceeds of Crime Bill ran into sustained opposition in the House from some law lords, with compromise being reached on the degree of discretion that courts could be allowed in relation to the recovery of assets. The government suffered sixteen defeats on the 2003 Criminal Justice Bill, where matters particularly in contention included (again) jury trials, with the government eventually agreeing to a compromise, as it did on the question of the admissibility of information about a defendant's earlier offences committed when that defendant was still a child. In 2006 prolonged ping-pong also took place on the Identity Cards Bill over the matter of compulsion, with the government's opponents arguing that the mandate given in the 2005 election manifesto had been for a voluntary scheme, and that the Bill effectively made the scheme compulsory. After four Commons votes reversing Lords amendments on this point, the former head of the civil service, Lord Armstrong of Ilminster, brokered a compromise, which was accepted despite continued resistance from the Liberal Democrats. The 2002 Nationality, Immigration and Asylum Bill was amended in the Lords partly as a result of Episcopal initiative, as mentioned in the previous Chapter. In 2004 a Lords amendment increasing the time limit for an appeal to be made by a failed asylum seeker was rejected by the Commons, and though the

Conservatives supported the Liberal Democrat Lord Goodhart when he moved that the House insist on its amendment, the government won the ensuing division by 137 votes to 127 (7 and 14 June 2004).

The anti-terrorism legislation introduced after 9/11 caused serious misgivings within and outside parliament. Partly this was because of the drastic powers contained in the bill, effectively suspending habeas corpus by allowing indefinite detention without trial, but also for the extent to which powers considered necessary to combat terrorism were extended to deal with crime generally. Some critics thought the Home Office had taken the opportunity presented by this emergency legislation to enact a range of provisions about which no genuine emergency existed. The scrutiny this bill received in the Lords was undoubtedly more thorough than that of the Commons. For a start peers spent more than twice as many hours as the Commons examining the bill, considering it over eight days, while the Commons dealt with it in three days. Furthermore peers dug their heels in on several points, defeating the government thirteen times, including a convincing rejection (by 234 votes to 121) of an amendment put forward as a compromise by the government following an earlier defeat on incitement to religious hatred, a subject then dropped from the bill. Two other defeats were on responses made by the government to earlier defeats – on retention of communications data, and on the sharing of information among law enforcement agencies. Although David Blunkett as Home Secretary claimed the government had reached agreement on 98 per cent of the bill, Philip Cowley spoke of the 'humiliatingly large number of concessions' the government had been obliged to make.[33]

When further legislation dealing with terrorism was introduced, the government ran into similar problems with the Lords. In response to a judicial ruling by law lords that indefinite detention without trial of foreign suspects was contrary to human rights, legislation allowing the Home Secretary to make 'control orders' was introduced in the 2004–05 session. This met with considerable resistance in the Commons (thirty-two Labour MPs voted against the second reading). By the time the bill reached third reading the government was promising sweeping amendment in the Lords. Indeed during third reading in the Commons, the Speaker intervened to require Charles Clarke, Home Secretary at the time, to speak about the bill in the form in which it then was in the Commons, and not about the changes yet to be introduced in the Lords! Amendments made independently by peers were mostly rejected under tightly programmed debates in the Commons. The Lords then became more stubborn, especially over amendments seeking a sunset clause. This led to a marathon stand-off between the two Houses, with the bill bouncing back and forward between them, and the Lords sitting for a record thirty-two hours on 10 March 2005, inflicting thirteen defeats on the government that day before compromise was reached. The compromise involved a further Terrorism Bill the following session, which included the new offence of 'glorification' of terrorism, which the Lords voted down twice, but by the time this Bill was going through, the mood of the country had changed after the July 2005 London tube bombings and the Conservative opposition was ready to abstain rather than inflict further defeat on the government.

This discussion points towards the fact that much of the rhetoric emphasising the need for the elected House to have its primacy recognised, and for the unelected House to acknowledge its subordinate position, is misplaced. In practice it is the government seeking primacy over both Houses. It is tempting to suggest that ministers frequently use the argument about Commons primacy as a smokescreen to obscure the issues actually at stake in disputed legislation, preferring simply to attack the House of Lords for its temerity in disagreeing with the government rather than answer the arguments it has advanced. This again is a matter we return to in the concluding Chapter.

Meanwhile we conclude this section by indicating how difficulties the Blair Government has faced in the Commons can at times be aggravated by defeats it suffers in the Lords. Some Labour MPs and peers were strongly opposed to the legislation to privatise the National Air Traffic Control System in 2000. The Lords amended this to delay any such sale until after the next general election. The Commons rejected this, but thirty-seven Labour MPs rebelled. The Lords then voted narrowly (132 to 125) to insist on such delay. Rather than face another perhaps more damaging Commons rebellion, a 'last minute compromise was cobbled together' involving a three month consultation before any sale could go through, and this was accepted by peers.[34] Similarly in the 1998–99 session the Labour Government faced some persistent rebellion within its own party ranks on the Welfare Reform and Pensions Bill, with dissent in the Commons being reinforced by the Lords, in particular through the veteran Labour campaigner in this area, Lord Ashley of Stoke, who instigated some very heavy defeats in the Lords (251 to 95 on one amendment concerned with incapacity benefit eligibility). Back in the Commons a compromise was put in place, but the Lords again rejected this by 260 votes to 127, before eventually accepting a further adjustment.

The legislative process is complicated and many faceted. Trying to ensure that all draft legislation is carefully scrutinised before it is enacted is a major parliamentary responsibility. It is certainly one that the present House of Lords contributes to in a substantial way. The effectiveness with which this is done depends on many factors, including the quality, experience and knowledge of the members of the House; the readiness and willingness with which those debating legislation can hear the views of those outside parliament, especially the leaders of relevant groups representing interested or affected members of the public; the readiness of government to listen; and the extent to which the two Houses work in a complementary or a competitive way. On this latter point it is noticeable that whenever the government wish to overturn a Lords amendment, ministers are inclined to present the issue as a Commons versus Lords matter, steering debate into competitive mode, rather than simply discussing issues of dispute on their merits. This is something discussed further in the concluding Chapter.

Effectiveness in deliberative role

Much of the work of the House is not directly concerned with legislation, as Table 4.2 has made clear. Debates on motions, statements and questions all fall into this category, as does much of the select committee work of the House, where the concern is to scrutinise the work of government and contribute towards ensuring the executive is held accountable for what it does and maybe for what it fails to do. It would be strange if a second chamber did not provide opportunity for debates and questions to the government. Parliament is not simply a legislature. As well as enacting bills, and thereby subjecting government policy to public debate and scrutiny, it is the purpose of parliament to call government to account. Non-legislative debate can be used to keep government on its toes so to speak.

There are two very different yet understandable reactions to debate in the Lords. One is to emphasise the very high quality of most of the debates that take place. To the speakers is attributed great wisdom, experience or expertise. They make speeches that are intelligent, thought-provoking and very well-informed. Debate is courteous and dignified. A professional pride ensures most peers take great care over their speeches, honing their arguments, and only speaking when they feel they really have something worthwhile to say. Such high quality debates must by definition be influential, or so it is thought. After all, ministers have to reply to them, so civil servants must read them, and surely therefore the sheer quality of what is said will exert an influence. A contrasting view emphasises that virtually no one pays any attention to non-legislative debate in the Lords. There may be occasional exceptions, perhaps when the media pick up on some particular participant – a former prime minister who takes issue with her own party, or a religious leader who attacks lax moral standards displayed by royalty, or when a peer who holds some public office chooses to answer public criticism through a debate in the House. But these are very much the exceptions. Generally all that is happening (so it can be argued) is that peers are talking to themselves; the chamber is a kind of wind-tunnel, or an echo chamber. Even if many speeches are carefully crafted and well-informed, so what? It is only peers themselves who notice.

Peers are certainly inclined to self-congratulation about the quality of their debates. When new peers who have had distinguished careers elsewhere make their maiden speeches, peers love to welcome them and express the hope that the House will frequently benefit from their wisdom and experience in the future. Reading the general debates that take place is often an educative exercise. They certainly offer a different style and approach to those that take place in the Commons. While the immediate political impact of peers' debates may be very limited, it is not unreasonable to think that a gentle seeping of opinion from the House into the world outside does take place, at least on some subjects.

Some peers have used their membership of the House to good effect in relation to particular subjects of which they are very well informed. The former permanent secretary at the Home Office, Lord Allen of Abbeydale, president of MENCAP among other commitments, frequently contributed on the needs of the mentally ill, and on the condition of the prison service. Another persistent contributor and user of questions in the House has been the Countess of Mar (an elected cross-bench hereditary peeress, thirty-first in line of succession), whose campaigning on behalf of farmers affected by sheep dip containing organophosphates earned her first the *Country Life* 'Parliamentarian of the Year' award in 1996 and the *Spectator* 'Peer of the Year' award in 1997. There are many other examples of individual peers who possibly over many years have persistently campaigned in the upper House, and whose use of debates and questions has been an important weapon in their arsenals. MPs of course do the same, and arguably MPs have the democratic credentials to do the job that peers do not have. But the House of Lords does have a diversity and depth of experience within its ranks that is not found in the House of Commons.

Debates on foreign affairs and defence bring this out. When the House debated the armed forces in 2002 Lord King of Bridgwater (formerly Tom King, Secretary of State for Defence) contrasted the two Houses, pointing out that four ex-Chiefs of Defence Staff were to speak in the Lords debate. Nor do the ex-chiefs pull their punches. In January 2004

Lord Bramall (one of four defence chiefs to speak) described the white paper as 'long-winded, repetitive . . . strong in lofty sentiment and virtuous expression of intent, but singularly ill-defined in detail'.[35] A year later when five former defence chiefs spoke, Lord King said he had never heard five former chiefs express such united scepticism. Sometimes it is the mix of expertise that is important. On 17 November 2003 a debate on the legality of armed forces operations in Iraq drew contributions from former law officers and judges as well as military figures and diplomats. Senior military and legal figures contributed to a debate in February 2006 on the advice given by the Attorney General to the army legal service and army prosecuting authority. As the relationship between the judiciary and the government became increasingly fraught, the House of Lords provided a focus for dispassionate and better-informed debate than was possible in the Commons (where some senior ministers had become almost abusive towards judges).[36]

In part it is the different approach to debate that distinguishes the Lords. Speeches tend to be less concerned with asserting party advantage, more concerned with well-informed argument – more cerebral and less populist. But to some extent different priorities are evident in the subjects chosen for debate. Introducing a debate on education and health care in prisons Lord Hurd of Westwell (Douglas Hurd) drew on his long experience of the Commons and as Home Secretary, saying that in his view the Lords had a particular responsibility for prisons 'not constitutionally, but because of the interests of members, and because the ordinary processes of politics in the House of Commons did not serve the interests of such areas well'.[37] The minister replying to the Queen's Speech debate on foreign affairs in 2004, Baroness Symons of Vernham Dean, spoke of the 'great expertise and most powerful advocacy and intellectual erudition' displayed in the debate, which had incidentally witnessed two former Conservative Foreign Secretaries explain why they considered the invasion of Iraq to have been a mistake.[38]

When the great guru of focus groups, Lord (Philip) Gould made his maiden speech in the House, he drew on his experience saying the House of Lords was respected by the public because 'it can achieve balance, transcend politics and play a crucial revising role'.[39] Perusal of specialist publications indicates attention being given to the deliberative work of the House. At least eight medically related journals and magazines reported the Science and Technology Committee report on Complementary and Alternative Medicine in 2000–01. When Lord Wilson of Dinton, former head of the civil service, made his maiden speech he referred to the respect in which the House was held, and described its oversight of the executive as 'crucial'.[40]

Select committees

It is these qualities that also give distinctiveness to the select committee work of the House. The 1968 white paper on Lords reform contained the suggestion that there might be a greater role for such committees, which until then had been relatively rare. Though the main proposals for reform of the House were aborted, it was not long before peers were developing in a significant way investigatory select committee work. This has taken a number of different strands. First were ad hoc select committees established to investigate a topic or perhaps a private member's bill. One of the earliest was a committee set up in 1972 to examine an Anti-Discrimination Bill introduced by the leader of the Liberal Party in the House; this helped push along opinion by establishing evidence of discrimination on gender grounds, and pointing the way to remedies. Over the years a string of such committees have reported – on a Bill of Rights in 1977; on the 'causes and implications of the deficit in the balance of trade in manufactured goods' in 1984; on the sentence for murder in 1989; and on medical ethics in 1993 following some highly publicised cases of 'mercy killing', a topic further considered in 2005 when the former Lord Chancellor, Lord Mackay of Clashfern, chaired a select committee on Lord Joffe's Assisted Dying for the Terminally Ill Bill. This took evidence from some 140 expert witnesses and visited four countries where euthanasia in some form was practised. Following the government's abortive attempt to introduce the offence of incitement to religious hatred in the 2002 Anti-Terrorism Bill the House set up a select committee to examine this knotty problem, which though not producing a unanimous report did allow views to be put on record and potential difficulties to be carefully explored. Generally now at least one ad hoc committee is in operation every session, and there is no shortage of peers coming forward with suggestions. Lord Lestor wanted a select committee on his bill dealing with prerogative powers of the crown, but could not gain enough support for this. In 2005–06 Lord Fowler chaired an ad hoc select committee on the BBC charter review, which as might be expected included a seeming galaxy of relevant experience.

A second strand to Lords committee work was the establishment in 1974 of the European Communities Committee to scrutinise draft Community legislation and other relevant matters. This rapidly became a major aspect of the work of the House. The need for such a committee arose at just the time that the upper House felt it had the capacity to undertake some new task. Many of the recently arrived life peers approached their parliamentary work with a greater professionalism than had been hitherto seen in the House. In the Commons greater emphasis was being given to select committee work, and this was something peers felt they could reasonably emulate. Furthermore, in the Commons membership of the EC was still a matter very fraught with political division, both within as well as between parties, and this made the task of providing scrutiny of Community legislation more difficult. The scrutiny process could so readily become victim to fundamental political quarrels about membership. Peers on the other hand were at that time overwhelmingly in support of membership, and approached the whole matter of scrutiny in a very practical way. Because the legislative process of the Community did not directly engage with national parliaments, the role of the latter could only be one of influence rather than direct power – a context with which the House of Lords was readily familiar in contrast to the self-perception of the Commons still inclined to cherish its alleged 'sovereignty'. These factors helped to shape the development of the scrutiny process in different directions in the two Houses. Whereas the Commons scrutiny committee focused on the need to report on the significance of each item of draft legislation, alerting MPs to those upon which further debate was considered desirable, the Lords committee operated differently. A pattern of subject-based sub-committees provided in-depth scrutiny of selected issues. By the late 1970s seven sub-committees mobilised over 100 peers into the scrutiny process. Furthermore the terms of reference of the Lords committee did not confine it to draft legislation but enabled it to examine other questions which it considered relevant, for example wider policy issues such as Community enlargement, fraud within the Community, or green papers dealing with matters still some way off draft legislation.

The labours of the committee were considerable. In most sessions it produced some two dozen reports, some of which were the result of very substantial inquiries and evidence gathering. The committee tended to have a well-developed 'European' outlook with good contacts in the Community institutions. Its approach was practical, flexible and pragmatic – a sub-committee dealing especially with legal issues and almost always chaired by a law lord, frequently engaged in correspondence with ministers on the legal aspects of Community legislation. A new post of Principal Deputy Chairman of Committees was created for a peer to become the full-time salaried chairman of this committee. Peers were rotated off the committee (or sub-committee) after a few sessions of membership (three prior to 1992, then four). This soon resulted in a significant proportion of the active members of the House having had first hand experience of scrutinising Community matters. It helped the House to develop an awareness and understanding of the Community.

In the early 1990s concern developed in the House of Lords that the EU Committee was pre-empting too high a proportion of the available resources of the House. A review of committee work led to a reduction in the number of sub-committees from seven to five, though this was keenly contested within the House, and subsequently the number was raised again to seven. When in 1989 the Commons Procedure Committee inquired into the process of scrutiny of EC legislation, it took evidence from the Lords Committee and clearly felt that peers had developed a very useful complementary approach to that of the lower House. During the 1990s, and especially following the 1997 election, the House of Commons made significant alterations to its machinery for providing scrutiny of European Union matters. In 2004 a suggestion came from the Modernisation Committee of the House of Commons for a new joint Parliamentary European Committee, but this was greeted without enthusiasm by the House of Lords.[41] Table 4.4 indicates the committee structure in 2006.

The main committee always conducts an examination of the annual work programme of the Commission, and following the six-monthly meetings of the European Council usually takes evidence from the Minister for Europe. The sub-committees are very much evidence driven; 'our key aim is to scrutinise draft legislation in order to add value to discussion on these proposals'.[42] They generally seek to work 'upstream' in the legislative process, believing that the earlier input is made, the greater the likelihood of it receiving attention. Lord Brittain of Spelthorne, formerly EU Commissioner, praised the work of the committee from a European perspective, quoting the former president of the Commission, Jacques Delors, as saying reports from the Lords committee 'represented the most serious critique of European policy emanating from any legislature in the European Union'.[43] The Lords Committee has provided a very good example of the second chamber developing a role to which for various reasons it was well suited, and doing so at a time when the House of Commons was again for various reasons unable to do this.[44]

Similar points may be made about the other sessional committees the House of Lords has established, which represents the third strand to its committee work. First was the select committee on science and technology, set up in 1980 just as the Commons decided to abandon its subject orientated committees (including one on science and technology) in preference for departmentally focused select committees. This is a smaller operation, usually working through two sub-committees. Typically these involve some twenty or so peers, several of whom are distinguished scientists or engineers. In its early years the committee

Table 4.4 The European Union Committee in 2006

Designation	Subject matter	Chairman	Number of members (including co-opted)	Recent reports
Main committee	Matters relating to the EU	Lord Grenfell	18	Further enlargement of the EU
Sub-committee A	Economic, financial and international	Lord Radice	10 (7)	Reinvigoration of the Doha development agenda
Sub-committee B	Internal market	Lord Woolmer of Leeds	10 (8)	Single markets in services and in energy
Sub-committee C	Foreign affairs, defence and development	Lord Bowness	10 (8)	Strategy for Africa
Sub-committee D	Environment and agriculture	Lord Renton of Mount Harry	10 (9)	Biofuels
Sub-committee E	Law and institutions	Lord Brown of Eaton-under-Heywood	10 (7)	The Fundamental Rights Agency
Sub-committee F	Home affairs	Lord Wright of Richmond	10 (7)	Economic migration and illegal migrants
Sub-committee G	Social policy and consumer affairs	Baroness Thomas of Walliswood	11 (9)	Lifelong learning strategy for mental health

appeared to have some difficulty in ensuring its reports were taken notice of within government, with replies sometimes being very late and when made giving little evidence that the issues concerned had been seriously considered. But the committee gradually earned a reputation not only for the authority of its reports based on the expertise within its membership, but also for its persistence. If it considered a government reply inadequate the committee was inclined simply to return to the subject of an earlier report. Ministers and civil servants for their part have been made aware that they are dealing with some of the most eminent scientists in the country, who have chosen to engage at least for the time being with the policy-making process from the vantage point of a parliamentary select committee. Nor has the committee been averse to tackling some of the most problematic of issues, or taking what in parliamentary terms are unorthodox views. One report recommended that doctors should be allowed to prescribe cannabis, a recommendation rejected very publicly by the government on the day of publication, much to the committee's annoyance.[45] Recent reports have considered the implications of growing resistance to antibiotics, the management of nuclear waste, genetically modified food and pandemic influenza.

In 1998 a select committee was established to examine the operation of the new Monetary Policy Committee of the Bank of England. This was an ad hoc committee but two years later it was re-established as a sessional (permanent) select committee 'to consider economic affairs'. This allowed the committee to select for examination from a wide range of policy issues, using economic analysis in what its first chairman, Lord Peston (a professor of economics at the LSE), described as its 'fact-finding, evidence driven consensual' approach.[46] Among recently considered subjects have been economic aspects of an ageing population in 2004, climate change in 2005 and the management of risk in 2006. This latter report argued that threats to personal liberty needed to be weighed more carefully when formulating public policy, and in support of this drew on case studies on passive smoking and the relative expenditure on road and rail safety.[47] In the 2005–06 session the committee was taking an active interest in plans being made by government to introduce new arrangements for the collection and reporting of official statistics with direct accountability to parliament. Lord Wakeham succeeded Lord Peston as chairman of the committee in 2004, when it consisted of a former governor of the Bank of England, two former Chancellors of the Exchequer, the former chairman of the Public Accounts Committee, two professors of economics, the former chairman of BT and five other business figures. A somewhat surprising development has been the use of a sub-committee each year since 2003 to examine the annual Finance Bill implementing the budget.[48] Care has however been taken to avoid encroachment on Commons financial privilege by tightly defining the terms of reference of this sub-committee to such matters as tax administration, clarification and simplification, not the proposed rates or incidence of tax. However this did not stop the Leader of the Commons, Jack Straw, from saying that in his view by establishing such a committee the House was making a 'quite deliberate claim to additional powers'.[49]

The final sessional committee is on the Constitution. Such a committee had been advocated by a number of peers before being recommended by the Wakeham Commission. It is charged with the task of reviewing all bills for their constitutional implications and with keeping the constitution under review. It was set up in 2001, chaired first by the Conservative peer, Lord Norton of Louth (the academic Professor Philip Norton) and then from 2005 by Lord Holme of Cheltenham, the Liberal Democrat peer who has had a long-standing interest in this area. Among significant general inquiries that it has made are 'Parliament and the Legislative Process' and 'Waging War, Parliament's Role and Responsibility'.[50] The committee generally produces about ten briefer reports every session on particular bills. Given the uncodified nature of the British Constitution, the committee acts as something of a constitutional watchdog alerting parliamentarians and others to proposals that may have unintended implications for the constitution. This is a role that many would argue is especially appropriate to a second chamber in a system where a parliamentary majority based on a first-past-the-post electoral system can at times use its power to achieve some seemingly attractive short-term goals, but without adequate sensitivity to longer-term constitutional implications.

A fourth strand in Lords select committee work has focused on the legislative process, and in particular the use of secondary legislation, an area of great expansion and growing significance. In the early 1990s a number of peers developed a sharp interest in this, including Lord Rippon of Hexham, who chaired the Hansard Society Commission *Making the Law* (1992). He initiated a debate on delegated legislation in the House in 1990. The concern of peers to subject the order-making powers contained within bills to more systematic scrutiny was met with typical lack of enthusiasm from government, the then Lord Chancellor, Lord Mackay of Clashfern, saying that such was the interest taken by peers in the powers contained within bills 'that no parliamentary draftsman . . . is unaware of your Lordships' attitude to these clauses'.[51] However the House did establish the Delegated Powers Committee in the 1992–93 session under the chairmanship of Lord Rippon, with lawyers and former government ministers being prominent members. Immediately after first reading of a bill the sponsoring department sends an explanatory memorandum to the committee explaining the purpose of powers contained within the bill. The committee then reports quickly so that its views can contribute to consideration of the bill concerned while it is going through the House. The committee quickly earned a high reputation, prompting substantial amendment to the 1993 Education Bill following its report which declared part two, dealing with student unions, a 'skeleton' bill.[52]

When the Conservative Government introduced its Deregulation and Contracting Out Bill in the 1993–94 session, the committee offered trenchant criticism, as did the Commons procedure committee. This resulted in some amendment being made to extend the possibility of parliamentary scrutiny of deregulation orders. The Lords committee then took on the additional task of scrutinising deregulation orders, and was rechristened as the Delegated Powers and Regulatory Reform Committee. Since 1994 it has had a Commons committee as a companion for that part of its work involving deregulation orders. In 1995 the committee rejected a deregulation order concerned with Sunday dancing, stating forthrightly that deregulation procedure was inappropriate for the proposal, that consultation had not been adequate, and that necessary protections were not maintained.[53] What was interesting about this was that the Commons Committee took a less robust line, stating only that it had found consultation inadequate, but not on the more fundamental grounds taken up by the Lords committee. The committee has been accorded very little attention outside interested circles within Westminster and Whitehall. However its existence is appreciated where it matters because it requires government departments to justify in writing every new provision by which delegated power may be exercised, and civil servants know that they may be required to substantiate the acquisition of these proposed powers in oral evidence to the committee, which will then publish its report in time to sharpen parliamentary scrutiny of the bill. The committee was spoken of as having established a reputation as 'the constitutional conscience of the House in relation to delegated powers'.[54] It is another example of the House of Lords developing a select committee role to which it was well suited, and one that has proved effective in the task it faced.

This committee dealt with the genesis of secondary legislation, and complemented a joint select committee, which since 1972 had provided technical scrutiny of draft instruments, drawing attention to any defects, unusual or retrospective use of powers or similar cause for concern. But this still left the consideration of the policy implications of SIs to other parliamentary processes, and given the number of instruments and their growing complexity, this was often not forthcoming because of the difficulty in finding parliamentary time. In 2003 the Lords therefore decided to set up a committee to consider the merits of SIs. This – the Merits of Statutory Instruments Committee – meets weekly throughout the session, and aims to report quickly on instruments so that where necessary, time exists for further parliamentary consideration within the forty-day period generally allowed. In 2006 the committee drew on its experience in examining some 2000 items of secondary legislation reporting on the management of secondary legislation by government departments, which it argued could be significantly improved.[55]

An area of growing activity in recent years has been joint select committees. When the Human Rights Act was passed in 1998 a joint committee was set up to keep human rights matters under review, to scrutinise draft legislation for human rights implications and to examine remedial orders that may be brought in under the Act. Also, as part of Labour's modernisation programme, the publication of bills in draft form has become more usual without ever becoming the norm that many have advocated. In some cases draft bills are scrutinised by already established select committees, but several have been the subject of specially set up joint select committees, and where this has been the case the Lords have contributed substantially. For example the 2002 Communications Bill was scrutinised by a joint committee chaired by Lord Puttnam, the 2003 Corruption Bill by a committee chaired by Lord Slynn of Hadley (a law lord), while Lord Carter, former Chief Whip, chaired the scrutiny committee on the 2003 Mental Incapacity Bill and the committee that examined the draft Disability Discrimination Bill in 2005.

One reason for using joint select committees is to obtain the right blend of experience and expertise for such scrutiny work. The Lords does contain members who can bring a deep understanding of some of the issues involved to such work. Given the scale of select committee work within parliament it has sometimes been difficult to find enough MPs available for such scrutiny committees, whereas the availability of peers has not been a problem. The select committee on the Disability Discrimination Bill was cut in size from sixteen to twelve because of the difficulty of finding MPs to serve. The attendance of peers at scrutiny sessions has also been less problematic. The MP who chaired the joint committee on the Gambling Bill said some peers had brought 'huge experience' to the subject, and that he was in no doubt joint committees were better than those drawn from one House only.[56] An additional benefit of such scrutiny committees is that some members of both Houses can engage in a more pertinent way with the content of a bill during its subsequent parliamentary stages, and do so with greater authority. When Lord Puttnam, who had chaired the joint select committee on the draft Communications Bill, moved an amendment designed to strengthen safeguards for consumers by reordering the duties placed on OFCOM, he spoke with the backing of other members of the committee, and in the resulting division the government was defeated by 179 votes to 74, with thirty-three Labour peers voting with Lord Puttnam.[57]

Select committee inquiries do enable evidence from interested parties, experts of various kinds and others, to be put on the record. Of course those who give evidence could find other outlets for their views, and many do, but there is a discipline about giving evidence to a select committee which may well be avoided elsewhere. Furthermore, having this activity take place within the context of parliament does enhance the public accountability of government in the areas concerned. Government appointed committees of inquiry report to the government, and it is then ministers and their advisers who are in control of the publication and public presentation of the report. A select committee is in a fundamentally different position. In practice and behind the scenes ministers may seek to control what select committees are set up, what subjects they tackle and then – if they produce unwelcome reports – ignore or marginalise them. But the report of a select committee is made to parliament where it may be debated, and the committee is able to organise the public presentation of the report. The Lords like the Commons has invested resources in developing its Committee Office to try and ensure better media coverage of reports. Members of committees can use other parliamentary procedures to follow up a report, or indeed to return and re-inquire and re-report on the same issue, examining the government's response or its failure to respond.

Back in 1991 the House set up a select committee to examine its own committee work, which became known as the Jellicoe Committee, after its chairman, Lord Jellicoe, a former Leader of the House.[58] This involved a more systematic analysis than had hitherto been made of the varied developments that had occurred and the growing pressure the House was experiencing for expansion of committee work. One of its recommendations was for a 'Steering Committee' to oversee select committee work. This led to the establishment of the Liaison Committee, which unlike its Commons namesake does not consist of select committee chairmen, but of party leaders and some backbench representation. This now allocates resources between select committees and makes recommendations for new committees. For example in 2005 it listened to representations from the current and former chairmen of the Constitution Committee in support of a new sessional (ongoing) committee, preferably a joint committee, to scrutinise regulatory bodies. At the same time the retired law lord, Lord Lloyd of Berwick, proposed an ad hoc committee on the interception of communications. The Liaison Committee did not agree to either because of resource implications,

though in the same report it did approve the lifting of the ceiling on
the number of members on each of the seven EU Committee sub-
committees from ten to eleven.[59]

Committees and the improvement of the legislative process

Much select committee activity in the Lords has been focused on trying
to improve the quality of the legislative process, and this has resulted in
a readiness for procedural experimentation and innovation. In the late
1980s the House seemed to be developing a collective conscience about
the state of the statute book, and the sluggishness and complacency of
parliament in the face of ever-escalating government demands for more
legislation, often ill-thought out, and in some cases requiring almost
instant repeal or drastic amendment. In January 1990 a retired law lord,
who had also been a Conservative minister, Lord Simon of Glaisdale, initiated a debate on the quantity and quality of legislation. Former
Conservative ministers who took part in the debate were heavily critical
of their own party in office; the government stood indicted of both
increasing the quantity and reducing the quality of legislation, a far cry
from what they had proclaimed when in opposition in the 1970s. In particular Lord Rippon had some fun quoting from a pamphlet written by
his colleague Geoffrey Howe in the 1970s entitled *Too Much Law?* in
which he complained: 'We are doubling the statute book once in every
fifteen years. It should be the first duty of parliament to resist the temp-
tation to add any more. We must make fewer laws and the laws fewer'.[60]

The Law Commission expressed frustration at seeing so little action
on a significant proportion of its reports, given its specific remit to make
proposals for law reform. In its early years reports had been speedily
implemented – twenty-eight of its first thirty within two years of publication. But by 1990 of thirty-three reports made since 1984 only eleven
had been implemented. In the House of Lords a retired law lord, Lord
Wilberforce, took up the Law Commission's case, and in successive years
during debate on the Queen's Speech he bemoaned the way law reform
was being ignored. In 1992 another law lord, Lord Brightman, suggested that the annual £3 million spent on the Law Commission could
hardly be justified if so many of its reports were left simply gathering
dust.

The House then established a new procedure designed to provide a
fast track through parliament for Law Commission bills, while ensuring
that matters that were controversial within such bills could be adequately explored. This was the Lords equivalent of Special Bill procedure
in the Commons. It involved a select committee taking evidence for

a limited period after second reading, thereby it was hoped enabling interested parties to bring their concerns before a parliamentary committee, which would then report the bill with suggested amendments to the House. Such bills would then hopefully go quickly through the Commons. But after very limited use this procedure was abandoned because of opposition in the Commons.

By the later 1990s the Law Commission was again bemoaning in its annual reports the Government's tardiness in introducing bills based on its reports. In 1997 and again in 1998 only one Law Commission bill was taken through parliament, with twenty-three reports outstanding, some of which had been expressly accepted by the government.[61] The Commission had itself commissioned research to show that relatively little parliamentary time was required for its bills.[62] The two bills enacted in 1996 had taken respectively thirteen minutes and sixty-five minutes of Lords time and one minute each in the Commons. It seemed ironic that with so much government legislation being of the legislate-as-you-go kind, these 'properly baked legislative cakes' should be left to go stale.[63] It is hard to say whether parliament really feels any clear sense of responsibility for the quality of the statute book. In so far as there are signs that it might these appear to have come from the House of Lords and not from the Commons. We return to this point in Chapter 6.

Conclusion

This Chapter has briefly analysed the work of the present House of Lords. Implicit throughout this Chapter has been the argument that a second chamber makes a very substantial contribution to the work of parliament. Furthermore, this Chapter has argued that in relation to the functions of scrutiny and holding the executive to account the Lords does add value to the work of the Commons. In particular its select committees have done this, and its floor of the House debates do ensure that alongside the high octane political partisanship manifested so readily in Commons debates, there is also from within parliament discussion that is characterised by very different qualities. Without attempting to evaluate one against the other one might simply say that both have their place.

Along with the need for the second chamber therefore, this Chapter has drawn attention to the way the present House of Lords has adapted and innovated its procedures, and how it has done so not as a rival or competitor to the Commons, but essentially as a complementary chamber. Its committee work and its legislative procedures have attempted to fill gaps, to do what the Commons is unable or unwilling to do at least for the time being. Nor has the House sought seriously to contest power with the Commons. Occasionally it has persisted with a difference of view, but always recognising and acknowledging limitations imposed both by the Parliament Acts and conventions. When considering the increasing frequency of parliamentary ping-pong on bills, it is well to remember that it takes two to play ping-pong. The reluctance of governments to give way to the second chamber has resulted at times in legislation being enacted that subsequently can be seen as defective on some of the very points where the Lords was trying to seek change. What is needed is a culture within Westminster and Whitehall that recognises the truth in Robin Cook's dictum: 'Good government requires good scrutiny', and one where parliament as a whole feels a greater sense of responsibility for the quality of legislation. This would enable the House of Lords to fulfil its role with greater confidence and enable the Commons and the government to be less touchy about the second chamber taking a different point of view.

But all this does not mean that the House is incapable of improvement. In its work of revising bills the House is above all a convenience to the government. And that is not what a parliamentary chamber is intended to be. It should be something more than that. The chamber is diligent but on the whole docile. It has fitted itself to a parliamentary culture in which the balance between parliament and government has tipped too far in the direction of government. Where parliament generally is too weak, simply emphasising that the Lords must be kept subordinate to the Commons, is inadequate as a guiding principle. The House of Lords has somewhat complacently acquiesced in this view, at least until recently. It has usually been very ready to offer itself a vote of confidence, and appears to think that if it did this often enough and loudly enough, then everyone else would recognise those virtues which peers could so clearly see in themselves. In so doing it has tended to confirm the complacency with which parliament views itself and its role. The question of reform really raises the larger issue of parliament's role within our political system. And this we return to in Chapter 6.

Notes

1 HL Deb. 12 Jul. 2005, cols. 1000–32; HL 92, 2005–06.
2 HL 111, 2001–02; HL 148, 2001–02; HL 162, 2003–04; HL 184, 2003–04.
3 HL Deb. 22 Mar. 1999, cols. 960–90; 23 Jan. 2001, cols. 135–61; 24 Mar. 2005, cols. 365–86.
4 HL Deb. 24 Jul. 2006, cols. 1544–50.

5 HL Deb. 26 Jan. 2005, cols. 1339–84.

6 HL 78, 1997–98; HL Deb. 30 Apr. 1998, cols. 389–440.

7 HL 144, 1997–98; HL Deb. 16 Nov. 1998, cols. 983–1017.

8 HL Deb. 9 Jun. 1998, cols. 889–90; HL 106, 1997–98.

9 Occasionally argument has broken out on the floor of the House about sending a bill to Grand Committee; in 2003 a Conservative backbench peer proposed that clauses in the Extradition Bill dealing with the 'European arrest warrant' should be taken on the floor of the House while the rest of the Bill might be dealt with in Grand Committee, but his motion to this effect was not supported by his own frontbench and lost on division. HL Deb. 6 May 2003, cols. 954–71.

10 HL 173-II, 2003–04, Q. 188.

11 HL Deb. 10 Nov. 2004, cols. 894–928, for opposition from the chairman of the Constitution Committee and others.

12 P. Richards, *Parliament and Conscience* (London, G. Allen & Unwin, 1970), esp. pp. 202–3.

13 HL 86, 2004–05; HL Deb. 10 Oct. 2005, cols. 12–32, 45–150.

14 See 'Untouched by Reform' in P. Giddings (ed.) *The Future of Parliament* (Basingstoke, Palgrave Macmillan, 2005). Also P. Cowley (ed.), *Conscience and Parliament* (London, Cass, 1998).

15 HL Deb. 12 Nov. 2003, cols. 1468–507. Giving evidence to the Joint Select Committee on Conventions, the former Chief Whip, Lord Carter, expressed the view that it would be 'very helpful if the Government were to take more notice of non-fatal motions' on SIs. HC 1212-I, 2005–06, Q. 40.

16 HL Deb. 21 May 2002, cols. 725–58.

17 HL Deb. 22 Feb. 2000, cols. 136–85; 6 Mar. 2000, col. 811.

18 HC Library Standard Note 'Acts & Statutory Instruments: Volume of UK Legislation', SN/SG/2911.

19 See for example HL Deb. 12 Jul. 2005, cols. 991–2 and 997–9, when Lord Peyton of Yeovil was prevented from asking a supplementary, resulting in some exchanges taking place on the floor of the House when questions were over.

20 See D. Shell, 'Questions in the House of Lords', in M. Franklin and P. Norton, (eds) *Parliamentary Questions*, (Oxford, Clarendon Press, 1993).

21 G. Drewry and J. Brock, 'Government Legislation: an Overview', in D. Shell and D. Beamish, (eds) *The House of Lords at Work* (Oxford, Clarendon Press, 1993).

22 HL Deb. 11 May 2004, cols. 151–5.

23 Joint Select Committee on Conventions, HC 1212-I, Q. 26.

24 R. Whitaker, 'Ping-Pong and Parliamentary Influence', *Parliamentary Affairs*, 59:3 (2006) 536–45.

25 See P. Cowley, *The Rebels: How Blair Mislaid his Majority* (London, Politicos, Methuen, 2005).

26 M. Russell, 'Views form Peers, MPs and the Public on the Legitimacy and Powers of the House of Lords', Constitution Unit paper, 2005.

27 Select Committee on Murder and Life Imprisonment, HL 78, 1988–89.

28 On all this see Lord Windlesham, *Responses to Crime, vol. 3, Legislating with the Tide* (Oxford, Clarendon Press, 1996) ch. 9.

29 *Ibid.* p. 103.

30 HL Deb. 1 Apr. 2004, col. 1449.

31 HC Deb. 8 Mar. 2003, col. 1296.

32 See statement following outcome of trial in Birmingham, HL Deb. 5 Apr. 2005, cols. 582–95.

33 P. Cowley, *The Rebels*, p. 93.

34 P. Cowley, *Revolts and Rebellions: Parliamentary Voting under Blair* (London, Politicos, 2002), p. 74.

35 HL Deb. 13 Jan. 2004, col. 494.

36 See 21 May 2003 on relations between the judiciary and the legislature, and 12 Feb. 2004 for six and a half hour debate on the Supreme Court judicial reforms.

37 HL Deb. 8 Dec. 2005, col. 803.

38 HL Deb. 24 Nov. 2004, col. 150.

39 HL Deb. 29 Nov. 2004, col. 309.

40 HL Deb. 26 Mar. 2003, cols. 822–23.

41 HL Deb. 16 Jun. 2004, cols. 756–68.

42 Lord Renton of Mount Harry, chairman of sub-committee D on environment and agriculture, *House Magazine*, Supplement, July 2006.

43 HL Deb. 26 Jan. 2004, col. 53.

44 See P. Giddings and G. Drewry (eds), *Britain in the European Union* (Basingstoke, Palgrave Macmillan, 2004); also chs. 5 and 7 in P. Giddings and G. Drewry, (eds) *Westminster and Europe* (Basingstoke, Macmillan 1996).

45 HL 151, 1997–98; also HL Deb. 3 Dec. 1998, col. 773.

46 HL Deb. 12 Nov. 2004, col. 1107.

47 HL 183, 2005–06; HL 12, 2005–06.

48 'An extraordinary step' according to Lord Tordoff, 'The Role of Select Committees in the House of Lords' in N. Baldwin (ed.) *Parliament in the 21st Century* (London, Politicos, 2005), p. 178.

49 Joint Select Committee on Conventions, HC 1212-I, 2005–06, see Q. 43 and Memorandum of Evidence from the Government, para. 72.

50 HL 173–1 & II, 2003–04; HL 236, 2005–06.

51 HL Deb. 14 Feb. 1990, cols. 1407–37; see also Select Committee on the committee work of the House, HL 35, 1991–92.

52 Select Committee on the Scrutiny of Delegated Powers, HL 11, 1993–94.

53 Select Committee on the Scrutiny of Delegated Powers, HL 102, 1995.

54 HC 152, 1995–96, appendix 2, para. 29.

55 HL 149, 2005–06.

56 HL 173–11, 2003–04, Qs. 168, 384.

57 See HL Deb. 23 Jun. 2003, cols. 11–25; analysis of vote from M. Russell and M. Sciara, 'The Lords, the Party System and British Politics', *British Politics*, 2:3 (2007).

58 HL 35, 1991–92.

59 HL 29, 2005–06.

60 For Howe's own rueful reflections on this after he had himself left government and reached the safety of the House of Lords, see HL Deb. 14 Dec. 1994, cols. 1295.

61 Law Commission Annual reports 1997 HC 565, 1997–98; 1998 HC 434, 1998–99.

62 P. Hopkins, 'Parliamentary Procedures and the Law Commission' (London, The Law Commission, 1994).

63 Lord Rippon of Hexham, *Making the Law: The Report of the Hansard Society Commission on the Legislative Process* (The Hansard Society, 1992), evidence at p. 496.

5

Second chambers elsewhere

Britain may have an unusual second chamber, but Britain is not unusual in having a second chamber. Though only a third or so of all national legislatures in the world are classified as bicameral, or two chamber, among large democratic states, bicameralism is normal. Half the member states of the European Union have second chambers. Bicameralism remains widespread in the Commonwealth countries and throughout the Americas, though less so in Africa and Asia. The proportion of legislatures that are bicameral rather than unicameral fell until the 1980s, but since then bicameralism has become more widespread, with significantly more countries creating or restoring second chambers than abolishing them.[1] This is an interesting trend to observe at the close of the century throughout most of which bicameralism appeared to be giving way to unicameralism. Second chambers were frequently associated with political systems that had yet to reach maturity as democracies. Typically, first chambers embodied genuine democracy, while second chambers frequently remained appointed (or even had hereditary membership), and few were directly elected. It seemed natural therefore to expect the number of second chambers to decline.

There have been a few well-known cases where democratic countries have deliberately abolished their second chambers, though these tended to be small in population terms. New Zealand, with less than three million inhabitants, removed its discredited second chamber in 1950; Denmark, with approximately five million people, abolished its second chamber in 1953, and Sweden, with some three million inhabitants, did so in 1971.[2] Other countries to take the unicameral path have been Kenya in 1966, Ecuador in 1979, Zimbabwe in 1990 and Peru in 1992. Elsewhere the inauguration of a new constitution has sometimes been the moment when a country has shifted from bicameralism to unicameralsim. This was true of Portugal in 1976, which with some ten million inhabitants currently remains the largest western democracy without a second chamber. Some countries have moved back and forward between the two, for example Turkey which went from unicameral to bicameral in 1961, and then back to unicameral in 1982. South Africa became unicameral for a short time in the early 1980s, then tricameral, before adopting a bicameral structure under its 1997 constitution. States that have created or restored second chambers include former communist countries in eastern Europe such as the Czech Republic, Poland, Romania, Belarus and Croatia. Elsewhere, for example Morocco and the Comoros islands, second chambers have been created over the last decade as part of a programme of constitutional reform.

The movement between single chamber and two chamber systems illustrates that second chambers are frequently contested institutions; they have not been taken for granted as first chambers have. This reflects the diversity of reasons for the existence of second chambers and the varied justifications that are offered for them. The very different forms that second chambers take provide further illustration of this point. Indeed, the variety is such that some argument exists as to which political systems are genuinely bicameral and which are not. Some have 'hidden' second chambers, that is, bodies that fulfil at least some of the functions attributed to second chambers, but receive no mention in the formal constitution of the country concerned.[3] The movement between unicameral and bicameral systems to some extent reflects changing understandings of the nature and most appropriate institutional expression of democracy.

The aim of this Chapter is to set the debate about the future of the British House of Lords in the wider context of a discussion about the principle and practice of bicameralism around the world. Why are second chambers so relatively widespread? Do they have features in common? Are there some that seem more effective and successful than others? Are there common themes that may be identified in the discussion of second chambers? Addressing such questions can help to stimulate analytical thought about the role and possible reform of the House of Lords. Not to look elsewhere is to be unnecessarily insular, but at the same time it would be a mistake to imagine that political institutions can be directly modelled from one political system to another. Every political system is unique, and the inter-relationships between institutions are matters of great subtlety. The fact that the sixty or so second chambers that do exist as part of national parliaments around the world demonstrate such diversity bears witness to this point. Examining second chambers is to be reminded of the denseness and intricacy of advanced political systems.

We may start with some general points about second chambers. First is the fact that they tend to be more diverse than first chambers. The latter are almost invariably directly elected, with members representing in principle an equal number of electors. By contrast second chambers, as we have noted, are composed in much more varied ways, with indi- rect election, appointment and even ex officio membership appearing as alternative routes to membership alongside direct election. Second chambers tend also to be smaller than first chambers; the average size of all second chambers is under 100, something less than half the average size of first chambers. Members of second chambers usually serve for longer terms than first chamber members, and their average age is invariably higher than that of first chambers. Some have a minimum age for membership that is greater than for first chambers, and a few countries with elected second chambers even have a higher minimum age for voters than for their first chambers.

These factors tend to give second chambers an air of seniority along- side first chambers, yet the paradox of second chambers is that despite the seniority of their members and their more exclusive feel, their power is normally less than that of first chambers. Usually second chambers are slightly more detached from governments than first chambers, and in parliamentary systems it is almost always the first chamber alone that has the power to remove a government. Frequently second chambers have a territorial or regional basis to their membership, seen most obvi- ously where there is a federal system. Indeed the relationship between bicameralsim and federalism is well attested, in that all large demo- cratic federal systems have two chamber legislatures. But a territorial basis for second chamber membership is often evident in non-federal systems too.

The federalist rationale for bicameralism was in effect invented by the founding fathers of the American constitution. But the idea of bicamer- alism pre-dated by a long way the Philadelphia convention of 1789. Two related precursors can be distinguished.[4] First is the notion, put at its simplest, that two is better than one, and that from diverse counsels wise decisions would arise. The Romans had two consuls so that one could check the other. They also had a council of elders known as the Senate, and this is the name borne by some two-thirds of modern day second chambers. This Roman thinking drew on Greek notions of the benefit of mixed government, made famous in Aristotle's analysis of kingship (rule of one), aristocracy (rule by the few) and polity (rule by the many). Government that was not mixed resulted in a perversion of each of these three, whereby kingship became tyranny, aristocracy became oligarchy, and rule by the many became democracy, or rule by the majority. Good government embaced at least two out of the three. Rulers should hear counsel from various sources, and power itself should be shared. This legacy from the ancient world may be recognised as a distant source of modern bicameralism.

Second however was the related notion that different classes or orders of society demanded separate representation. We have already noted that in Britain the division of parliament into two separate Houses reflected such a view. The aristocracy and at one stage the Church too required representation distinct from that of the knights of the shires and the burgesses. In most European countries in the middle ages three or even four chambers existed to represent different classes, though these Estates General fell at times into disuse, depending on the degree to which monarchy attained an absolutist character. By the nineteenth century, almost everywhere, these had been replaced by two chamber bodies, the second chamber being seen as representing landed and privileged classes and thereby exerting some restraint on the unpredictable and possibly dangerous power conferred on the more democratic chamber. In some countries, of course, revolutionary fervour led to the rejection of all but a unicameral people's assembly, but where this occurred, for example in France in 1790 and 1850, and Greece in 1860, a return to bicameralism usually followed.

As popular election became the normal way in which first chambers were composed, so second chambers based on aristocratic or more privileged membership began to disappear. At the commencement of the twentieth century Hungary, Portugal, Austria and the component states of Germany all still had hereditary second chambers, as did Britain and Japan. But by the time of the second world war such chambers had disappeared in Europe, apart from Britain, and just after the war the Japanese hereditary chamber was also removed. Britain became curious for its retention of such a body, though the new constitutions of some former colonies included in various cases provision for hereditary chiefs in their legislatures.

This notion that second chambers represented certain groups in society has lived on in the view that a bicameral structure provides the means for representation on a different basis to a first chamber. Occasionally this has been expressed in some form of functional representation, but more frequently in the idea that second chambers can represent territory within a state while first chambers represent the population.

Britain is an unusual case in that instead of old institutions being replaced they have been retained and adapted as we saw in Chapter 1. Neither revolution nor territorial adjustment brought any necessity for reinvention of the state. For this reason Britain's pathway to democracy was gradual and partial. Democratic features were added to the system while its former ancient institutions remained. The country became a democracy, but also a constitutional monarchy. The House of Lords survived, almost at the interface between hereditary power and popular will.

Elsewhere bolder steps towards democratic forms were taken. In the late seventeenth century revolutions in both America and France gave birth to fundamentally different conceptions of what democracy entailed. In France the sudden and violent overthrow of the former system, the *ancien regime,* was accompanied by an emphasis on the sovereignty of the people which of course had to be incarnated in a single place. The will of the people must be implemented with as little hindrance as possible. With the aristocracy and the monarchy out of the way, there could be no place for a second chamber either. The indefatigable constitution maker of revolutionary France, Abbe Sieyes, dismissed the idea of a second chamber with the oft-quoted words: 'If it agrees with the first chamber it is superfluous; if it disagrees it is obnoxious'. Frequent constitutional change followed over the next century in France, with unicameralism being experimented with when revolutionary fervour ran high.

In North America a very different understanding of democracy emerged. The great majority of the delegates who convened at Philadelphia in 1787 came from states whose legislatures were bicameral. In their deliberations a unicameral congress was at first proposed, but the desirability of a bicameral congress was quickly accepted, even if initially the Senate was to be a body elected by the House of Representatives. Later a compromise plan to have a lower House proportionate to population and an upper House comprised of two senators from each state regardless of population was accepted. The Federalist Papers provide ample testimony to the reasoning that led them to favour bicameralism.[5] The need for checks and balances was spelt out in Paper 51, with Paper 62 building on this and expounding the reasons for having two chambers. A second chamber was deemed necessary as a constitutional safeguard for the people, and was seen as desirable in order to provide an opportunity for second thoughts in the legislative process. Furthermore a second chamber would ensure more consistent and soundly based legislation because it would enable contributions to be made by those with wisdom and experience, qualities that may be lacking in the popularly elected first chamber.

What is striking today re-reading the Federalist Papers is the unabashed way in which the need for checks and balances is traced back to the underlying conception of human nature, and the consequent dangers of untrammelled power belonging to any one person or single group. The Senate was established therefore partly to safeguard the position of the states, but also to provide restraint upon the potential abuse of power by a populist government. Its role as a guarantor of state rights has been eclipsed by its role as a powerful part of Congress, not only a potential check on the presidency and the lower House, but also as a forum where policy initiatives may be taken and compromise negotiated. The American Senate remains the example *par excellence* of a powerful second chamber.

One understanding of democracy emphasises the need for strong government to implement whatever is defined as the popular will. Another emphasises the need for checks and balances, for restraint, on government to prevent too great an accumulation of power, which if it occurs, quickly leads to unaccountable power. Between these two parameters the practical details of democratic political systems have to be worked out. If the emphasis is placed upon the desirability of 'strong' government, with an executive sure of getting its way, then either unicameralism or a weak second chamber will seem appropriate. If the emphasis is placed on the dangers of populism and concentrated power, then the desirability of having a stronger second chamber able to exercise real restraint will be recognised.

The thinking of the founding fathers of America was very much in terms of restraint being exercised on the popularly elected first chamber. Throughout the nineteenth century political thinkers often stressed the dangers of democracy. The danger of power concentrated in the hands of a party majority, controlling both government and the elected chamber of parliament, were felt to be very real. This line of thought has been followed to the present day, for example in Lord Hailsham's critique of British democracy as 'elective dictatorship'. But under modern political conditions the role of second chambers in providing checks and balances is not generally rated highly. Instead such checks are looked for elsewhere, perhaps from a formal constitutional point of view the judiciary, or the necessity to hold a referendum, or the more political checks imposed by a competitive party system or perhaps in the tension between the executive and the lower chamber of the legislature, or even in the part played by organised groups outside the formal political system.

It is for these reasons that the role of second chambers has become generally less significant in the modern period. Many second chambers are not held in high esteem, and discussion about reform of second chambers is widespread. If they do exercise restraint this is as likely – perhaps more likely – to be seen as a threat to democracy than as a support to democracy. Yet there is also an awareness in advanced democracies of the complexity of modern government and of the need for policy to be fine-tuned to take account of the intricacies of society. It may be that contemporary second chambers have a role in exerting influence rather than wielding power, as bodies bringing wisdom and diverse experience to bear upon policy making rather than political will and popular demand. Maybe populist democracy needs to be balanced by a more deliberative form of democracy. Before pursuing such thoughts further, we will look a little more closely at the diversity of second chambers that do exist in the world today.[6]

The USA

The most obvious rationale for a second chamber is in a federal system. Here the American model is supreme. A first chamber – the House of Representatives – represents the people proportionately, and a second chamber represents the states or other constituent units. In the American case the states are represented evenly, so that both California and Wyoming are represented by two senators, though California has a population over sixty times as great as Wyoming. But the Senate has never been viewed primarily as the defender of state rights. It has become a powerful institution, central to the working of American government, with well-defined powers, designed to balance the presidency and the House of Representatives. It was designed to be composed of mature citizens whose judgement could be trusted. It was therefore given particular responsibility in respect of foreign policy and in regard to senior public appointments. When its credibility was in decline, it was strengthened through the seventeenth amendment passed in 1913. This replaced the original method of appointment of senators, indirect election through state legislatures, with direct popular election. Today each senator is elected for a six-year term, with one-third coming up for re-election every two years, at the same time as the entire House of Representatives is elected. The Senate is less than a quarter the size of the House, and this together with the longer term senators serve, gives the Senate an air of exclusivity. Congressmen frequently aspire to become senators, but never do senators aspire to be members of the House. Around a half of senators are former congressmen.

The American Senate is today the example *par excellence* of a powerful second chamber. It is a model that has been followed elsewhere in terms of its structure, but it remains unique. No other country has established a body that so obviously enjoys greater power and status than the first chamber. But it is an individualist body, and this gives rise to the chief criticism of the American political system, its propensity for gridlock. The emphasis in checks and balances can go too far in the direction of checks.[7]

Such a pattern of equal representation of units with very varied populations is also found in Argentina, Mexico and Switzerland. Elsewhere the number of representatives has been adjusted to take account of different population levels, though not necessarily with the same concern for evenness as generally found in first chambers. In India seats in the Rajya Sabba, or upper house, are allocated roughly according to population, and in most of Europe unequal representation has been the norm.

The German Bundesrat

The German second chamber, known as the Bundesrat, is in formal constitutional terms cast as the body representing the states, or Lander. Representation is not equal. But whereas the sixteen Lander vary in population from over twenty million to less than half a million, the number of representatives each has in the Bundesrat varies only between three and six. The state governments choose the sixty-nine members of the Bundesrat, who are usually members of the state government cabinets, generally including Lander prime ministers. Most of the work of the Bundesrat is done in committees and these are very often attended by civil servants who act on their ministers' instructions. The sixteen state delegations sit and vote en bloc. They change as the Lander governments change. The Bundesrat has been described as having an 'institutional kinship' with the European Union Council of Ministers.[8] It may be more correct to see the Bundesrat as an instrument of government, an institution through which state governments negotiate with the federal government, rather than as a parliamentary body.

The Bundesrat is not an institution under threat, nor even one about which the question of reform is frequently raised. Its *raison d'etre* is to protect the Lander interests, and to this end it has a right of veto over all legislation effecting the Lander. Such bills are known as consent bills, and constitute about half of all legislation. And in the German case this power is actually used; it is not a dead letter; for example in 1995 it rejected the federal budget and later it insisted on amendments to the Treaty of European Union.

Though its role is to defend the Lander interests it has also become a focal point for opposition parties. As party control in the Landers change so does the composition of the Bundesrat. It becomes a means for Lander governments to exert influence on the federal government's policy making. It is not a meekly acquiescent institution. In fact it is responsible for far more changes to draft legislation than is the Bundestag.

The Australian Senate

The Australian Senate represents the states evenly, with twelve senators from each of the six states, irrespective of their population, and four more senators representing two territories. Here the senators are directly elected, half every three years, on a party list form of proportional representation, giving individuals six-year terms, though Uhr points out the electorate essentially do no more than confirm the choice made within states by party officials.[9] The Australian Senate was originally intended to be a chamber of review, acting to protect the interests of the states. But the constitution imposed no particular tasks upon the Senate. The alteration of the electoral system to make it proportional in 1948 has brought minor parties into the Senate, which has meant that since then it has been exceptional for either the governing party or the main opposition to control the Senate. Minor parties have not been slow to seize the opportunity to influence the outcome of policy-making contests. As a result the Senate has become a much more significant player on the political scene.

And the Senate does have real power in that it can veto or amend legislation, though in respect of financial legislation it can only suggest amendments or reject such bills. In 1975 its readiness to withhold supply precipitated a general election which turned the then Labour Government out of power. In 1993 it forced the Labour Government headed by Keating to withdraw its proposed budget and revise it. Furthermore the Senate insisted that in future senators should be included in pre-budget negotiations with the government. The Australian Senate has in recent years become a more significant player in the whole political process. It has developed a role in relation to delegated legislation, and also established a committee to watch for the civil liberties implications of legislation.

These three second chambers, those of America, Germany and Australia, all have a clear rationale in representing the states in what are federal systems. But it is of interest to note that in all three cases their development in practice has taken them away from the role of protecting state interests, and made at least two of them much more obviously institutions through which the party struggle is played out. The very fact that they have a secure legitimacy derived from their constitutional role in federal systems has given them the confidence to exercise their powers, to throw their weight around. This in turn has obliged the parties to focus attention on their role, and in effect to seek to work through them in order to advance their own power seeking ambitions.

The Canadian Senate

The Canadian Senate was established as an entirely appointed body, currently composed of 104 senators. Provinces are not represented equally, though each of the broad regions of the country does have the same number of senators. Originally senators were appointed for life by the crown, but an age limit of seventy-five was later introduced, and appointment is now by the federal prime minister, though there have been some experiments with elections. The Senate has been described as 'the most written about and least studied of Canadian political institutions'.[10] For many years it has been the target of criticism for its moribund character. It has been seen as a very convenient source of patronage. Although theoretically having powers almost co-equal to the lower House, modelled on the British House of Lords prior to the Parliament Act, the Senate was for many years too aware of its own vulnerability to use its powers. Successive governments took it for granted. When the Senate was discussed it was either to advocate its abolition, or to look to a reformed Senate to resolve the most acute problems Canada faced, how to strengthen a federal system under increasing separatist tension. However, recent years have seen something of a revival in the role of the Senate, occasioned by the swing of the electoral pendulum and opposition efforts in such circumstances to make use of the Senate.[11] For this reason the Senate has become a more significant body over the last twenty-five years.

Demands for reform of the Senate have proliferated. In particular there have been calls for a triple E senate, one that is elected, equal and effective. Equal representation of the provinces would create huge imbalances and is unlikely to be agreed upon. Election would be a means of escape from the present discredited system of appointment, but would bring with it no doubt the close attention of party whips, and the possibility at least that the senate would become as partisan as the lower House. Effectiveness is fine as a slogan word, but what it might mean in practice is much less clear.

The French Senate

The 321 members of the French Senate are elected indirectly by electoral colleges representing the 36,000 local communes grouped into 100 departments. Most of the members of the electoral colleges are local councillors but regional councillors and members of the lower House are also represented. The overall effect of a complex system is to over-represent rural France. 'The Senate reflects the geography of France, its land and communities, whereas the National Assembly represents its demography and the current state of public opinion'.[12] Furthermore, senators are elected for nine-year terms, one-third at a time. But because they are elected by those who themselves have been elected perhaps three years earlier still, there is a pronounced time lag in the representative character of the Senate. Most of those elected are worthy local citizens, often also serving concurrently as mayors and councillors. Very few are women; few are young, many work in agriculture. The parties of the right and centre-right predominate in the Senate. The institution has become synonymous with a cautious, reflective, conservative approach. It has a power equal to the national Assembly, though if the government chooses to intervene in disputes between the two Houses the last word goes to the lower House. Nor does the Senate have the power to censure the government, though it can probe the executive.

The Senate has become in general more significant and is responsible for large numbers of amendments made to bills, these frequently reflecting the practical experience of its members in the warp and woof of local life. It has also become something of a watchdog for ensuring legislation is correctly formulated and consistently based on a principled approach. Compared to the Chamber of Deputies it 'is more knowledgeable about all types of legislation and more insulated from the whims of public opinion'.[13] It concerns itself especially with rights and freedoms, and uses with some alacrity its power to refer matters to the Constitutional Council. Perhaps France's turbulent history has helped to give the Senate a special place in the minds of the people, as an institution helping to bring moderation, reason and principle to bear on the passion and populism that epitomises so much of the nation's politics.

The Italian Senate

The Italian Senate is unusual in that it is elected at the same time and in a very similar way to the lower chamber. Furthermore, in theory it has co-equal power and can not only veto legislation but dismiss the government. But in practice the lower House is recognised as being the more powerful. Even though the Senate is smaller, and in various respects is recognised as the senior body, it does not have the same political clout. According to Pasquino this is because the leadership of the main parties is concentrated in the lower House party leaders.[14] While deputies can be elected at the age of twenty-five, senators have to be over forty, and the right to vote in Senate elections is limited to those over the age of twenty-five, whilst for elections to the lower House voters only need to be eighteen. It contains a few ex officio lifetime members including ex-presidents, and each president is now allowed to nominate up to five other lifetime members, being persons who have brought 'honour to the Nation'. Since 1993 three-quarters of the seats in each region are filled by election in single-member constituencies, with the remainder filled on a proportional party list basis by region.

The Irish Seanad

Ireland presents the leading example of a vocationally based senate. The present Irish Seanad dates from the 1937 constitution, and was probably only included to increase the likelihood of referendum approval for the whole constitutional package. Prior to this the 1920 constitution had included an Irish Senate of peers, bishops, and others appointed to represent professional groups. This is a model that has frequently been advocated elsewhere, including Britain. For a time Spain had a second chamber partly composed by functional representation, and the Bavarian upper house in Germany is composed this way. In Ireland five panels representing aspects of national life largely elect the Seanad, to which are added six members representing the Irish universities and eleven members appointed by the prime minister. However the electorate are not members of the public. Rather, in this 'complex, arcane and incomprehensible' system the electorate are the newly elected lower house (the Dail), the outgoing Seanad and local councils, something like a thousand individuals all told.[15] Members elected via the panels are almost invariably party nominees, and once elected they readily take a party whip. The eleven members appointed by the Taoiseach ensure that the government of the day has a majority in the chamber.

The Seanad has little formal power. It can suggest amendments to legislation, but the Dail can ignore these after ninety days. Occasionally it has had an impact, for example in summer 2001, obliging the government to withdraw a particularly badly thought out proposal to ban the publication of opinion polls during election campaigns. It can suggest amendments to legislation but the Dail can overturn these after a six-month delay. The tradition by which the Seanad has been a chamber to which Dail members may go upon retirement is giving way to a practice by which at least some folk seek to make their reputations in the Seanad before entering the Dail. But this is not facilitated by the low profile the Seanad has. The only group that regularly produces members who catch the public eye has been the university senators, among whom was Mary Robinson, subsequently president of the republic. An all-party review group considered constitutional reform in 1997, but its recommendations for change were very modest.[16]

Conclusions

Two myths about second chambers must be dispelled. One is to say that they are on the way out, that there is a trend towards unicameralism in the modern world. This is not so. A few countries have abolished their second chambers, but in the post-war world as many have instituted constitutions with second chambers. The second myth is that where they do exist second chambers are becoming weaker and ever more marginal bodies. This is not generally the case, though again there are exceptions. Some have lost ground and in recent years have become weaker bodies. But others have become more significant. The role of second chambers has to be seen in the context of the role of parliaments generally, many of which have declined in importance.

Second chambers may continue to exist for dubious reasons. One should not try to pretend that the motivation for including second chambers in new constitutions, or retaining them in existing constitutions, is altogether pure and transparent. Second chambers generally afford opportunities for patronage to party leaders and to prime ministers in particular. Politicians who call for their removal might well at some point in their career begin to recognise the sheer attractiveness of themselves moving in honoured retirement within the portals of the chamber they have earlier denounced. Leaders of smaller parties may see in second chambers the possibility of gaining a toehold of party representation otherwise denied to them. Within parties second chambers may offer opportunities for embodying a balance between factions or regions that otherwise does not readily appear attainable. The creation of a second chamber may be a convenient way of appeasing some group, as was the case with the Polish Senate in 1989. Again, one should recognise the importance of sheer inertia in retaining institutions. This has been emphasised in Chapter 1 above in relation to the UK, but clearly elsewhere too the practical difficulties inherent in abolition or substantial reform can be very great. It is noticeable that even where new constitutions are introduced, and perhaps much emphasis is given to the making of a fresh start, very often in practice older and familiar forms are adopted. At least this seems to be true in regard to second chambers. The German Bundesrat owes much to its predecessors that brought the German states together. The French Senate (and the Spanish) likewise bear many marks of earlier second chambers in their respective countries. Second chambers may have high symbolic value in providing reassurance to peoples troubled by change. This they may do while being relatively cost free in terms of their capacity genuinely to restrain government.

There has been a tendency simply to look at second chambers as if they are appendages to first chambers. They are viewed as a sort of historical hangover. If they retain any power, this is on sufferance so to speak, and the only thing that has to be thought about is how to ensure the first chamber gets its way. Parliaments are thought about as if they were unicameral. It may be argued that this simply reflects the de facto unicameralism of most systems. There may be a second chamber but it is not really relevant, other than in a bit of detailed work revising bills. It is essentially seen as an adjunct, an appendage, possibly like the human appendix, awaiting removal, or maybe as a seemingly useless organ, awaiting evolutionary developments that will ensure its disappearance. In bicameral systems, the second chamber ought to be considered in its total parliamentary context. It is part of a whole, and needs to be analysed in that way.

Second chambers may be composed in three broadly different ways. These are direct election, indirect election, or appointment, though of course several second chambers combine two of these methods. Mughan and Patterson in their survey of sixty-one second chambers found nineteen in which all members were directly elected, with fifteen more where indirect election or a combination of direct and indirect elections constitutes the membership.[17] Generally elections to second chambers are from constituencies that are wider than those used for first chambers. This may help resolve the difficulty inherent in having two chambers composed by direct election, both then claiming democratic legitimacy when in contest with each other. In federal countries the basis for election may seem obvious. Yet it is noticeable that where this is the case, the second chamber concerned may no longer be an effective safeguard of state rights, for example in Australia and America. In some cases the whole country is made a single constituency for electoral purposes, for example the Philippines, Paraguay and for the elected elements in the Mexican and Japanese second chambers. In Italy most members are elected on a first-past-the-post basis but almost a quarter are the 'best losers', giving an element of proportionality. Only in the Czech Republic are second chamber members elected in single member constituencies, while first chamber members are elected by proportional representation in multi-member seats. Indirect election is practised for a few second chambers, and this can take very different forms, as the examples of Ireland, France and Germany given above illustrate. In Argentina and South Africa provincial assemblies or regional parliaments make appointments to the second chamber. In Spain assemblies in autonomous regions appoint some of the members.

Functional representation is unusual. Ireland is the best known example, but Slovenia under its 1992 constitution has a second chamber elected by interest groups. Part of the Bavarian second chamber in Germany is so constituted, and in Morocco under the 1996 constitution a second chamber two-fifths of which is elected by professional associations was introduced, with the other three-fifths being elected by regional electoral colleges consisting of local bodies.[18]

Appointment is much less common. The Canadian Senate as we have seen is entirely appointed. Mughan and Patterson found seventeen of their sixty-one second chambers had an all-appointed membership; most of these were former British colonies, especially in the West Indies, though other examples were Jordan and Thailand. Elsewhere part of the membership of the second chamber may be appointed, for example in Chile and Malaysia. In Italy a small number of individuals may be appointed and this is also the case with the second chamber in India. Ex officio membership is accorded to a few individuals in some second chambers, for example ex-presidents of the state in Italy, Venezuela and Chile. Ex officio membership is of course also a method used for appointments in Britain – in respect of bishops and (at least hitherto) judges. Having mixed forms of membership does not seem to have created particular problems.

Those who have written and theorised about second chambers have tended to typify them according to their degree of power and the similarity or otherwise between their membership and that of the first chambers to which they are linked.[19] But such analysis can be misleading. Power may be defined as symmetric with that of the first chamber if both have similar powers, or asymmetric if the second chamber has much less power. But the question that must arise in categorising bicameral parliaments in this way is: to what extent is reliance placed on formal power or actual power? A constitution may confer similar formal powers on two chambers, but the practical reality may be that the second chamber has very little capacity actually to use the powers it has been given. Both the Canadian Senate and the Italian Senate have powers symmetric with their first chambers, but both are among the weakest and least creditable of second chambers. Russell suggests that perceptions of legitimacy among both the public and the political class need also to be taken into consideration, and in a way this is reinforcing the point that it is the capacity to use power that is crucial.[20] Some second chambers with relatively weak powers, such as the French Senate and the British House of Lords may have become much more effective as 'chambers of influence' rather than power. The reasons for this may be complex, but at root they lie in the relative legitimacy an institution possesses, as well perhaps as the place its members occupy in the parties that they represent.

Lijphart's other key variable focuses on the membership of second chambers, and the degree to which this is congruent or incongruent with the first chamber. Congruency of membership has generally been measured simply in terms of relative proportions of members adhering to the same political party within two chambers. If the proportions are very similar then this is taken as establishing a high degree of congruency, and such is taken as an indication of the likelihood of a weaker second chamber. Clearly party balance is a vital variable. But there are other dimensions to congruency that merit examination. A second chamber that has a different party complexion to the first chamber may be expected to express different views. But these may still be the views of the party leaderships found in both chambers. Increasingly parties are being dominated by professional politicians, folk who devote their entire time to politics. And increasingly too such folk are career politicians in the sense that they have always been first and foremost aspirants to a full-time job in politics. If first chambers are perhaps inevitably bound to be dominated by such folk, is there not a good case for arguing that second chambers should be so designed as to mobilise into politics and into membership of parliaments people who have quite different experiences and professional backgrounds? The result may be that in terms of party membership there is a congruence between the two chambers, but in terms of viewpoints and perspectives there is a divergence.

To some extent this may already be seen in the fact that second chambers tend to have older members serving longer terms. The second chamber may represent a different political generation. Or there may simply be many more members who have had substantial experience in professional and business life utterly removed from the world of professional politics. In principle second chambers can be thought about as institutions which provide for a greater diversity of parliamentarians than first chambers alone are likely to provide. This may of course be an advantage of appointment as a method of constituting a second chamber. Groups under-represented in a directly elected chamber can be especially targeted for appointment, though the political will to bring this about may be lacking.

Second chambers can add depth to representation within parliament. They not only afford an alternative route into parliament, and one that may less easily fall victim to the centralised control that parties so readily espouse, but they also afford contact points for organised groups outside of the mainstream political parties. They can therefore add value to the representative function of parliament. They can enrich its representative quality. It may of course be objected that in so doing they are as likely to frustrate the will of the people as expressed in elections to the first chamber. This simply takes us back to the basic understanding of democracy. A pluralist democratic system may welcome the enrichment to the democratic process that a second chamber provides. Legitimacy is not solely derived from election. Some forms of appointment that bring into second chambers individuals whose experience or personal qualities command respect may do more to enhance legitimacy than direct election.

The low esteem in which directly elected chambers are now widely held needs to be pondered. Almost a hundred years ago Lord Bryce suggested there were three sources of authority in relation to parliamentary bodies, traditional respect, representative character and personal merit or intellectual eminence.[21] The Wakeham Commission on the House of Lords made a similar point in robust style.[22] The fact that the enrichment is focused on parliament and not on some extra-parliamentary and corporatist inclined body is a further reason for welcoming it. Prime ministers, once they have got used to the comforts of power, may wish to vanquish as far as possible the sources of opposition to their will that they encounter. This may include a preference for a tame parliament, and a unicameral parliament is on balance more likely to be easily tamed than a bicameral one. But what one might call gentle opposition, focused in a reasoned way through a mature second chamber, can be a real benefit. Such a chamber can be cautionary for a president or prime minister, it can warn of impending difficulties or of possible impracticalities in policy. It can flag up problems that lie ahead. It can offer advice, but with a bit more edge than advisers ensconced within the executive machine itself.

Alongside their role in representational terms, there is also therefore a role in terms of influence, particularly in revising legislation in detailed ways to meet particular needs Patterson and Mughan speak of this as a 'redundancy' role. It is a matter of bringing influence to bear and causing adjustments to be made to policy and to legislation. Frequently this detailed work fails to attract significant attention. The influence exerted by any parliamentary chamber may at times be difficult to recognise, but this is especially true of second chambers because these are much less likely to be in the political limelight. Sometimes it is the ability to apply particular experience and expertise to a situation that counts. There are simply new facts to examine, and for whatever reason the second chamber is better placed to focus these facts and the arguments which they give rise to than the first chamber. Sometimes it is the more traditional role of causing delay and allowing time for second thoughts that is significant. Popularly elected houses can give way to popular pressure very quickly. The demand for the 'government to do something about' a situation places irresistible pressure upon ministers who feel they must respond. Legislation becomes less about sound law-making, more about appeasing public opinion. Sometimes more careful assessment can result in the conclusion that proposed legislation simply will not do what is intended, or pretended. A second chamber can attempt to impose delay, though of course it may not be listened to. That depends on the relative standing the second chamber possesses.

Finally there is the constitutional role a second chamber can fulfil. In some systems a second chamber simply by being there imposes an extra hurdle which must be surmounted before constitutional change can be implemented. In some cases objections from a second chamber cannot be over-ridden, but in others some special procedure can achieve this, for example a heightened majority in the first chamber or a referendum. Second chambers can fulfil a more general constitutional role in the attention they give to particular matters. The Australian Senate has taken a particular interest in human rights questions. The French Senate shows special interest in the principles on which legislation is based. The same might be said of the British House of Lords. It is to the reform of the second chamber in Britain that we devote the final Chapter.

Notes

1 L. Massicotte, 'Legislative Unicameralism: A Global Survey', in N. Baldwin and D. Shell, (eds) *Second Chambers*, pp. 151–70 (London, Frank Cass, 2001). Massicotte found that from 1950–79, nineteen second chambers were abolished and seventeen were created or restored, while from 1980 to 1999, six were abolished and twenty-five were created or restored.

2 L. D. Longley and D. Olson, *Two into One: The Politics and Processes of National Legislative Change* (Columbia, Westview Press, 1991).

3 P. Norton, 'How Many Bicameral Legislatures are There?', *Journal of Legislative Studies*, 10:4 (2004) 1–9; A. Lijphart, *Patterns of Democracy: Government Forms and Performance in Thirty-six Countries* (New Haven and London, Yale University Press, 1999) pp. 201–3 considers the cases of Norway and Iceland.

4 See D. Shell. 'The History of Bicameralism', in N. Baldwin and D. Shell (eds), *Second Chambers*. Also G. Tsebelis and J. Money, *Bicameralism* (Cambridge University Press, 1997), esp. ch. 1.

5 A. Hamilton and J. Madison, *The Federalist* (London, Everyman Library edition, J. M. Dent, 1964).

6 For comparative analysis see especially M. Russell, *Reforming the House of Lords: Lessons from Overseas* (Oxford University Press, 2000); and S. C. Patterson and A. Mughan (eds), *Senates: Bicameralism in the Contemporary World* (Columbus, Ohio State University Press, 1999).

7 B. Sinclair, 'Co-equal Partner: The US Senate', in S. C. Patterson and A. Mughan (eds), *Senates*.

8 W. J. Patzelt, in Patterson and Mughan (eds), *Senates*.

9 See J. Uhr, 'Explicating the Australian Senate', *Journal of Legislative Studies*, 8:3 (2002) 3–26.

10 C. E. S. Franks, 'Not Dead Yet, but Should it be Resurrected?' in Patterson and Mughan (eds), *Senates*.

11 D. Docherty, 'The Canadian Senate: Chamber of Sober Reflection or Loony Cousin?', *Journal of Legislative Studies*, 8:3 (2002) 27–48.

12 J. Mastias, 'A Problem of Identity: The French Senate', in Patterson and Mughan (eds), *Senates*.

13 Tsebilis and Money, *Bicameralism*, p. 149.

14 G. Pasquino, 'The Italian Senate', *Journal of Legislative Studies*, 8:3 (2002) 67–78.

15 M. Laver, 'The Role and Future of the Upper House in Ireland', *Journal of Legislative Studies*, 8:3 (2002) 49–66.

16 *Report of the Constitution Review Group* (Dublin, Stationery Office, 1997).

17 Patterson and Mughan (eds), *Senates*, esp. ch. 1.

18 J. P. Ketterer, 'From One Chamber to Two: The case of Morocco', in Baldwin and Shell (eds), Second Chambers.

19 See esp. A. Lijphart, *Patterns of Democracy*, ch. 11.

20 M. Russell, 'What are Second Chambers for?', *Parliamentary Affairs*, 54:3 (2001) 442–58.

21 J. (Viscount) Bryce, *Modern Democracies*, vol II (London, Macmillan, 1921), p. 445.

22 *A House for the Future*, Report of the Royal Commission on the House of Lords, (2000), Cm. 4534; para. 10.6, discussed further below at pp. 153–5.

6

Reforming the second chamber

This book has concentrated on what the present House of Lords is and what it does. But it would be odd if no attempt was made in conclusion to address the question of reform. At the time of writing (summer 2006) the future of the House is uncertain. The Labour Government in office since 1997 certainly intended to bring about a more thoroughgoing reform than has yet been achieved. Manifesto commitments remain unfulfilled. Neither the government nor the Conservative or the Liberal Democrat opposition parties profess contentment with the status quo. On the contrary, all parties want to bring about further reform. But for reform to take place there either has to be a degree of consensus between the major parties, or there has to be a clear commitment and clear leadership from the governing party. Neither of these conditions has been fulfilled. A consensus that might have been sufficient to bring about reform could have emerged around the time of the Wakeham Commission, but that opportunity was soon lost.

Whatever ambition the Blair-led Government once had for fundamental reform seems now to have faded. Frustration has replaced ambition. Simply removing the remaining hereditary peers would now seem quite an achievement! After the 2005 election the government launched a joint select committee to examine the so-called 'constitutional conventions' relating to the House. This appeared an attempt from a ministerial point of view to try and keep the House in its place, namely subordinate to the Commons and unthreatening to the government. It is indeed ironic that one obvious result of the reform imposed by the Blair Government has been to make the House of Lords a more assertive and confident chamber, and one the further reform of which now looks much more difficult to achieve than it did before the removal of the hereditary peers. Part of the reason why the government has arrived at this position is because there have been serious differences of view on this subject within the cabinet and the parliamentary party. That has always inhibited realistic policy making in this area. But it is also fair to say that those differences have festered because of the prime minister's own vacillation on the whole subject. It is a matter about which he gives no impression of having thought very deeply.

This Chapter will begin by trying to explain the rather sorry saga of Lords reform under Labour. This involves some retrospective examination of Labour's emerging policy on the Lords prior to 1997, and an analysis of the rather twisted course of events since then. Second, this Chapter will offer some discussion of the major ideas for reform that have been considered over this period, before finally trying briefly to locate the whole debate in the wider context of parliamentary reform and the position of parliament in relation to government and society.

Labour's policy on the Lords

As has been noted in Chapter 2, Labour has always been to some degree schizophrenic about the House of Lords. Obviously as a radical left of centre party, traditionally representing the working class, it could hardly do other than have a policy either for outright abolition or fundamental reform of a second chamber, especially one that remained dominated by an aristocratic class. But in practice Labour in office almost invariably found it could work with the House of Lords and that the chamber was a useful place to help get legislation sorted out. Furthermore, like other governments, Labour realised that reforming the Lords would be both time consuming, pushing other desirable legislation off the agenda, and divisive within its own party ranks. As Chapter 2 made clear the 1968 debacle over the Parliament (No 2) Bill reinforced this feeling. Thereafter Labour policy oscillated between doing nothing (both 1974 manifestos), and outright abolition (1983 manifesto).

The party gradually rowed back from the 1983 unicameralist stance, proposing that by 1992 – in the context of a much more developed policy of overall constitutional reform – that a new elected second chamber be created. This would have had power to delay for a parliament (until after a general election) any legislation that affected the constitution or citizen rights.[1] On the face of it this represented a stronger commitment to bicameralism than had ever before been made by the party. A report from the Institute of Public Policy Research (a 'think-tank' closely associated with the Labour Party) filled out possible detail, calling for a 300-strong Senate with thirty appointed members and 270 elected members.[2]

But following the 1992 election Labour's plans for constitutional reform took a different direction, focusing on specific changes rather than a fundamental re-ordering of the constitution. These plans included a two stage reform process for the Lords. This was attractive in that it involved a supposedly simple first step – the removal of all hereditary peers, something for which the party would have a clear electoral mandate and which would be popular among party members. This would leave an all-appointed House, obviously not a tenable long-term solution, but by acting quickly and decisively on the removal of hereditary peers momentum would be generated and a stage two reform to create a more democratic second chamber could follow. Or so it was thought. This view was not without its critics from within the Labour Party, one of whom described it as 'a short-sighted and opportunist way to proceed'.[3] It was feared that once the hereditary peers had gone, there would be little incentive to drive through further reform. The chamber would settle comfortably into being a body entirely composed of appointees, and prime ministers would continue to savour the joys of patronage as they remained the crucial gatekeeper controlling the flow of new entrants.

But to counter such sceptics 'New Labour' emphasised the party's commitment to further change. The joint Labour–Liberal Democrat Commission on constitutional reform was clear that a 'democratic and representative second chamber' was the proper way forward.[4] The Plant Commission established to advise the party on electoral reform put forward ideas for appropriate electoral systems for both chambers.[5] As new party leader Tony Blair emphasised Labour's commitment to reform, saying in a major speech on the constitution in 1996: 'We have always favoured an elected second chamber'.[6]

The House of Lords Act 1999

Labour was swept into office in 1997 with a clear mandate for this two stage reform process. But the clarity of the manifesto commitment was not matched with any firmness of underlying purpose within the government. A cabinet committee mulled over possibilities in the early months of 1998. Lord Richard, leader of the Labour peers since 1992 and Leader of the House from 1997, was given the go-ahead to consult secretly with the Conservative leader in the Lords, Lord Cranborne. The possibility of a 'big-bang' reform was mooted, with Labour holding off removal of the hereditary peers in return for Conservative agreement on the introduction of a partly elected House.[7] Lord Richard made little secret of his desire to see a stronger second chamber, and that to him meant a chamber the majority of whose members were directly elected, as he later argued in his book *Unfinished Business*.[8] But other members of the cabinet were certainly getting cold feet about such radicalism.

This was the background to Lord Richard's sudden dismissal from the government in July 1998. In a subsequent interview he voiced his concerns about the pace of Lords reform, saying: 'If all the government is going to do is to abolish the right of hereditary peers to sit and vote and then kick the second stage into touch it will be a great missed opportunity'. When asked what the prime minister's views on the subject were, he replied rather revealingly: 'I've no idea what the prime minister's views are. I've never talked to him about it. I don't think his mind has been engaged with this in any concentrated way'.[9] Clearly Lords reform, though firmly on the agenda for the government, was not considered of sufficient complexity or importance to require prime ministerial attention!

In the dying days of the 1997–98 session peers held a two-day debate on the reform of their House, in which over 100 speeches were made.[10] Baroness Jay, now leading for the government, reiterated a determination to move ahead with stage one, but also announced that a Royal Commission would be set up to consider further reform. The desirability of having some kind of strategy for what happened after stage one had taken place was now becoming apparent. Without this there may be more difficulty with stage one than ministers had earlier thought. The Queen's Speech in November 1998 as expected announced the forthcoming bill, 'to remove the right of hereditary peers to sit and vote in the House of Lords', as 'the first stage in a process of reform to make the House of Lords more democratic and representative'.

Meanwhile Lord Cranborne's behind the scenes discussions had continued and before the House of Lords Bill was debated in parliament, news of the deal he had made with the prime minister (behind the backs of his shadow cabinet colleagues) had leaked out. This resulted in Cranborne's dismissal, and considerable Conservative Party confusion. It was the deal that led to the 'Weatherill amendment' resulting in the retention within the House of ninety-two hereditary peers. Lord Weatherill, as a former Speaker in the Commons and in 1998 the convenor of the cross-bench peers, was considered a helpful and neutral enough person to front-up the arrangement. But though widely publicised the government did not want the amendment added to the Bill until late in its parliamentary passage. It was to be a carrot awarded to Conservative peers for good behaviour.

When the Bill was debated at second reading in the Commons in early February, it was greeted without enthusiasm. From the Labour point of view the Weatherill amendment was a very significant compromise, a tactic that could only be justified on the grounds that the arrangement would last a short time. In a formal sense it certainly was a breach of the manifesto's clear commitment to remove hereditary peers. It was a decision thrust upon the party, and one the implications of which were never properly debated, certainly not by MPs. Nor arguably was it necessary. The idea that the Conservative opposition in the Lords had to be bought off in this way was almost certainly fanciful. Were threats to massacre government legislation realistic in the face of Labour's clear manifesto commitment, huge parliamentary majority and continued very high approval ratings in the country? If Blair mistakenly believed this, his lack of understanding of the Lords was matched by that of the Conservative leader, William Hague, who in trying to stop the deal entirely misunderstood the mood of the Conservative peers, who were not surprisingly very supportive of a proposal that would allow almost 100 hereditary members to remain. Within both parties the Commons leadership had little understanding of how the party in the Lords really felt or was likely to behave. Whereas many leading peers have served in the Commons and know a good deal about the dynamics of life in the lower House, this is not reciprocated.

By the time the Bill had completed its passage it had been further amended to provide for replacement of elected hereditary peers as they died, a feature that had certainly not been part of the Cranborne/Blair deal. And before the Commons had debated the Weatherill amendment, the Lords had drawn up a new standing order for the election of hereditary peers and those elections had all taken place. The Bill was debated at great length in the Lords, with all kinds of avenues of imagined uncertainty being explored, but the outcome was never in serious doubt. It was finally passed by 221 votes to 81, late on 26 October, a day that had seen the largest ever attendance at the House, though most of the 752 recorded as having been there that day had probably gone home before the vote. The following month the Commons did as it was told and on 10 November, the penultimate day of the session, retrospectively ratified the amendment that had already resulted in the election of hereditary peers.

The Royal Commission on the future House

As the Bill had commenced its passage the government announced the establishment of the promised Royal Commission to consider the longer-term future of the House.[11] Its terms of reference laid much emphasis on the need to retain the pre-eminence and primacy of the House of Commons. The decision to appoint such a body was probably made in an effort to invest the whole issue with a greater sense of importance than the government had hitherto appeared to give it. Lord Wakeham, a Conservative peer, a former Leader of both the Commons and of the Lords, and a man with a reputation as a political fixer, agreed to chair the Commission. This implied that the prime minister was keen to see the Commission produce an agreed report that would help mobilise a consensus behind a politically realistic stage two reform.[12] The request to the Commission to report within a year, an unprecedentedly tight time schedule for such an exercise, suggested there was within government a sense of urgency about the matter. Removing hereditary peers without having any alternative plan for the House was no longer considered prudent politics.

Meanwhile the Conservatives lost little time in abandoning their previous policy of making no change to the House. In 1998 their party leader, William Hague, set up a commission under the previous Lord Chancellor, Lord Mackay of Clashfern, which in 1999 reported in favour of a chamber largely if not entirely elected, from which both existing hereditary and life peers would be excluded.[13] This never became official Conservative Party policy, though subsequently the party leadership showed a surprising readiness to support a largely elected House.[14] Lord Hurd was one of the members of the Mackay Commission, and as its work finished he became a member of the Wakeham Commission. The Conservative opposition was not at this stage making itself any sort of obstacle to Labour's professed policy of making the Lords a more democratic body.

The Wakeham Commission's report was 'launched to almost universal derision' in January 2000.[15] It broadly endorsed the existing functions and powers of the House, though it followed the government in emphasising the importance of the House of Commons retaining 'primacy'. Constrained by its terms of reference it never really got to grips with the larger question of how to locate the role of the second chamber in a parliamentary system where the power of the governing party in the Commons was so dominant. As far as composition went, the report's recommendations relied heavily on appointments, all to be made by a 'totally independent' commission, with the prime minister and the government excluded. This it believed would result in an end to political patronage and could result in a House 'broadly representative of British society' (including at least 30 per cent female, and with fair ethnic minority and broader religious representation). The independence of appointed members would be reinforced because all would serve fifteen year non-renewable terms.

But the Commission was aware that an all-appointed House would hardly have satisfied public or parliamentary opinion. So it put forward three possible models for an elected element, ranging from sixty-five 'elected' members to 195 in a total House of approximately 550 members. A majority of the Commission supported a middle option, with eighty-seven members elected by one-thirds, simultaneous with the five-yearly elections to the European Parliament.

Such a House would have much the same powers as before, though the Commission seemed confused over its recommendations on delegated legislation, at one point recommending a three-month delaying power, but then suggesting this would be a three-month period during which the Commons could over-ride any Lords objection to an SI, over-looking the fact that MPs could do this any time after the Lords had objected, potentially reducing the three month delay to a few hours. The Commission endorsed ideas for more select committee work by the House.

In a curious sort of way the reaction provoked by the report appeared to give momentum to the demand for an elected second chamber. Over the following year the tide of parliamentary and media opinion seemed to flow that way. Commission members reported that they had found the public not only keen on direct elections as the main route into the second chamber, but also keen to keep politics out of the chamber. Trying to reconcile these two aspirations was clearly problematic! But confidence in any system of appointment had reached a low ebb. To try and invest the appointments process with more credibility the prime minister announced the setting up of the Appointments Commission in May 2000, though the subsequent performance of the Commission did little to win support for the idea of a second chamber heavily reliant on appointed members (see above, pp. 60–3)

Lord Wakeham warned that the Commission's report was a carefully balanced set of proposals that should not be 'cherry-picked'. The government professed not to be doing this, and Labour in its 2001 election manifesto said that it would implement the Wakeham proposals 'in the most effective way possible'. (See appendix).

Muddle and confusion

Six months on from the election, in November 2001, the government put forward its official response to the Wakeham Commission report. This was done in a white paper optimistically entitled *Completing the Reform*.[16] A House one-fifth elected, with elected members probably serving renewable five-year terms, and elections taking place on a closed party list system, was proposed. This was a significant departure from Wakeham; any elected members found uncongenial to the party whips would slide down the party list – and then probably quite quickly out of the House. More serious however was the proposal that party leaders would directly nominate over half the membership of the House, again for renewable terms, either of one parliament or two; the white paper was not sure which, but this meant the absolute maximum period for nomination would be ten years, and it could easily be much shorter. This would have allowed party leaders to rid themselves of any who wavered too far from the party line, as well as excluding any party member they wished to exclude.

If the Wakeham report had a poor reception, the government's proposals fared much worse.[17] Both Houses debated them (9 and 10 January 2002). In the Lords debate Lord Wakeham led the five peers who had been members of the Commission in rebutting the government claim that these proposals were in line with the Commission's recommendations. Though intended by ministers to lead to legislation later that session it soon became clear no bill embodying these ideas would get through either House.

Meanwhile the Commons select committee on Public Administration had launched an inquiry on Lords reform. One of its early witnesses, the backbench Labour peer Lord Lipsey, referring to the ill-fated white paper, said governments would do well to recognise when their proposals were like 'a dead duck on its back with its feet in the air'. In February the committee published its report, nicely entitled *Continuing the Reform* (which certainly sounded less presumptuous than that of the ill-fated government white paper, *Completing the Reform*).[18] Based on a confidential survey of MPs, the committee concluded that the 'centre of gravity' of parliamentary opinion lay with a 60 per cent elected House. It proposed that 20 per cent should be party nominees and 20 per cent independently nominated. Bishops and existing life peers should leave, and all members serve single non-renewable terms of two parliaments. Election should be by single transferable vote in large regional constituencies, using open party lists. The report included discussion on powers and a proposed timetable for a phased introduction of change. It became a much quoted document. An Early Day Motion in the Commons calling for a 'wholly or substantially elected' second chamber had by this time gathered over 300 signatures. The government realised it had to withdraw its proposals.

Having done this the government in July 2002 remitted the whole matter to a joint select committee composed of twenty-four members drawn equally from Lords and Commons, to 'consider issues relating to House of Lords reform'. This produced a report in December, offering seven different options on composition ranging from fully elected to fully appointed.[19] Both Houses held debates in late January, and then voting on the options took place in early February.[20] However the week before the votes, the prime minister 'slammed a big fat torpedo' into the strategy when at Question Time he forcefully expressed his clear preference for an all-appointed chamber, posing the antithesis between a revising chamber or a rival chamber, and indicating that in his view any elected element would make the second chamber a rival to the Commons.[21] Although it was a free vote, the whips were apparently urging Labour MPs to 'support Tony', and themselves voted heavily for the all-appointed option.[22] The Lords predictably opted for an all-appointed House by 335 votes to 110, and by similar margins voted all the other options down. The Commons however voted against every alternative, though it was the 80 per cent elected and 20 per cent appointed option that came closest to success, being rejected by just three votes, 284 to 281. Analysis of these votes showed that a clear majority of MPs supported a largely elected House, while the fully appointed option was decisively rejected (by 323 to 245). Apparently four Conservative MPs mistakenly voted the opposite way to that which they intended on the 80 per cent elected option; had they known what they were doing, that option would have been approved![23]

Clearly muddle and confusion was partly responsible for this outcome. But equally it was apparent that support for direct elections to the second chamber had waned. Several MPs who had signed the Early Day Motion calling for a substantially elected House in the previous parliament had now voted for an all-appointed House. One reason for this was probably the effort made by an all-party campaign led by Lord Norton of Louth and Sir Patrick Cormack, emphasising the case for an appointed second chamber. According to an article written by Lord Norton this had found increasing favour among MPs and peers of all parties. In opposing election to the Lords, the prime minister had both 'caught a wave as well as added to it'.[24] Likewise Lord Irvine of Lairg and the prime minister had both come out strongly against a so-called 'hybrid' chamber, which was another way of opposing any elected members unless the chamber was to be entirely elected (which few supported).

The joint committee bravely sought to emphasise the degree of consensus that did exist on the role, powers and functions of the House, but in July the government accepted that in the absence of any consensus on composition, it would now 'concentrate on making the House of Lords work as effectively as possible in fulfilment of its important role'.[25]

In September 2003 the government published yet another consultation document and the new Lord Chancellor, Lord Falconer, simultaneously announced that the remaining hereditary peers would be removed and the Appointments Commission put on a statutory basis.[26] In effect the government had now run out of patience. The hereditary peers were replenishing themselves through by-elections; the House was becoming stroppier and there seemed very little hope of any substantial reform taking place. Predictably the response to this from other parties was hostile. The hereditary peers remained in the House precisely in order to provoke further reform. If they were removed without this taking place, an entirely appointed chamber would be the outcome. This was not a solution favoured by any group, other perhaps than peers themselves. There was much talk of broken pledges over the proposed removal of hereditary peers before stage two reform was reached. Robin Cook, the former Leader of the Commons, now on the backbenches, wondered why the government was going 'ahead with the measure that was least popular among Members of Parliament'.[27] The Queen's Speech a few weeks later announced forthcoming legislation to reform the House in this way. But again parliamentary debate in both Houses made clear how difficult this would be to enact. In the event no such bill was ever introduced though the abandonment of the proposal was not announced until the following April. So for the second year running the government's proclaimed intention to legislate had had to be shelved.

Meanwhile, the Constitutional Reform Bill had been introduced and the House of Lords was coming to terms with the prospect of losing its judicial role, and the ex officio presence in its midst of serving senior judges, and of losing the Lord Chancellor as its presiding officer. At the 2005 election, Labour's manifesto again promised the removal of remaining hereditary peers and another free vote on composition, but it also included a commitment to seek the codification of 'the key conventions of the Lords', and legislation to place 'reasonable limits on the time bills spend in the second chamber' (see Appendix). In 2006 another joint select committee was established to examine the so-called key conventions, and at the time of writing this committee is taking evidence.[28] One is tempted to suggest that 'codifying conventions' is code for tying the House of Lords down a bit. After all, if conventions are codified, with some definite rule in the shape of a standing order or legislation embodying the conventions, then they cease to be conventions; they become rules with some definite mechanism for enforcement. That seems to be the direction the development of the constitution is moving in, but it seems unlikely in this case to be one that will find widespread acceptance.

The Conservative and Liberal Democrat Parties both officially advocate a substantially elected second chamber, though it is fair to say that within both parties, especially the Conservatives, there is a sizable and vocal minority, especially among peers themselves, who strongly oppose this policy, and wish to keep the House largely or entirely appointed. No one can make safe predictions about the future course of reform. And once again in such circumstances the easiest option is to keep talking but do nothing! A change of prime minister may however bring a sudden new impetus and even an imposed settlement.

When Labour came to office in 1997 no one imagined that nine years later the House of Lords would still contain almost 100 hereditary peers, along with some 600 appointed members the great majority of whom had arrived in the House at their party leader's say-so. Nor would it have seemed credible that after two further election victories, Labour would face a House that had become more assertive and more awkward to the government than had ever been the case since the 1909–11 crisis. The real worry for the government is that the effect of their mishandling of this whole issue has been to boost the collective confidence and deter-mination of peers so much that at least in relation to reform of their own House they will simply dig their heels in rather than accept proposals that fail to strengthen the legitimacy of their chamber. This is not an easy conundrum for ministers to resolve.

So, one lesson to learn from this saga is that reform of the Lords should not be seen as a simple or straightforward matter. Rather it is a subject that demands and requires serious thought and disciplined application. In the introduction to his 1918 report on the future of the second chamber, the chairman, Viscount Bryce, wrote: 'The problems we had to deal with presented difficulties which can hardly be appreci-ated except by those who have steadily applied themselves to prolonged study of the issues involved'.[29] This point needs emphasis because there is a deceptive looking simplicity about the matter of Lords reform. Most people, be they electors in the street or MPs at Westminster, have their opinion about how the House should be changed. It is not infrequently said that everything worth saying on the subject has been said already – several times over. But talking about the subject is not the same as think-ing through the objectives and the practicalities of reform. The incentive to do this has rarely been present. There are always more urgent matters to attend to in politics. This is true of the leadership of both the larger parties. To quote Lord Norton (again), this time giving evidence early in 2002 to the Select Committee on Public Administration on the whole question of reform, and no doubt reflecting on discussions with party leaders: 'Politicians have demonstrated hidden depths of shallowness'.[30] Senior politicians need to get a grip on the subject. Most are preoccu-pied with the Commons. Many who eventually reach the Lords confess when they get there how little they had hitherto understood or appreci-ated its ethos and its work.

Constitutional change

There is no reason to suppose that change in the future will not come about as has happened in the past. If this is so, the House of Lords will not be abolished, and no entirely new second chamber will be created. Instead, there will be more gradual and incremental change. Significant reform has usually been the result of crisis, for example the 1832 Reform Act and the 1911 Parliament Act. Where that has not been the case, reform has been imposed by the government of the day, and then accepted by successor governments, as for example happened with the Macmillan Government reforms to the Lords, the Life Peerages Act in particular. That appears at present the most likely long-term outcome of the devolution programme carried through by Labour after 1997. It may also be the outcome in relation to Labour's creation of a new Supreme Court. The other model for change is the gradual, almost imperceptible accumulation of small adjustments that eventually leads to a new pattern or new or different kind of relationship, which then becomes recognised as normative for the functioning of the constitution. Arguably, this was illustrated by the change that occurred in relation to the House of Lords after the 1911 Parliament Act, whereby it became accepted that an implication of the Act was that the Lords should not persist in resisting the will of the Commons, even though the Parliament Act was there precisely in order to cope with such a divergence of opinion – a development that is now under challenge.

   That the removal of hereditary peers would change the nature of the House was accepted by the government's leading figure in the Lords, the Leader of the House, Baroness Jay, as the House of Lords Bill was being enacted. Lord Strathclyde, the Conservative leader who succeeded Lord Cranborne, drew out some of the implications of this in a lecture delivered on the day the hereditary peers left the House. To him the former constitutional settlement had now been altered by this Act; 'a plough has been drawn across the settled landscape of the constitution', and as a result new boundary lines had to be drawn, not least between the two Houses and between government and parliament.[31] This would take time but it was clear that to the Conservatives the rules of the game had been changed. In particular Lord Strathclyde argued the practice of not voting against delegated legislation merited critical rethinking. The following year the Lords did vote down two SIs, thus deviating from a settled practice (see above, p. 95). By 2005 Lord McNally, leader of the Liberal Democrat peers, rather shocked ministers by saying in the Queen's Speech debate: 'I do not believe that a convention drawn up sixty years ago on relations between a wholly hereditary Conservative-dominated House and a Labour Government who had forty-eight per cent of the vote should apply in the same way to the position in which we find ourselves today'.[32] A little while later Lord Wallace of Saltaire, deputy leader of the Liberal Democrat peers, was more emphatic, telling the joint select committee on conventions: 'It is our strong and settled view that the Salisbury–Addison Convention was a historical negotiation between the Labour Party in the Commons and the Conservative party in the Lords, and not relevant to the entirely different circumstances we are now in, several generations later'.[33] Since the 1999 House of Lords Act the understanding of the way the House works has changed, and the government's concern about this can only be heightened by the fact that these comments both came from the leadership of the 'pivotal' party with the swing votes within the politically balanced House. There is an ineluctable character to the process of constitutional change. Quite where the present evolving understanding of the appropriate role of the House will eventually settle is far from clear. But it is changing.

Maybe there will be an attempt to legislate for further reform. The most likely form that this would take while Labour remains in power would be for the removal of the remaining hereditary peers, and the creation of a statutory process or commission to handle appointments to the House. But any attempt to do this without introducing an elected element to the membership of the House would be bitterly fought by the Liberal Democrats. And the Conservatives, whatever else they may support, are bound to oppose any unilateral attempt to remove the remaining hereditary peers without replacement in any way.

Principles to guide further reform

Amidst the process of change, whether it comes slowly or otherwise, certain principles need to be kept in mind. First, the second chamber must not usurp the unique position of the first chamber within the constitution. Putting the matter this way makes clear that what is being spoken of is the making and unmaking of governments. A party comes to power through winning a majority in the elected House, and to remain in power it is necessary to retain the confidence of the elected House. The second chamber has nothing to do with the matter. For the second chamber to pass a motion of no confidence in the government would be a meaningless exercise from a constitutional point of view. This is the crucial point about the so-called primacy or supremacy of the Commons. The latter terms have often been re-iterated since 1997, but when they are unpacked they mean different things to different people.

Sometimes they are interpreted to mean that the second chamber should back off whenever it runs into disagreement with the first, that it should simply ask the first chamber to 'think again' and then fall silent.

But this is not what the primacy of the first chamber means in a constitutional sense, however convenient such an understanding may be in a political sense to the government of the day. The necessary primacy of the first chamber is safeguarded by the Parliament Acts. A second chamber in a parliamentary system should not be in a position to block government bills indefinitely, or in some other way prevent the government from implementing its basic programme. This is partly a matter of ensuring a government can fulfil its election manifesto, but it is not simply a matter of the past manifesto of the party in power.[34] After all, events move on and manifestos become dated and even irrelevant. Furthermore the danger of overemphasising the manifesto is that it becomes a tool of party management rather than a means of setting before the electorate a clear and simple statement of the main principles and policies a party intends to follow if elected. A government has to use its judgment about what it ought to do in face of new circumstances, and a government knows that it will have to answer for this when it next faces the electorate.

If primacy in this constitutional sense belongs to the first chamber, the second principle that must be recognised in relation to Lords reform is that some real formal power must remain with the second chamber. This power must not be so drastic that it is incapable of use. That has been the problem in the past with the Lords veto over delegated legislation. But nor must the powers the second chamber possesses be so slight that their use can pass almost unnoticed. The power proposed by the Wakeham Commission for the Lords in relation to delegated legislation ran this risk. The second chamber could vote an SI down, but the Commons could at *any* point within the next three months vote to overrule that, without even the necessity for a debate on the matter. The view of the second chamber could have been set aside within hours of it being expressed. That is not a sufficient power. In practice the Commons has frequently reversed Lords amendments with minimal debate. Tight programme motions already on occasions give no time for some Lords amendments to receive any attention on the floor of the House when returned to the Commons. There is always the possibility at present that when this happens the Lords will dig its heels in and bounce the matter back again to the Commons. Indeed, peers have sometimes emphasised this point in debate when ping-pong has been getting under way. On other occasions ministers in the Commons have focused their remarks less on the substance of the issue in dispute, more on the temerity of the House of Lords in daring to persist with disagreement. The second chamber needs sufficient power to ensure that its views are taken seriously by government.

This leads us to a third point which concerns the special position of constitutional legislation. Given the nature of the British constitution there are difficulties here, in that there is no clear way of determining (or at least no clear authority to make a ruling) as to what is 'constitutional' and what isn't. Constitutional issues may lurk behind a bill without for a time being identified. But this practical difficulty does not alter the substance of the point, that a second chamber ought in principle to have particular responsibilities in relation to constitutional legislation. The House of Lords now has a select committee on the constitution which seeks to identify in all bills any matter that may be considered constitutional. This is a useful process. The House is developing a nose for constitutional matters. Not infrequently peers remind themselves in debate that constitutional issues merit special attention. This is not to say they may not also get special attention in the Commons too, but the elected House generally has a single party, the governing party, holding a majority of the seats. And this makes it *prima facie* less suitable as a constitutional watchdog than a second chamber that is more politically balanced and more independent of the executive. The bill dealing with the extension of postal voting upon which extended ping-pong took place in 2003 was discussed briefly at page 108, where the comment of the junior minister asserting that it was the Commons that was accountable for parliament's decisions and not the Lords was quoted. On the same bill the deputy prime minister said: 'I find it completely unacceptable that the Lords should make judgments on the planning and procedures for the European and local elections. It should not be up to unelected people to make such decisions. We have greater moral authority'.[35] On this matter, though inevitably complex, it seems reasonable to say that the position being taken by the Lords had more support from the Electoral Commission than the position of the Commons. In the event one party, in one House of Parliament, was asserting the right to make new electoral arrangements that were opposed by the other parties in the Commons and by the Lords. A compromise of sorts was reached, though mainly through the Lords eventually giving way after five rounds of ping-pong.

The point of substance illustrated by this example concerns the role of the second chamber in regard to matters that are constitutional. At present the Lords has no greater powers over such matters than over any other bills, with the exception that any bill to extend the life of a parliament (that is, postpone an election) is still subject to an absolute veto by the Lords under the Parliament Acts. If the present government are serious about legislating to codify 'conventions' concerning the role of the House, then attention should certainly be given to some means of affording special powers to the House in relation to constitutional matters, perhaps a capacity to delay such a bill for two years, or until after an election, or to force a referendum. Perhaps this will become a role for the new Supreme Court, though most politicians would probably prefer that it didn't. An alternative would be to vest the Speaker of the Commons with the responsibility of designating bills that affected the constitution, (as at present it is the Speaker who designates Money bills, though designating constitutional bills would be much more problematic).

A fourth principle would be that a reformed House must have sufficient legitimacy to be able to use the power it possesses. The Commons derives its legitimacy from its directly elected character. The Lords has for many years been uncertain where it derives its legitimacy from, or indeed whether it possesses any genuine legitimacy at all. Power that cannot be used (or used only in some very extreme circumstance) is not an effective power. The Wakeham Commission commented: 'Throughout the twentieth century the House of Lords was inhibited by its lack of confidence. The reformed second chamber must be free of such debilitating inhibitions'.[36] Much of the discussion about Lords reform has assumed that in the age of universal suffrage legitimacy can only be conferred by election. But legitimacy is primarily a quality afforded by others to an institution. It is not therefore something fixed, something that automatically arises as a result of certain procedures (such as elections) being followed. It may well be that direct election is the most normal way of conferring legitimacy. However, even that may be questionable. The first-past-the-post electoral system was a more obvious means of conferring legitimacy on the House of Commons when over three-quarters of the electorate voted for the two main parties than when less than 40 per cent do so. The legitimacy of the Commons may be rather more threadbare than MPs generally assume. But it is also true, in relation to the second chamber, that direct election is not the only means of conferring legitimacy. A system of appointment that brings in members that are recognised as having relevant expertise and experience and perhaps personal distinction may generate legitimacy. The Commons claim to be 'representative' rests on the very important fact that it is elected. That is one understanding of the word 'representative'. But it is not the only understanding. There has been a growing debate about other dimensions to representation. Gender, ethnicity and age are just some of the qualities identified as relevant to this debate. In principle a system of appointment can meet requirements for representation understood in this way. This point is further considered below in relation to discussion about the composition of the second chamber.

Fifth, the second chamber should in principle be composed in such a way that no single party has an overall majority, and so that it retains an independent element, as represented in the present House by the crossbench peers. Both these features, which are of course related, are considered valuable aspects of the present House. It is nonsense to imagine the second chamber can somehow be made into a politics-free zone, but it would be unfortunate if party politics became as dominating in the second chamber as it has become in the first. The second chamber needs a degree of independence. It needs to be able to stand apart a little from government and from the all-encompassing party struggle that so dominates the Commons. This is not just a matter of style and appearance; it is not merely for cosmetic reasons. It is a necessary feature to enable a second chamber to bring a distinctive perspective to its work of scrutiny and revision of bills.

There are several ways in which this independence can be attained. One is to ensure a sizable crossbench element is maintained in the House, and that points to the need for a proportion of members, not less than a third, to be appointed rather than elected. But at least as important is the desirability of structuring the House so that an independence of outlook also characterises party nominees whether they arrive by election or appointment. Such independence is largely taken for granted in the existing House of Lords because membership is for life. But in a modern working parliamentary chamber, lifetime membership has too many drawbacks in terms of swollen size and age structure, and also perhaps in the pressures it places on the elderly to continue attending to please party whips when they should be granted a discharge! Lengthy terms, perhaps non-renewable, would probably have a very similar effect in promoting independence. The Wakeham Commission recommended twelve-year terms. The important point is that members must be able to do their work free of concern about whether their party will be happy to see their re-election or re-appointment. Parties will still remain dominating aspects to the life and way of working of the second chamber. But the argument here is that their position in the chamber should not become any greater than it now is, and there is certainly a danger that an accidental by-product of reform would be to do exactly that.

A final principle that follows from the above is that expertise and experience of a kind not readily found in the Commons should be mobilised into the service of parliament through second chamber reform. As well as representing society in ways that appear difficult for the first chamber to achieve (notably in respect of gender and ethnicity), a second chamber can draw on a much wider range of experience than is now typically to be found in directly elected first chambers. The House of Commons has become increasingly dominated not only by full-time professional politicians, but by those who have made a career of politics, probably from a relatively early age. In a sense such folk are the most unrepresentative of people. Only a tiny proportion of the electorate devote themselves to politics in the way that politicians must. Most immerse themselves in other activities, their employment and their leisure pursuits, which take them in many different directions. Of course politicians are by no means homogeneous. But there is room for greater diversity, and there is advantage to be gained from a broader variety of experience and expertise being brought to bear within the second chamber. It is the mingling of politicians with this broader range of experience and expertise that gives the present House of Lords one of its valuable characteristics. It would be desirable to retain a second chamber that can bring together experts and politicians, and join their thinking up (in both directions), especially in relation to policy issues that lie outside normal inter party debate and perhaps involve difficult ethical questions. The value of this can be seen in the membership of select committees, and indeed some of the recent joint select committees set up to examine draft bills (see above, p. 122).

It is perhaps a mistake to think this is a particularly new phenomenon. The Bryce Commission in 1918 made a very similar point about the desirability of breadth of experience in a second chamber. In his book *Modern Democracies* published in 1921 Bryce wrote that second chambers should be reservoirs of 'special knowledge and ripened wisdom' and that they should possess a moral authority based on the personal eminence of their members, and should therefore be able to enlighten and influence the people through their debates.[37]

One of the difficulties with democracy is that it places heavy responsibilities on the electorate without necessarily providing them with the means to discharge these in a truly responsible way. A healthy democracy needs informed debate at its centre. One might hope that the media facilitate this, but for all sorts of reasons the state cannot oblige the media to do so, and in any case the media is subject to such competitive pressures that it seems unrealistic to expect it to make such a contribution. However, parliament can contribute to this education of the public. It should as Bagehot said, 'teach the nation what it does not know'.[38] Both chambers might do this, but the populism involved in competitive party politics inhibits the extent to which informed opinion can be the driver of debate in the Commons. A second chamber with expertise and experience of a more varied kind can help to serve the public in a different way.

Election or appointment?

Much debate about the future of the second chamber sharply polarises election and appointment. But elections can take many forms, as can methods of appointment. For example, the Wakeham Commission had a model involving what it called 'complementary voting', under which votes at a general election would be totalled up by party regionally, and a proportionate number of candidates on a closed party list would be declared elected to the second chamber. Voters need not even be aware that their votes for MPs were actually also resulting in the 'election' to the second chamber of individuals chosen by their party, in a way that they – the voters – could not influence let alone alter. The difference between election of this kind and party appointment could be very slight in practice. One of the reasons given for suggesting such a method of election was to avoid low turnouts supposedly caused by voter fatigue, but there are two responses to voter fatigue. One is to make voting easier, for example by using a single vote to chose members of more than one chamber, though this may well be considered objectionable on democratic grounds, denying genuine choice to the voter. The other approach is to make voting recognisably more worthwhile. Reform of the second chamber should seek the latter route.

Most proposals for reform of the House have recommended it contain both elected and appointed members. This was true of the Wakeham Commission and of the report made by the Public Administration Select Committee, as discussed above. An all-party group of senior MPs (including Robin Cook and Kenneth Clarke) in February 2005 produced a report recommending a 70 per cent elected and 30 per cent appointed House.[39] Such mixed membership has obvious advantages, creating the opportunity to produce a more socially and professionally representative chamber, as just discussed, but also giving opportunity for election on a basis different from the Commons, perhaps representing regions and enabling smaller parties to compete more fairly.

But voices have been raised against such mixed membership, with in particular the prime minister and the Lord Chancellor, Lord Irvine, decrying the notion of a 'hybrid' House in early 2003. In a way this is strange because the existing House has always been a 'hybrid' House in the sense that members have arrived there by different routes, some appointed, some by succession, and a few in modern times for ex officio reasons. Hybridity is nothing new. One reason for expressing concern is the fear that elected members would claim a greater legitimacy than appointed members. But that would in part depend on the manner of appointment. A more open and transparent method of appointment, exemplifying greater independence from the Executive would help to restore confidence. There are few things that have done more damage to the credibility of the existing House than the impression that peerages are given out in return for money donated to political parties, or on the basis of personal friendship. It would certainly be desirable to create a statutory appointments commission with a defined remit and a genuine independence.

Another fear is that having elected members will result in a House that rivals the Commons. This was emphasised by the prime minister when he made his intervention just before the 2003 unwhipped votes on the composition of the House. But if elections are by thirds and members serve twelve-year terms, very seldom would more than a third of the elected members be able to claim a more recent mandate than MPs could claim. A further concern about having elected members is the possible encroachment on the MPs' constituency role. That is of course a common feature of many democracies, and indeed within the UK electors already have members of the European Parliament, as well as local councillors alongside MPs. In Scotland and Wales there are also the members of devolved bodies. These arrangements have caused some tensions and difficulties, but they have not been such as to erode the established constituency role of the MP. In any case in any advanced democratic society a multiplicity of representation is inevitable, and there is no reason why it should not also be thought of as welcome.

Conclusion[40]

The House of Lords has proved itself to be a highly adaptable institution, and also one that has been of genuine significance to the Constitution. Throughout the centuries of its existence, it has undergone change. That has certainly been so over the last sixty years during which it has worked its way back from the margins of political life and become more significant again within the political system. At the time of writing, the House has once more become the centre of controversy. The eventual outcome of this is uncertain. Its membership has been partially reformed, with the clear understanding that this process is incomplete and that further changes must take place. There is no settled will in parliament or in the country about what ought to be done with the House.

An important concern is the need to restore parliament's public esteem. This, of course, is primarily a matter for the Commons. But the Lords does have a role to play. The second chamber is part of a single institution, parliament, whose reputation depends on both chambers working in complementary style, together fulfilling the tasks which only parliament can properly fulfil. Parliament's reputation depends ultimately on its effectiveness. It is the body which on behalf of the people and the nation holds the executive to account through scrutinising its activities. It is the forum in which government must explain itself. It is the institution which can uncover the detail of government's policies and which can display the contrast between the thinking of the government and that of the alternative – the opposition. It is the place where draft government legislation can be analysed before it is formally enacted. It is the place where the clash of political opinion can define the choice faced by the electorate at election time. Reform of the second chamber must enable it to contribute more effectively to parliament's vital tasks.

One of these is parliament's role as the legislature. Laws are made through parliament and in this sense parliament is the custodian of the statute book, the body of extant law that operates within society. It seems a trite observation to make, but parliament needs to take its responsibility as the legislature more seriously. An immense amount of legislation is enacted, much of it in a hurried way. This is a perennial complaint, but it remains perennial precisely because parliament simply lacks the capacity to impose a tighter discipline on the whole legislative process. Parliament needs to consider what its responsibilities are for the condition of the statute book, thinking of itself perhaps as the regulator of the statute book. The House of Lords already takes a significant share of the parliamentary work of scrutinising draft legislation, almost certainly now the major share. This has become more true with the regularity of programming bills in the Commons. But there is probably a further role for a second chamber here. Much that is on the statute book is irrelevant or arcane. The implementation of much legislation that parliament has passed should be monitored. The second chamber can contribute resources to these tasks. This should be an area for inter-House cooperation. The Houses need to work together in a complementary way to help restore public confidence in parliament.

This is where the emphasis on maintaining the primacy of the Commons can become so misleading. Most of the time this translates as primacy of the executive. It is not the balance between Lords and Commons that needs urgent attention and correction. It is the balance between the executive and parliament. Commons and Lords need to play complementary roles in altering that relationship, 'shifting the balance'.[41] Making the executive more genuinely accountable through parliament to the electorate would help to restore the reputation of parliament, and the second chamber undoubtedly can have a part to play in this.

Finally, the reform of the Lords needs to go with the grain of other constitutional change. This is not simply a matter of connecting with other obvious constitutional change, such as devolution, though that does have a place. But more profoundly our constitution is gradually responding to the development of a more pluralist and more complex democracy. The old class-based party system, which dominated so much of the twentieth century, is fading. The two-party system is weakening as third parties achieve greater prominence at national and regional level. The first-past-the-post electoral system may remain for the House of Commons, but practically everywhere else it is disappearing. The concentration of power at Westminster, with a single party in control of a legally sovereign parliament, is being eroded, as are the widely understood conventions about how this power might appropriately be exercised. Britain may remain more unitary than federal, but it is no longer the unitary state that it was: a kind of asymmetrical quasi-federalism is in place. Fundamental judicial review may still be absent, but judicial review has steadily grown in scope, and this development is likely to continue, assisted by the creation of the Supreme Court.

It is in this context that we need to think about the future of the House of Lords. It is naive to go on arguing that British democracy depends on some form of unambiguous accountability, whereby the electorate know exactly which set of politicians to hold responsible for what, because only a single party wields power through a House of Commons that wields untrammelled supremacy. British democracy is more complicated in both its form and its expression. It is not an all or nothing question of a House of Commons majority. Democracy is not simply a matter of a dubiously produced majority having the right to get its way. It is a matter of checks and balances, of government taking the initiative but having to negotiate and adjust as it evolves its policies. It is in this context that a second chamber has a vital role to play.

Notes

1 See R. Blackburn and R. Plant, *Constitutional Reform: The Labour Government's Constitutional Reform Agenda* (London, Addison Wesley Longman, 1999); M. Evans, *Constitution-Making and the Labour Party* (Basingstoke, Palgrave Macmillan, 2003).

2 Jeremy Mitchell and Anne Davies, *Reforming the Lords* (London, Institute for Public Policy Research, 1993).

3 D. Leonard, 'Replacing the Lords', *Political Quarterly* 66 (1995) 287–98.

4 Report of the Joint Consultative Committee on Constitutional Reform, in Blackburn and Plant, *Constitutional Reform*.

5 Report of the National Executive Committee Working Party on Electoral Systems, (The Plant Report), Labour Party, 1993.

6 T. Blair, 'A New Agenda for Democracy: Labour's Proposals for Constitutional Reform', 7 Feb. 1996, Labour Party Press Release.

7 See E. Crewe, *Lords of Parliament* (Manchester University Press, 2005), ch. 4 for an account of this.

8 I. Richard and D. Welfare, *Unfinished Business: Reforming the House of Lords* (London, Vintage, 1999).

9 *New Statesman*, 30 July 1998. See also his wife's account in J. Jones, *Labour of Love: The Partly Political Diary of a Cabinet Minister's Wife* (London, Politicos, 1999) esp. p. 274.

10 HL Deb. 14 and 15 Oct. 1998; for Bs Jay see cols. 929–31.

11 *Modernising Parliament: Reforming the House of Lords* (1999), Cm. 4183.

12 Other members were Gerald Kaufman and Douglas Hurd; two trade unionists, Bill Morris and Baroness Dean; the former cabinet secretary Lord Butler of Brockwell; the former Clerk of the Parliaments, Sir Michael Wheeler-Booth; the Bishop of Oxford, Richard Harries; Professors Anthony King and Dawn Oliver; and Ann Beynon from Wales and Kenneth Munro from Scotland.

13 The Report of the Constitutional Commission on options for a new Second Chamber (chairman Lord Mackay of Clashfern), published by Douglas Slater, 1999. Lord Hurd was also a member of this Commission and subsequently of the Wakeham Commission.

14 Iain Duncan Smith, *Sunday Telegraph*, 13 Jan. 2002, argued for an 80 per cent elected House.

15 The Royal Commission on the House of Lords, *A House for the Future* (2000) Cm. 4534. Comment made by Mary Ann Sieghart, summarising media reaction on Radio 4, 22 Jan. 2000.

16 *Completing the Reform* (2001) Cm. 5291.

17 Robin Cook's account of Lord Irvine's attendance at a PLP meeting in early January to consider the proposals also vividly conveys the hopelessness of any attempt to implement them. See R. Cook, *Point of Departure* (London, Simon & Schuster, 2003), pp. 76–7.

18 Fifth Report, Select Committee on Public Administration, *The Second Chamber: Continuing the Reform*, HC 494. Ld Lipsey HC 494-II, Q123.

19 Joint Select Committee, *House of Lords Reform*, HL 17 and HC 171, 2002–03.

20 HL Debs. 21 and 22 Jan. 2003; HC Debs. 22 Jan. 2003; votes were on 4 Feb. 2003.

21 The quotation is from R. Cook, *Point of Departure*, p. 274. HC Deb. 29 Jan. 2003, cols. 877–8.

22 P. Cowley and M. Stuart, 'Parliament: More Bleak House than Great Expectations', *Parliamentary Affairs*, 57 (2004), 303.

23 See I. McLean, A. Spirling and M. Russell, 'None of the Above: The UK House of Commons votes on reforming the House of Lords, February 2003', *Political Quarterly*, 74 (2003): 299–304.

24 P. Norton, 'Reforming the Lords: A View from the Parapets', http://www.revolts.co.uk/cat_articles.html.

25 Joint Committee, HL 155 and HC 1027, 2002–03, paras 5–6.

26 Department of Constitutional Affairs, *Next Steps in Lords Reform* (2003).

27 HC Deb. 18 Sept. 2003, col. 1093.

28 Joint Select Committee on Conventions, HC 1212, 2005–06.

29 *Report of the Conference on Reform of the Second Chamber*, Chairman Lord Bryce (1918), Cd. 9038.

30 Evidence to Public Administration Committee, *ibid*, HC 494-II, 2001–02, Q. 132.

31 Lord Strathclyde, lecture to Politeia, 30 Nov. 1999.

32 HL Deb. 17 May 2005, cols. 20–1.

33 *Ibid*, Q. 158, 27 Jun. 2006.

34 One of the consequences of giving excessive attention to manifestos is that these documents tend to become overloaded with detail because party leaders see this as an easy way to minimise internal party dissent after an election, and give themselves the authority to carry through their policy ideas. In so doing manifestos become cluttered with matters which diminish their value to an electorate seeking a clear and understandable statement of the major policies and principles the party stands for. Labour's 2005 manifesto included at p. 110 the statement: 'We will legislate to place reasonable limits on the time bills spend in the second chamber – no longer than 60 sitting days for most bills'.

35 HC Deb. 8 Mar. 2003, col. 1296.

36 *Ibid*, para 10.8.

37 Viscount Bryce, *Modern Democracies*, vols. 1 and 2 (London, Macmillan, 1921).

38 W. Bagehot, *The English Constitution* (London, 1867, Fontana edition, 1963), p. 152.

39 *Reforming the House of Lords: Breaking the Deadlock* (London, The Constitution Unit, 2005). The other MPs were Paul Tyler, Tony Wright and George Young. See HC Deb. 23 Feb. 2005, cols. 71WH-95WH for debate on this report.

40 This section draws on D. Shell, 'The Future of the Second Chamber', *Parliamentary Affairs*, 57:4 (2004) 852–66.

41 This was the title of a major report on strengthening the Commons select committees; House of Commons Liaison Committee, *Shifting the Balance*, HC 300, 1999–2000.

Addendum

The saga of possible House of Lords reform has continued to unfold since the text of this book was completed in August 2006. Of particular significance has been the appearance of a further White Paper, House of Lords: Reform[1] in February 2007. This was the outcome of all-party consultations led by Jack Straw, Leader of the Commons. Reviewing the options for reform, this came out unequivocally in favour of a 'hybrid' House, arguing that this was desirable in order to enhance legitimacy while also retaining a strong non-party element. Tentatively the Paper proposed a 50:50 split, with 20 per cent of the reformed House being appointed non party-political members, 30 per cent appointed party-political members and the remaining 50 per cent being elected. After reviewing various methods for election, the Paper proposed using the European Parliament regional constituencies, with partially open lists and elections by thirds held simultaneously with the five-yearly European elections. Both appointed and elected members of the reformed House would sit for fifteen-year-non-renewable terms. A new statutory Appointments Commission would be established, which would be required to make appointments, taking account of the balance of votes cast for parties at the last general election, though Prime Ministers would still be allowed to appoint Ministers directly to the House, and to nominate up to ten former public servants per parliament. A House of 540 members was envisaged, with 90 elected members being replaced at each election and 84 appointed members being replaced in each round of appointments (36 non party-political and 54 party-political).

Regarding functions and powers, the Government did not envisage any significant change. Earlier, in November 2006, the Joint Committee on Conventions[2] (referred to in chapter 6 above) had made its final report, unanimously agreeing that current conventions on relations between the Houses were working satisfactorily and that these could not be codified, though it did warn that if the composition of the House were to be changed then the conventions may no longer hold. The Government White Paper accepted this report, but emphasised that in its view the current conventions were the correct ones for a reformed House to work with, at least initially.

In order to avoid what he described as the 'train wreck' that took place in 2003 when MPs voted down every proposal regarding the composition of the House (see above p. 157), Jack Straw proposed that MPs on a free vote, express preferences using an alternative vote procedure on a ballot paper. This ruffled the feathers of traditionalists in the House and the proposal was quickly withdrawn. But unlike 2003, the Commons did give clear support to a largely or wholly elected House, surprisingly approving the all-elected option by a 113 majority and the 80 per cent elected option by a majority of 38, with all other options being rejected. However, in the Lords a few days later peers voted heavily in support of an all-appointed House (361 to 121) and decisively rejected all other options.[3] So the Houses reached diametrically opposed views. But among MPs supporting the all-elected option were many known opponents of an elected House. Their support for this option can only be interpreted as a wrecking tactic, designed to make any measure of reform less likely. Indeed, an all-elected House does present difficulties for the Government in that it would mean the exclusion of bishops and the almost certain near elimination of the crossbench element, the latter being a clear breach of the generally agreed principles in relation to a reformed chamber. The Government's response to these votes was simply to express its determination to bring forward comprehensive proposals for reform of the House, in line with the will of the Commons. Immediately after the transition to Gordon Brown's premiership, a Green paper, The Governance of Britain,[4] was published which reiterated the Government's intention to 'develop reforms for a substantially or wholly elected second chamber', in line not only with the will of the Commons but of the Conservative and Liberal Democrat 2005 election manifestos. But Labour is deeply divided, and at present the great majority of Conservative MPs and peers do not support their frontbench on this issue.

All this underlines how difficult reform is likely to be. Certainly no legislation is likely until after Gordon Brown has secured fresh endorsement – presumably for a largely elected House – in a general election. But there would then be plenty of room for argument, not only over the precise proportions of elected and appointed members, but over matters such as the form of election, the frequency of elections, the manner in which appointments to the House were made, to say nothing of the whole transitional arrangements, including not only the exclusion of existing elected hereditary peers, but the pruning of life peers as new arrangements were phased in.

Meanwhile the existing House of Lords continued to play a robust role in relation to government legislation. The greater assertiveness of the House has received widespread recognition, and while assertiveness should not be equated with effectiveness, there is no reason to believe the House is not also gradually developing its effectiveness in terms of scrutiny and enhancing the accountability of government. The existing House is receiving greater recognition for its role from the Commons, the media and the public. In terms of party balance and the inclusion of a significant crossbench element it is seen to be representative of the electorate in a way that the Commons is not.

Perhaps the 1999 Act removing most hereditary peers, seen at the time as a temporary measure pending further reform, will take its place alongside the 1911 Parliament Act, again a supposedly temporary measure pending further reform, but in the event an Act that had no sequel in terms of altering the basis on which the House was composed for over 80 years. It would be easy to envisage further reform that would diminish the effectiveness of the existing House, but on the other hand if it is left alone and party leaders become increasingly preoccupied with ensuring they only send reliable party loyalists to the House, then its value within the parliamentary system could once again diminish.

Notes

1 *House of Lords: Reform*, Cm 7027 (2007).
2 Joint Committee on Conventions *Conventions in the UK Parliament*, HL 265 and HC 1212 (2005–06).
3 HC Deb 7 Mar 2007, cols. 1601–33; HL Deb 14 Mar 2007, cols 742–59.
4 *The Governance of Britain*, Cm 7170 (2007).

Appendix
Party manifesto statements on the House of Lords: 1979–2005

1979

Labour

No one can defend on any democratic grounds the House of Lords and the power and influence it exercises in our constitution. We propose, therefore, in the next parliament, to abolish the delaying power and legislative veto of the House of Lords.

Conservative

Now Labour want not merely to abolish the House of Lords but to put nothing in its place. This would be a most dangerous step. A strong second chamber is necessary not only to revise legislation but also to guarantee our constitution and liberties.

Liberal Democrat

The House of Lords should be replaced by a new, democratically chosen, second chamber which includes representatives of the nations and regions of the United Kingdom and UK members of the European Parliament.

1982

Labour

We shall . . . Take action to abolish the undemocratic House of Lords as quickly as possible and, as an interim measure, introduce a bill in the first session of parliament to remove its legislative powers – with the exception of those that relate to the life of a parliament.

Conservative

Labour will want to abolish the House of Lords. We will ensure that it has a secure and effective future. A strong second chamber is a vital safeguard for democracy and contributes to good government.

1987

SDP/Liberal Alliance

The alliance if empowered by the British people, will . . . reform the House of Lords.

1992

Labour

Further constitutional reforms will include those leading to the replacement of the House of Lords with a new elected second chamber which will have the power to delay for the lifetime of a parliament, change to designated legislation reducing individual or constitutional rights.

Liberal Democrat

We will maintain a second chamber as a Senate, primarily elected by the citizens of the nations and regions of the United Kingdom. It will have power to delay all legislation other than money bills for up to two years.

1997

Labour

The House of Lords must be reformed. As an initial, self-contained reform, not dependent on further reform in the future, the right of hereditary peers to sit and vote in the House of Lords will be ended by statute. This will be the first stage in a process of reform to make the House of Lords more democratic and representative. The legislative powers of the House of Lords will remain unaltered. The system of appointment of life peers to the House of Lords will be reviewed. Our objective will be to ensure that over time party appointees as life peers more accurately reflect the proportion of votes cast at the previous general election. We are committed to maintaining an independent crossbench presence of life peers. No one political party should seek a majority in the House of Lords.

A committee of both Houses of Parliament will be appointed to undertake a wide ranging review of possible further change and then to bring forward proposals for reform.

Conservative

Fundamental proposals which have not been thought through – such as opposition proposals on the House of Lords – would be extremely damaging. We will oppose change for change's sake.

Liberal Democrat

We will create an effective and democratic upper house. We will over two parliaments transform the House of Lords into a predominantly elected second chamber capable of representing the nations and regions of the UK and playing a key role in scrutinising European legislation.

2001

Labour

We are committed to completing House of Lords reform, including removal of the remaining hereditary peers, to make it more representative and democratic, while maintaining the House of Commons' traditional primacy. We have given our support to the report and conclusions of the Wakeham Commission, and will seek to implement them in the most effective way possible. Labour supports modernisation of the House of Lords' procedures to improve its effectiveness. We will put the independent Appointments Commission on a statutory footing.

Conservative

We will strengthen the independence of the House of Lords as an effective revising chamber by requiring new members to be approved by an independent appointments commission. We will set up a joint committee of both Houses of Parliament in order to seek consensus on lasting reform in the House of Lords. We would like to see a stronger House of Lords in the future, including a substantial elected element.

Liberal Democrat

We will replace the House of Lords with a smaller directly elected Senate with representation from the nations and regions of the UK. The Senate will be given new powers to improve legislation. We will transfer the judicial functions currently undertaken by the House of Lords to a new Supreme Court.

2005

Labour

In our first term we ended the absurdity of a House of Lords dominated by hereditary peers. Labour believes that a reformed upper chamber must be effective, legitimate and more representative without challenging the primacy of the House of Commons.

Following a review conducted by a committee of both Houses, we will seek agreement on codifying the key conventions of the Lords, and developing alternative forms of scrutiny that complement rather than replicate those of the Commons; the review should also explore how the upper chamber might offer a better route for public engagement in scrutiny and policy-making. We will legislate to place reasonable limits on the time bills spend in the second chamber – no longer than sixty sitting days for most bills.

As part of the process of modernisation, we will remove the remaining hereditary peers and allow for a free vote on the composition of the House.

Conservative

Proper reform of the House of Lords has been repeatedly promised but never delivered. We will seek cross-party agreement for a substantially elected House of Lords.

Liberal Democrat

Reform of the House of Lords has been botched by Labour, leaving it unelected and even more in the patronage of the prime minister. We will replace it with a predominantly elected second chamber.

Official sources

References to Hansard are in the form of HL Deb. for House of Lords and HC Deb. for House of Commons, followed by date and column number. Written statements have ws after the column number; Westminster Hall debates have the letters WH after the column number.

References to select committee reports are in the form: HL followed by the number of the report concerned and the session in which it appeared, eg HL 16, 2003–04. The above are available at the Houses of Parliament website, where a great deal of further information is also now available: http://www.parliament.uk/.

References to government papers give the command paper reference number, followed by the year of publication.

Select bibliography

Adonis, A. *Making Aristocracy Work* (Oxford, Clarendon Press, 1993).

Bailey, S. (ed.) *The Future of the House of Lords* (London, Hansard Society, 1954).

Baldwin, N. and Shell, D. (eds) *Second Chambers* (London, Frank Cass, 2001).

Baldwin, N. (ed.) *Parliament in the 21st Century* (London, Politicos, 2005).

Blackburn, R. and Plant, R. *Constitutional Reform: The Labour Government's Constitutional Reform Agenda* (London, Addison Wesley Longman, 1999).

Bogdanor, V. (ed.) *The British Constitution in the Twentieth Century* (Oxford University Press, 2003).

Bromhead, P. A. *The House of Lords and Contemporary Politics 1911–1957* (London, Routledge, 1958).

Bryce, J. (Viscount) *Modern Democracies*, vol. II (London, Macmillan, 1921).

Butler, D. and Butler, G. *British Political Facts 1900–2000* (Basingstoke, Macmillan, 2000).

Cook, R. *Point of Departure* (London, Simon & Schuster, 2003).

Cowley, P. *Revolts and Rebellions: Parliamentary Voting under Blair* (London, Politicos, 2002).

Cowley, P. and Stuart, M. 'Parliament: More Bleak House than Great Expectations', *Parliamentary Affairs*, 57 (2004) 303.

Cowley, P. *The Rebels: How Blair mislaid his majority* (London, Politicos, Methuen, 2005).

Crewe, E. *Lords of Parliament* (Manchester University Press, 2005).

Dickson, B. and Carmichael, P. (eds) *The House of Lords: Its Parliamentary and Judicial Roles* (Oxford, Hart Publishing, 1999).

Evans, M. *Constitution-Making and the Labour Party* (Basingstoke, Palgrave Macmillan, 2003).

Franklin, M. and Norton, P. (eds) *Parliamentary Questions* (Oxford, Clarendon Press, 1993).

Giddings, P. (ed.) *The Future of Parliament* (Basingstoke, Palgrave Macmillan, 2005).

Giddings, P. and Drewry, G. (eds) *Westminster and Europe* (Basingstoke, Macmillan, 1996).

Giddings, P. and Drewry, G. (eds) *Britain in the European Union* (Basingstoke, Palgrave Macmillan, 2004).

Hailsham, Lord *Elective Dictatorship* (London, BBC Publications, 1976).

Hamilton, A. and Madison, J. *The Federalist* (London, Everyman Library edition, J. M. Dent).

Home, Lord. *Report of the Review Committee on the Second Chamber* (London, Conservative Political Centre, 1978).

Jenkins, R. *Mr Balfour's Poodle* (London, Heinemann, 1954).

Jones, C. and Jones, D. L. (eds) *Peers, Politics and Power* (London, Hambledon Press, 1968).

Jones, J. *Labour of Love: The Partly Political Diary of a Cabinet Minister's Wife* (London, Politicos, 1999).

Judge, D. *Political Institutions in the UK* (Oxford University Press, 2005).

King, A. *Does the UK Still Have a Constitution?* (London, Sweet & Maxwell, 2001).

Lijphart, A. *Patterns of Democracy: Government Forms and Performance in Thirty-six Countries* (New Haven and London, Yale University Press, 1999) pp. 201–3.

Longley, L. D. and Olson, D. *Two into One: The Politics and Processes of National Legislative Change* (Columbia, Westview Press, 1991).

McLean, I., Spirling, A. and Russell, M. 'None of the Above: The UK House of Commons Votes on Reforming the House of Lords, February 2003', *Political Quarterly*, 74 (2003) 299–304.

Morgan, J. *The House of Lords and the Labour Government 1964–70* (Oxford University Press, 1975).

Norton, P. (Lord Norton of Louth) 'Cohesion without Discipline: Party Voting in the House of Lords', *Journal of Legislative Studies*, 9:4 (2003) 57–72.

Oliver, D. *Constitutional Reform in the UK* (Oxford University Press, 2003).

Patterson, S. C. and Mughan, A. *Senates: Bicameralism in the Contemporary World* (Columbus, Ohio State University Press, 1999).

Richard, I (Lord Richard) and Welfare, D. *Unfinished Business: Reforming the House of Lords* (London, Vintage, 1999).

Rippon of Hexham, Lord *Making the Law: The Report of the Hansard Society Commission on the Legislative Process* (The Hansard Society, 1992).

Rush, M. (ed.), *Parliament and Pressure Politics* (Oxford, Clarendon Press, 1990).

Russell, M. *Reforming the House of Lords: Lessons from Overseas* (Oxford University Press, 2000).

Russell, M. 'What are Second Chambers for?', *Parliamentary Affairs*, 54:3 (2001) 442–58.

Russell, M. 'Views from Peers, MPs and the Public on the Legitimacy and Powers of the House of Lords', Constitution Unit paper, 2005.

Russell, M. and Sciara, M. 'The Lords, the Party System and British Politics', *British Politics*, 2:3 (2007).

Shell, D. *The House of Lords* (Hemel Hempstead, Harvester-Wheatsheaf, 1992).

Shell, D. and Beamish, D. (eds) *The House of Lords at Work* (Oxford, Clarendon Press, 1993).

Shell, D. 'Labour and the House of Lords: A Case Study in Constitutional Reform', *Parliamentary Affairs*, 53:2 (2000) 290–310.

Shell, D. 'The Future of the Second Chamber', *Parliamentary Affairs*, 57:4 (2004) 852–66.

Tsebelis, G. and Money, J. *Bicameralism* (Cambridge University Press, 1997).

Weston, C. C. *English Constitutional Theory and the House of Lords 1556–1832* (London, Routledge, 1965).

Whitaker, R. 'Ping-Pong and Parliamentary Influence', *Parliamentary Affairs*, 59:3 (2006) 536–45.

Windlesham, Lord *Responses to Crime, vol 3, Legislating with the Tide* (Oxford, Clarendon Press, 1996).

Official reports

(listed chronologically)

1918: Report of the Conference on Reform of the Second Chamber, Chairman Lord Bryce, Cd. 9038 (1918).

1948: Parliament Bill, 1947, Agreed Statement on conclusion of Conference of Party Leaders, Cmnd. 7380 (1948).

1968: House of Lords Reform, Cmnd. 3799 (1968).

1999: *Modernising Parliament: Reforming the House of Lords*, Cm. 4183.

2000: *A House for the Future*, Report of Royal Commission on the House of Lords, chairman, Lord Wakeham. Cm. 4534.

2001: *The House of Lords: Completing the Reform*, Cm. 5291.

2002: *The Second Chamber: Continuing the Reform*, Fifth Report Select Committee on Public Administration, HC 494-I and II, 2001–02.

2002: *House of Lords Reform*, First Report, Joint Committee on House of Lords Reform, HL 17 and HC 171, 2002–03.

2003: *House of Lords Reform*, Second Report, Joint Committee on House of Lords Reform, HL 97 and HC 688, 2002–03.

2003: *Constitutional Reform: Next Steps for the House of Lords*, Department for Constitutional Affairs.

2006: *Joint Select Committee on Conventions*, First Special Report, HL 189 and HC 1151, 2005–06, and HC 1212, 2005–06 for subsequent evidence.

Index

Activity of House of Lords 86–8
American Senate 134–7
Appellate peers *see* Law Lords
Appointments Commission 58, 60–3,
    155, 158
Attendance of peers 69–72, 87
Australian Senate 138

Benn, Tony 33, 64
Bicameralism 130–6
Bill of Rights (1689) 7
Bishops 10, 43, 48–9, 53–5, 70
Bryce Commission (1918) 11, 34–6,
    146, 159, 166

Canadian Senate 139
Carrington, Lord 22, 72–3
Constitution of UK
    Modernisation of 3–4
    Reform of 1–4, 160–1, 163–4
    Unwritten character 4–6
    Westminster model 10–11
Constitution, Select Committee
    120
Constitutional crisis (1909–11)
    13–14
Constitutional Reform Act (2006) 56,
    158
Conventions of the Constitution Select
    Committee 30, 149, 158
Cost of House of Lords 79
Cranborne, Lord 74, 77, 80, 151–3
Crossbench peers 27, 32, 49, 57, 59,
    68, 71, 74–7, 101, 165

Death Penalty abolition 22
Debates in House of Lords 89, 96–7,
    112–14
Delegated Powers Committee 120–1

Economic Affairs Committee 119–20
European Communities Committee
    115–18
European Parliamentary Elections Bill
    (1999) 24–6, 104
Expense allowances 31, 78

Financial privilege 7
French Senate 139–40

Government Bills 98–112
Government representation in House of
    Lords 72–4
Grand Committee 88, 90–1
Great Reform Act (1832) 8, 12

Home Committee (1976) 42–4
Honours lists 47–8, 58–9, 62
House of Lords Act (1999) 17, 26–7,
    151–3
Hunting Bill (2004) 27–9

Irish Seanad 130–6
Irvine of Lairg, Lord 75, 106, 157,
    167
Italian Senate 140–1

Jay, Baroness 27, 152, 160
Jellicoe Committee 123

Law Commission Bills 124–5
Law Lords 43, 48, 55–7, 70, 109
Leader of the House 72, 87
Leave of absence 31–2, 48
Legislation in the House of Lords
    91–4
Liaison Committee 123–4
Life Peerages Act (1958) 32, 36
Life peers 57–8
Lord Chancellor 56, 73, 90
Lord Speaker 67, 87

Mackay of Clashfern, Lord 115, 120,
    154
McNally, Lord 29, 160
Measures 95–6
Merits of Statutory Instruments
    Committee 121–2
Ministerial salaries 79
Modernisation of procedures 88–90

Opposition frontbench 74, 77
Oral questions 97

Parliament Acts (1911 and 1949) 11,
    14–15, 24–30, 92, 102, 160
Parliament (No 2) Bill (1969) 37–40
Party balance in House 68–9, 103
Party organisation in House 72–5
Peerage Act (1963) 32–3
Peers
    Activity levels 69–72
    Average age 67
    Elected hereditary 48–50
    Ethnic minority 67
    Hereditary 13, 17, 33–4, 48–52
    Irish 9, 52
    Life 57–67
    Register of interests 79–80
    Scottish 9, 52

Spiritual *see* Bishops
    Women 32, 66–7
    Working 47, 59–60
Plant Committee 151
Political Honours Scrutiny Committee
    62
Private members bills 93–4
Public Administration Select
    Committee 62–3, 156

Questions
    For written answer 87
    Unstarred *see* debates
    see also Oral questions

Richard, Lord 151–2
Roseberry Committee (1908) 36
Royal Commission *see* Wakeham

Salisbury convention 20, 29–30
Second chambers 142–7
    see also Bicameralism
Select Committees 35, 115–24
Sexual Offences (Amendment) Bill
    (2000) 27
Science and Technology Committee
    117–19
Southern Rhodesia Sanctions Order
    (1968) 22, 38
Statutory instruments 94–5, 160
Strathclyde, Lord 160

Thatcher, Margaret (Baroness) 42,
    44–5, 59, 68, 71, 106

Wakeham Commission (2000) 35, 55,
    120, 146, 149, 153–6, 164–7
War Crimes Act (1990) 24
Weatherill, Lord 152–3
Whips 71, 73–4, 76–7